Heritage Marketing

THE LIBRARY
WRITTLE COLLEGE
CHELMSFORD   CM1 3RR

D0549964

Heritage Marketing

Shashi Misiura

ELSEVIER

AMSTERDAM • BOSTON • HEIDELBERG • LONDON • NEW YORK • OXFORD
PARIS • SAN DIEGO • SAN FRANCISCO • SINGAPORE • SYDNEY • TOKYO
Butterworth-Heinemann is an imprint of Elsevier

Butterworth-Heinemann is an imprint of Elsevier
Linacre House, Jordan Hill, Oxford OX2 8DP
30 Corporate Drive, Suite 400, Burlington, MA 01803

First published 2006

Copyright © 2006, Elsevier Ltd. All rights reserved

No part of this publication may be reproduced in any material form (including photo-
copying or storing in any medium by electronic means and whether or not transiently
or incidentally to some other use of this publication) without the written permission of
the copyright holder except in accordance with the provisions of the Copyright,
Designs and Patents Act 1988 or under the terms of a licence issued by the Copyright
Licensing Agency Ltd, 90 Tottenham Court Road, London, England W1T 4LP.
Applications for the copyright holder's written permission to reproduce any part of
this publication should be addressed to the publisher

Permissions may be sought directly from Elsevier's Science & Technology Rights
Department in Oxford, UK: phone: (+44) 1865 843830, fax: (+44) 1865 853333, e-mail:
permissions@elsevier.co.uk. You may also complete your request on-line via the
Elsevier homepage (http://www.elsevier.com), by selecting 'Customer Support' and
then 'Obtaining Permissions'

British Library Cataloguing in Publication Data
A catalogue record for this book is available from the British Library

Library of Congress Cataloguing in Publication Data Control Number: 2005931199

ISBN-13: 978-0-7506-6318-2
ISBN-10: 0-7506-6318-9

For information on all Butterworth-Heinemann
publications visit our website at http://books.elsevier.com

Typeset by SPI Publisher Services, Kundli
Printed and bound in Great Britain by MPG Books Ltd, Cornwall

Working together to grow
libraries in developing countries

www.elsevier.com | www.bookaid.org | www.sabre.org

ELSEVIER   BOOK AID
            International   Sabre Foundation

Contents

Preface

> Brideshead today would be open to trippers, its treasures rearranged by expert hands and the fabric better maintained than it was by Lord Marchmain.
> (Evelyn Waugh (1959) Preface. *Brideshead Revisited*. Penguin, London)

Heritage Marketing: Principles and Practice is the very first applied marketing textbook that addresses the unique application of marketing principles to the 'heritage industry'.

The idea for this book came to me in the summer of 2003, both by re-reading a favourite novel, *Brideshead Revisited* (see quotation above) and by chance of a television programme which mentioned the love of Indian architecture by the British Royal Family and nobility, particularly in the reign of the Prince Regent, and how this manifest itself in the building of Royal Palaces and the acquisition of art and artefacts. Two examples that illustrate this past phenomenon are the creation of 'Brighton Pavillion', a famous landmark in the UK (which is featured in this book) and the lesser known 'Sezincote House' in Gloucestershire, which is much more than a building in both the venacular and Indian style – it is also about India's religious heritage which is captured in the spirit of the place by the internal and external layout, other design features and spiritual curios gathered from India.

I managed to get some way with my research on the relationship between Indian architecture and its representation in British Royal Palaces but felt that it might be more appropriate to look more widely at the link between heritage and marketing before focusing on one particular, albeit complex, aspect. Little was I prepared for the complex nature of this subject, which has taken many months to research and prepare for publication.

Before my research began, I was very surprised to discover that there is currently no book on the market that explores the relationship between marketing and heritage (and indeed what literature there is can be found scattered all over the place). I was therefore delighted that Reed Elsevier were willing to support me, once we had identified that there would be a demand. Indeed, the book seems to coincide with an unprecedented growth in interest among the public in general (more on this later) and students and practitioners in particular, on all aspects of 'heritage'. In the case of the latter two this is evident in the increasing number of new courses available at Colleges, Universities and private providers as well as new and specific jobs, for example for 'Heritage Managers'.

In this book, although I will be sensitive to debates surrounding the (debated) concept of heritage from (in no particular order!) geographers, conservationists, archaeologists, historians and other academics and experts, my main aim is to explain and illustrate (mainly through examples and case studies), how various aspects of heritage can be marketed successfully. The 'heritage industry' covers anything and everything connected with the past (well, almost!) but I have chosen to focus on a few specific sectors that are the most appropriate for students of heritage studies, marketing, business, tourism, leisure and hospitality/catering studies. The first main area explored is heritage tourism (for students of marketing generally and specifically those studying leisure and tourism), food and drink heritage (for general marketing students and especially those engaged with the study of hospitality/catering) and also on how companies are increasingly using aspects of heritage as part of their marketing strategies in the competitive arena, this will be of interest to general business students as well as other student groups. Practitioners will find both the theory and examples, through the 'insights' and case studies offering a wider and deeper knowledge of various sectors in the heritage industry.

The book is ostensibly about the role of marketing and how the process of this academic discipline stimulates demand by capitalizing on the positive attitude of actual or potential heritage consumers. However, the heritage marketer must manage demand so that the 'product' in question is not swamped (this applies in particular to tourist 'products'/'attractions'), as this is unlikely to be in the interests of anyone.

The 'heritage consumer' (just like any other) must be fully understood in terms of the benefits that he/she seeks to achieve from consumption of the product, service or brand. What motivates a consumer to have a relationship with something from the past, either nostalgically or nostophobically, or in other emotional terms? In this book the segmentation variable 'psychographics' will go a long way toward helping us understand, and get closer to, the heritage consumer.

I will use examples from the built environment, natural world, literature, food and drink, sport, art, people, music, festivals/events, religion and spirituality, from all around the globe, to illustrate how heritage is marketed, recognizing that there may be links between one or more of the above, as well as relationships between them and issues of education, conservation, preservation and restoration.

I do hope that you enjoy reading and studying from this book, as much as I have enjoyed preparing and presenting it.

Shashi Misiura
July, 2005

Acknowledgments

I am very grateful to Tim Goodfellow, Commissioning Editor at Butterworth-Heinemann/Elsevier for his very warm response to what was initially no more than a few random thoughts. I am indebted to his continuing support and hope that all at Elsevier will be pleased with the results of my effort.

I also wish to thank Dr David Storey and Dr Heather Barrett for their kind listening ears and for enabling me to test my drafts on their students of Heritage Studies at University College, Worcester and also to my own students of Business Management who have patiently analysed case studies and absorbed numerous heritage-related examples in Marketing lectures.

I am extremely grateful to many people, too numerous to mention, who have kindly given me information for use in the book, either as illustrative examples, 'insights' or case studies. In particular, I would like to thank personnel at: 'The Museum in the Park', Stroud, Gloucestershire; Mr Peter Lacey, Headmaster at the King's School, Gloucester; The Thermae Bath Spa Project, Bath, Avon; The Coca-Cola Company, Atlanta, USA; Buccleuch, Scotland; The Ritz Hotel, London; The Admirable Crichton, London; Puerto de Culturas, Cartegena, Spain; and Hershey International, USA.

This book is dedicated to my son.

Introduction

Heritage Marketing addresses the issues facing students and practitioners in applying the generic principles of marketing to the heritage industry, which is both large and complex; indeed the notion of heritage is very much a debated concept. It is an *applied marketing textbook*.

The book is *international* in its outlook, using examples from many countries, including the UK, USA, Australia, South Africa, India and many European countries, including newly industrializing ones such as those in the Baltic States, Eastern and Southern Europe.

Heritage Marketing is divided into six chapters and each will have the following:

- Introduction, including definitions.
- Contents, explanations, examples and discussion.
- 'Insights', short and long case studies to amplify and illustrate applied marketing heritage concepts and issues.
- Case studies for students to work on either individually or in groups and which will act as a facility for further discussion.
- Summary.
- Discussion Questions and Activities.
- Recommended Reading.

Chapter One is an introduction to the applied nature of this textbook and looks specifically at the concept of heritage and its relationship to marketing. Funding heritage, especially the built environment (historical buildings, etc.), is explored in detail, both in the context of the UK and other countries. The work of the National Trust, UK, English Heritage and The Heritage Lottery Fund and are just some of the organizations closely related to built heritage (and other aspects of heritage) that will be featured in 'Insights'.

Chapter Three is an extensive and crucial investigation of the target markets for heritage, both consumer and business to business. The chapter will include a section on market and marketing research applied to the heritage sector. Insights and case studies will feature examples from many countries, including The Netherlands, Scotland, Italy and Spain, and will deal with many aspects of heritage: sporting heritage, historical houses and their heritage, heritage hotels, museums, cultural heritage, education and heritage and the multiplier effect generated by restoring buildings or regenerating areas, together with a consideration of how a heritage sports event such as the Olympic Games can contribute significantly to the economic fortunes of a country.

Chapter Four is one of two chapters on heritage 'products', in this case heritage tourism. The chapter will begin with an understanding of the (controversial) debate surrounding heritage tourism and how practitioners in particular must address and balance issues of conservation, regeneration, preservation, sustainability and restoration with marketing efforts. A wide range of examples drawn from spiritual and religious heritage, heritage towns and cities, cultural events such as festivals, literary, music and others will reinforce the concepts presented. A lengthy end of chapter case study on the Thermae Bath Spa project will draw together many strands of the debate which students can then explore further through the questions that follow.

Chapter Five is the second of the two on 'products' and looks in depth at marketing food and drink heritage – this will be of particular interest to students/practitioners of hospitality and catering but also to students of marketing and tourism and leisure as it will deal with many aspects of this subject that relate to others already dealt with in the book, such as segmentation and tourism – a key element of this chapter will be to understand the concept of branding food and drink for differentiation through the use of heritage.

Chapter Six has as its focus a number of different companies, such as Royal Worcester and Morgan Cars, who at a corporate level trade on their heritage – understanding and creating uniqueness for competitive advantage and maintaining this position is a key feature of this chapter.

List of case studies

List of insights

Chapter 1

Heritage marketing – an introduction

A definition of marketing

> Marketing is the management function that is involved in identifying, anticipating and satisfying customer requirements, profitably.
>
> (Chartered Institute of Marketing, UK)

Marketing is therefore concerned to identify suitable target markets or audiences for a product or service (which may be developed or enhanced, once the needs of the market have been understood) by using the process of market segmentation (this is explored in detail in Chapter 3).

The principle of anticipation comes from economics and states that 'demand is always in anticipation of supply'; this means that, to a certain extent, one cannot know whether the product or service will be 'successful' until it has been 'consumed' (or perhaps enquiries made about it, orders taken, reservations made and so on). There is therefore an element of **risk** in presenting something to the marketplace.

Satisfying the market can take on many different forms and may be known by other marketing terms (such as 'adding value') and is part of the targeting process through the appropriate use of marketing communications. This principle has been 'extended' in recent years by aligning it to other disciplines such as information technology and creating new concepts such as customer relationship marketing; this will be explored later in the book. However, recent literature on marketing suggests that a new paradigm is now largely guiding thinking on practice and this is branding, a topic that will be covered in this book.

The only part of this definition that some concerned with marketing a heritage product, service or brand might not consider appropriate is profit, because the motive for marketing may be, for example, to enable the regeneration of a locality, conservation of a landscape, preservation of a property or for many other reasons, rather than to generate a profit in the commercial sense. However, some not-for-profit organizations are comfortable with the fact that they must create a 'surplus' in order to survive/grow, which is effectively the same as making a profit and, indeed, may be generated from the same types of activities performed by commercial organizations, such as operating shops, bars and restaurants alongside the (possibly free entry) heritage site or attraction. In the context of the marketing of food and drink connected with one or more aspects of heritage, I cannot think of a single example where this product is marketed for reasons other than commercial gain, or profit-making.

The essence of the heritage marketing process, then, is to find out what the customer wants and to deliver it, subject to any constraints that might prevail, such as the need to protect parts of a heritage site or historic property because of the increased wear and tear resulting from the extra footfall stimulated through marketing initiatives. This example is typical of the balance that many heritage providers must achieve, particularly in relation to the built environment, i.e., the marketing activities should be designed to stimulate demand and satisfy the consumer but not to the detriment of that which needs to be preserved for future generations. Similarly, food and drink that is marketed because of an aspect of heritage (such as the quality of the water in the Scottish Highlands that gives Scotch Whisky a distinct flavour) must not ultimately be aimed at the mass market but at niche market(s) in order to retain a degree of exclusivity and 'premiumness'. Profit can be made from extra margins that can be levied on these types of goods and, in the long run, repeat purchase and advocacy by consumers that creates brand loyalty.

In short, 'the aim of marketing is to know and understand the customer so well that the product or service *fits* him/her but allows the organization to achieve its goals' (Dibb and Simkin, 2002).

The customer therefore will be central to our understanding of heritage marketing as we explore how the past is reflected in the present for all types of advantage, commercial and non-commercial or quantitative and qualitative. Figure 1.1 gives a summary of the generic principles that will be applied in the context of heritage marketing.

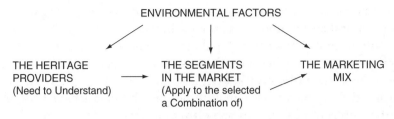

Figure 1.1 A Summary of the generic principles that will be applied in the context of heritage marketing.

The growth of marketing as an academic discipline and its relationship to heritage

Marketing is a relatively new academic discipline, having emerged and developed from the general worldwide era of production in the nineteenth century, through the specific sales era in the 1920s to the marketing era that has been the case since the 1950s when significant advances were made by commercial organizations, for example, the multinational Unilever. Some writers on the history of marketing argue that the founding father was Edison, who was the first to recognize the commercial potential for his inventions.

From the definition above, we begin to see that marketing has its foundations in the more traditional academic disciplines of economics, psychology and sociology, all of which are focused on the individual to a great extent and have offered much to our current understanding of consumer behaviour.

Since the 1980s much more attention has been paid to concepts such as *segmentation* as a way of advancing our understanding of consumers and, in particular, their lifestyle choices, with influential work from many authors, in particular Wedel and Kamakura (2000). In the latter two decades of the Millennium, issues such as quality, customer service and service issues generally have been the focus of attention which has led to a paradigm shift in favour of 'relationship marketing', though quickly superseding this is the notion of branding and brand loyalty, as briefly mentioned above.

The marketing of heritage seems to coincide with the birth of marketing as an academic discipline in North America in the 1950s, although there is evidence of heritage tourism existing in many parts of the world since time immemorial (more on this later), i.e., well before there were any techniques for awareness-raising through to branding, customer loyalty programmes and service issues.

In the 1950s, the USA and Canada wanted to engage audiences with their national and natural conservation policies, which gave rise to marketing plans and specific promotional activities. This process was adopted in the UK, particularly by those involved with promoting rural areas, especially to educate the masses in conservation, as it was increasingly being recognized that the natural environment was under threat.

Institutions in the 'business' of making aspects of heritage available to the general public around the world have seemed to lack focus and direction, although museums (the best known association that people have in mind when asked about the physical manifestation of heritage), have been around since the eighteenth century in one form or another.

> During the 1950s and 1960s, collections were either moveable or site-based. Museums usually had displays in glass cases, the occasional warder as a security guard and a curator behind the scenes. The analogy with a prison was very real. The strong impression given was that the visitor was privileged to be allowed entry. In fact, there was an underlying assumption that those who visited museums, historic houses or stately homes . . . would have the necessary knowledge and cultural understanding from their formative years of schooling to make explanation beyond the detail superfluous. The reputation of museums as dark and dreary, fusty, musty places dates from this time and took a long while to dispel. Relatively few people had cars so access to the countryside and other towns remained limited.
>
> (Millar, 1999)

During the 1970s conservation became increasingly important to a variety of different stakeholders. Local history societies and amenity groups were raising funds and providing volunteer labour to save places and artefacts from the fast-disappearing agricultural and industrial landscape in a rapidly changing economic climate. Machinery, mills, houses, canals, coastline and woodlands were saved from destruction in the wake of new development. The phenomenon of a nation's heritage under attack was recognized by Colin Amery and Dan Cruickshank in their seminal work *The Rape of Britain*, published in 1975. They concluded that the destruction during the nineteenth century paled into insignificance compared with the licensed vandalism of the years 1950–75.

Between 1975 and the early 1980s there was a growing concern by political leaders in many countries about their national heritage, mainly at this time in terms of the built environment, which led to the shaping of policy to begin a large-scale preservation process. In the UK, this gave rise to the National Heritage Act (1980), which in general is concerned with the preservation of that range of property defined therein as 'the heritage', but it also seeks to secure public access to ensure that 'the heritage' is available for cultural consumption and to see that it is displayed as such.

In the 1980s, partly to coincide with the growth in mass-market tourism, the leisure and tourism industries began to exploit heritage sites around the world *en masse*, and turned them into 'attractions' for commercial gain. By the 1990s, these attractions and others gained momentum and they, in turn, lobbied harder for a complex and sophisticated system of funding which now operates for many heritage sites in most countries. This system of funding operates on a plural model, i.e., they achieve grants from a range of stakeholders including government, tourist boards, charities or from revenue generated through their entry charges and other enterprises.

During the 1980s there were rapid changes in the way heritage organizations saw themselves in relation to their prospective customers.

> The external environment was taken seriously [see Chapter 2]. This included making provision for tourists from the region, the rest of the UK and overseas; ensuring the interests of members of the local community or communities of interest were looked after through Friends groups and membership organisations and establishing links with educational institutions, particularly schools, with an emergent agenda of lifelong learning. **Interpretation** and education became key 'front of house' activities ... fierce debates revolved around issues of signage, information panels, the nature and type of labelling for displays and the right kind of exhibitions to attract a wider audience. There was an increasing need for a variety of information and interpretative/educational publications both for use on site and to take away as souvenirs. Audio-visual theatres provided an historical introduction and background information on the project through dual slide projection or video–new technology at the time. Warders became stewards; guides provided educational tours; education officers focused largely on the organisation of school groups and INSET training for teachers; demonstrators/live interpreters offered the possibility of an entertaining engagement with a past way of life or awareness of environmental issues such as CFC's. Jorvik (in York) set the trend for a whole new style of interpretation including smells and animatronic models, a ride and a chance to view the archaeological dig and accompanying finds at the end.
>
> (Millar, 1999)

In 2003, a series of major developments took place in relation to international cultural policy and law that have significance for the heritage tourism sector as a whole and for museums in particular.

In 2003, the Dealing in Cultural Objects (Offences) Act was passed by the British Parliament, following the UK Government's ratification of the 1970 United Nations Educational, Scientific and Cultural Organisation (UNESCO) Convention; there was also the creation of a new international convention aimed at protecting and promoting the world's intangible cultural heritage (ICH).

The 32nd General Conference of UNESCO in 2003 saw governments from around the world voting to adopt the International Convention for the Safeguarding of the Intangible Heritage. Modelled on the 1972 World Heritage Convention, the new treaty is the culmination of efforts aimed at widening the scope of international cultural policy beyond the sites and landscapes covered by the 1972 Convention.

There have been attempts to have intangible heritage recognized and protected by international law for some time. The first recognition of this came through the adoption of a UNESCO recommendation aimed at safeguarding traditional culture and folklore. The 1989 recommendation was not legally binding and had a limited focus on 'traditional cultures'. The limitations of this have been acknowledged and have given rise to a new Convention which is also legally binding and which incorporates a wider definition of intangible cultural heritage. The Convention defines intangible cultural heritages as practices, representations, expressions, knowledge, skills – as well as the instruments, objects, artefacts and cultural spaces associated with them – that communities, groups and, in some cases, individuals recognize as part of their cultural heritage.

The Convention requires countries that sign it to work nationally with communities, groups and non-governmental organizations to prepare national inventories of ICH and to report on their efforts to protect ICH at regular meetings. These meetings will be responsible for monitoring progress in implementing the Convention.

In summary, the last 30 years in particular have seen 'an extraordinary and it seems, ever-growing enthusiasm for the recovery of the national past – both the real past of recorded history and the timeless one of tradition' (Samuel, 1989). The section above has established that one important driving force in heritage marketing, apart from qualitative reasons (for example, to educate), is to raise revenue. This is because, on the whole, in spite of the funding arrangements that many countries now have in place and the initiatives that many heritage sectors have taken in order to raise revenue, the vast majority of heritage enterprises are still underfunded. Nevertheless, much evidence points to the fact that all around the world, an interest in all aspects of heritage is at an all time high amongst most groups in societies and that, because of the present shape of the external environment, this is set to continue and grow.

Heritage providers (whether this is in the heritage tourism sector, the food and drink associated with the heritage sector, sporting heritage sector or any other), just like any commercial business have to appeal to the **motivations and aspirations** of their customers and all activities must be coordinated (**customer/quality/relationship marketing**) with attention to detail. Heritage, in other words a relationship with the past that can be gained in many different ways, is aspirational, i.e., something that someone (a consumer) wants, and marketing is the process by which it can be made available, either at a personal, local, national or international level.

New developments in heritage marketing

The vast majority of literature on heritage, apart from the philosophical and intellectual, has concerned itself with heritage tourism, a sector that has undoubtedly grown globally and, most importantly, has created much-needed revenue and employment for 'poorer' nations, i.e., other than those in the developed West (although these, too, have benefited in many ways from this new source of income). Countries such as Jamaica and, more recently, the newly industrializing ones in Eastern Europe and the Baltic States such as Hungary, Poland, the Czech Republic and Estonia, are all busy exploring aspects of place marketing. In addition, they are also considering how other aspects of their heritage can be marketed, both for commercial gain and also in terms of generating a 'feel good' factor amongst the indigenous population (qualitative reasons). The marketing of heritage, especially heritage tourism, must be a finely balanced set of activities, as there is little point in alienating the local populus in favour of (possibly short-term) heritage tourism. There are also wider issues of national identity and how this should be perceived, nationally and internationally, that are very much tied-up with the notion of heritage.

There is currently very little written about the relationship between food and drink heritage and marketing, or how companies are increasingly using one or more aspects of heritage in their generic stance, or specifically in promotional material, either for the organization itself or for one or more of its brands. Both of these issues will be addressed in this book, alongside heritage tourism.

Food and drink heritage has been linked to heritage tourism for some time. However, it seems that now, more than ever, consumers are looking for these cultural aspects to be more closely related in a package deal or are willing to travel for food and drink heritage's own sake. For example, the Spanish tourist authorities have learned that consumers want to eat Spanish food (and not the 'bland' diet that they had previously been offered) to experience that part of the country's heritage as well as other cultural aspects such as music and dance, together with an appreciation of what its built environment (architectural heritage, both 'old' and 'new') has to offer. This growing phenomenon has given rise to niche market opportunities that heritage (and general) tourism marketers are only too pleased to exploit, not least because demand can be stimulated for 'off-peak' seasons and times of the year (for example city breaks with a built environment or other cultural emphasis, such as a music or food festival, can take place outside of the peak summer months). Other interesting developments in relation to heritage food and drink are also emerging. For example, it is now possible to purchase through the Internet, i.e., from any part of the world, any number of vines in a French vineyard, the product of which will be delivered to the customer's door. We shall return to a fuller discussion of food and drink and heritage later in the book.

New heritage attractions are opening all the time, some in purpose-built buildings that will become heritage attractions in their own right, in time, just as 'period' buildings in which we find many museums and galleries are in the present. In order to address this very issue, New City Architecture is a new public exhibition hosted by the Corporation of London and British Land that explores the City of London's buildings and public places. The focus for this exhibition is the City's people, places and buildings in the context of the development of London during the last 20 years. The exhibition will showcase 21 schemes, both newly built and proposed, to provide a rare opportunity to preview the City's emerging group of tall buildings. The criteria in selecting the buildings has been design excellence in creating new and sustainable space. The chosen schemes and their individual architectural merits will be made accessible through models, drawings, computer images and full-size sections.

Another example of new developments is the Ford Rouge Factory Tour in Detroit, USA, which re-opens this year after 20 years. The Ford Motor Company is partnering with America's history attraction, The Henry Ford, which will operate the new visitor centre and plant tour. The all-new state-of-the-art presentation venue offers two multiscreen theatres, numerous touch-screen interpretive displays and an 80-foot-high observation deck overlooking the world's largest 'living roof' on the Dearborn Truck Plant. The centrepiece of the visitor experience is a seven-screen circular theatre combining video, lighting, heat, fog, fans and misters to create an immersive environment for the film *The Art of Manufacturing*.

In the UK, the River & Rowing Museum's collection is unique and combines three aspects of heritage: the natural features and distinctiveness of the River Thames, the historic town of Henley-on-Thames and the international heritage sport of rowing. The collection ranges chronologically from artefacts of prehistoric times to modern photographs, and in size from badges to boats used in Olympic events. The museum has been faced with a problem that taxes most: how to maintain and make accessible a growing collection where there are real constraints of physical space. The answer in this case has been to set up a Collections Access project that digitizes the museum's entire collection of over 13 000 objects, making the information available to visitors via kiosks in the galleries and Internet users through the online programme.

The museum came up with their own segmentation of the online user market and defined these as 'paddler', 'swimmer' and 'diver'. Paddlers want only to 'dip their toes' into the information available; swimmers' expectations are for more details on the content; and divers can go deep into the information and access databases and other detailed information. Celebrities such as local resident Sir Steve Redgrave were invited to select their favourite objects which are presented as virtual tours, giving visitors the chance to engage with that person's thoughts and opinions; these tours are available in the museum's galleries and online and have proven to be an important starting point for many visitors.

Many museums and other heritage sites and attractions will often use a relevant link to create a temporary or special exhibition in order to extend the product offering that has nothing to do with commercial activities as described above, but for which there may be a (additional) charge as a result of its uniqueness and the cost of setting it up. One example of this is the special exhibition that has been mounted at the Imperial War Museum to commemorate the 60th anniversary of the D-Day landings that marked the beginning of the end of the Second World War. The exhibition demonstrates the planning and build-up to the invasion and also events that took place on the day itself. This is achieved in the main through oral history recordings of personal experiences of people involved with the attack; film footage, photographs, diaries and letters from the museum's collections have also been incorporated to amplify the history, as well as original models used by the planners of the operation, water-stained maps and equipment used by soldiers, a communion set and notebook that had been carried by an army chaplain and an assortment of medals. The exhibition was launched to coincide with a major drama-documentary shown on the UK's BBC1.

An introduction to heritage for marketers

> The elements in my music come from the memory of my feelings, the music I loved in the past, and also from popular and classical music . . . my Mother used to play the piano and I always remember hearing the sound of the piano coming from the house; it's very connected to my memories of childhood.
>
> (Ludovico Einaudi, International Pianist, Milan, Italy, 2004)

A very brief definition of heritage is **that which is inherited from the past**. '. . . Heritage is a process by which things (and indeed non-material things) come into the self-conscious arena when someone wants to conserve/collect them. So anything (or even nothing) can become heritage, but not every thing is' (Ashworth and Howard, 1999).

Heritage is created by establishing a number of principles, processes and practices; different academics and experts in vastly contrasting (or complementary) fields will produce *values* that accrue around the concept of heritage (it is not the purpose of this book to represent these views in any great length but to recognize that the overall value created will be of significance in marketing the heritage product or service, a point that we will return to later, both in this chapter and the next).

Heritage (however this is defined by individuals or others on their behalf) is considered by most people to be an important part of their lives. It is therefore crucial to recognize at the outset that what individuals and groups mean by heritage and what they want to preserve in terms of personal, local, national or international heritage is not necessarily immediately obvious. It can require a great deal of sensitivity to establish the facts, as well as the use of creative techniques that may not be employed to their full extent at present, such as ethnographic approaches as part of a research methodology; this is partly because heritage as a generic notion is still being understood. 'The past in question – the "heritage" which conservationists fight to preserve and retrieval projects to unearth, and which the holiday public or museum visitors are invited to "experience" – is in many ways a novel one' (Hobsbawm, 1983).

The notion of heritage is very contentious and the arguments in the ever-expanding literature rage on, notably amongst historians, many of whom have a great distaste for the idea of heritage, although this view has been challenged: 'If historians despise heritage fakery, heritage disdains historians' truth fetishes' (Lowenthal, 1996a).

David Lowenthal is one of the first academics to champion the idea of heritage as a **celebration of the past**, whereas the majority of historians (and other academics) have poured scorn on this notion, for a variety of reasons. The main one seems to be that people are deluding themselves when it comes to the past and that, rather than hanging on to a fictitious ideal or something imagined, they would be better dealing with the reality of their present situations and of what is to come in the future. The past therefore is something that people are hiding behind because they cannot face up to current existence. 'Protective illusion . . . has been central to the obsessive construction of both enterprise and heritage cultures in these post-imperial days [in Britain]' (Robins, 2004).

Conversely, Sir Roy Strong, in his introduction to Patrick Cormack's *Heritage in Danger* argues that 'the heritage represents some form of security, a point of reference, a refuge perhaps, something visible and tangible which, within a topsey-turvey world, seems stable and unchanged' (1978: 17).

Where there might be some acceptance of heritage being represented in museums, exhibitions or other spheres of public life, this has been argued as a sanitized and commodified presentation that bears little resemblance to the overall context.

Other writers suggest that the appeal of tradition is very much a feature of modern nations but that there is too much ready acceptance by the general public of that which is advocated by powerful leaders in the name of heritage. They use this as a way of justifying present social arrangements through a reference back to ways of life the origins of which are so remote that they apparently need no justification, they have simply always 'been there'.

However, not all the literature is critical and there is definitely a growing body of knowledge that is concerning itself with the positive benefits of heritage. 'Tradition and heritage are factors that enhance the "quality" of life of particular places and make them attractive locations for investment. An emphasis on tradition is important in the development of tourism as a major industry.' These two points identify major **causative effects** of the heritage industry, i.e., there is undoubtedly a causal link between the heritage place sector in local economies and the regeneration of these areas; the development of heritage foods has bolstered either a non-existent growing or manufacturing industry or contributed to it's growth; and in terms of the tourism sector, heritage has played a key role in attracting consumers to a region, country or locality.

Heritage can manifest itself in almost endless ways, for example visits to heritage sites is a growth area, interest in other cultural aspects of a country will stimulate demand for short or long visits and perhaps even a desire to reside in a particular country permanently. For example, recent research (2003) has estimated that 20% of UK people will live abroad on retirement by the year 2020 and, in 2003, 1 million were already doing so.

Insight 1.1: African-American heritage in the USA

A growing awareness of the contributions of African-Americans to the heritage of the USA is manifesting itself in almost every town and city through a range of general marketing initiatives and specific promotional material such as brochures, booklets and maps. For example, 'Alabama's Black Heritage' booklet identifies numerous sites associated with these aspects of the past across the state, by county. Other places market themselves as follows:

- Florence is the birthplace of the music legend W.C. Handy and he is commemorated every year with a week-long jazz and blues festival.
- Montgomery has many places associated with the civil rights movement, one of which is the Rosa Parks Museum. Macon has a Tubman African-American Museum.
- Junction City, Leavenworth has 'Buffalo Soldier' exhibits and monuments – the well-known and highly regarded all-black cavalry unit which fought in the Civil Right movement.
- Nicodemus is a declared National Historic Site where every July Buffalo Soldier interpreters (actors) stage a re-enactment of the fighting. Nicodemus is also the only all-black town in the USA, just west of the famous Mississippi River.
- Wichita has the Kansas African-American Museum and Lafayette and Lake Charles have issued a brochure for the public entitled *The Soul of SouthWest Louisiana* that guides people to connected African-American sites.
- Statewide (New York) also has promotional material in the shape of a brochure called *Explore New York State's Diversity* which includes a list of African-American events. New York City also has many Harlem spiritual, gospel and jazz tours.
- Westchester County has one of the USA's African-American Heritage Trails and in North Carolina, the statewide booklet *The Rich Black Heritage of African-Americans in North Carolina* lists many activities, events and celebrations that commemorate black citizens.
- Durham in North Carolina has 28 heritage sites and five music and arts festivals. New Bern has 32 sites that offer a deep look into the past connected

with its African-American citizens. Wilmington has an African-American Heritage Festival, an African-American Heritage Trail and the Upperman African-American Cultural Center.

- The Ohio Historical Society's website identifies many locations that are associated with the Underground Railroad, and Cincinnati has The National Underground Railroad Freedom Center, a 158 000 square-foot museum and learning center.
- Clermont County has a Freedom Trail and sites associated with the abolitionist movement, whilst Wilberforce has The National Afro-American Museum and Cultural Center.
- In Pennsylvania, Sugar Grove holds an Underground Railroad Convention every June when actors re-create and play the roles of notable figures associated with this building venture, notably Frederick Douglas.
- In South Carolina, *Charleston Black Heritage* is a visitor guide that presents a series of articles from the College of Charleston.
- Virginia has many cities connected with African-American heritage, such as the Booker T. Washington national monument and heritage trail in Hardy, and in Norfolk many festivals celebrate African-American heritage, such as the 'soul-food' cruise.

Cultural pursuits that attract consumers and residents include food and drink, language, art, literature or literary connections (the Balearic island of Majorca is associated with Robert Graves who wrote *I Claudius* there, Cuba is associated with the American writer E. Hemmingway and the Caribbean with the British playwright Noel Coward), music, flora and fauna, landscapes (sometimes collectively understood as the 'natural environment'), etc.

Some academics argue that the past is no longer the exclusive privilege of the upper classes or social elite and is increasingly being made accessible to all sections of society. 'The new version of the national past . . . [offers] more points of access to "ordinary people" and a wider form of belonging. Indeed, even in the case of the country house a new attention is now lavished on life "below stairs" (the servants' kitchen) while the owners themselves (or live-in trustees) are at pains to project themselves as leading private lives – "ordinary" people in family occupation. This new version of the national past is not only more democratic than earlier ones but also more feminine and domestic' (Robins, 2004: 13). In relation to the former point, there are indeed many examples of heritage attractions where the evidence of all layers of the social strata are depicted, either through models, room settings that demonstrate a 'typical' event such as the hard work in preparing a banquet for those 'upstairs', story boards, trails, photographs, paintings and so on. This idea has been the main focus for Jamaican heritage tourism where the indigenous population has wanted to show, particularly through art forms, the relationship between masters and slaves and the relative differences in the ways that these two sets of lives were lived. In other

Caribbean islands, different aspects of heritage are emphasized in the promotional literature, for example the wildlife, flora and fauna of Antigua, the seascape of St Lucia and the architectural heritage of the Dominican Republic.

With respect to the other major product grouping that we shall have as a focus, namely food and drink (in the UK the image of the 'cloth-capped' boy delivering bread; more recently an actual rather than imaginary figure from the past in the use of 'The King', i.e., Elvis Presley), many notions of heritage are used in advertising campaigns, mainly in **psychographic emotional** terms, mainly through the use of **nostalgia** (we shall be returning to this point but for the moment will contend with the fact that nostalgia filters out unpleasant aspects of the past – this links into the section on history and heritage, below).

One aspect of heritage in the UK that is increasingly being recognized by consumers (creating a demand-pull), practitioners and other stakeholders (in particular funding agencies) is sporting heritage.

In 2002, a conference was held by English Heritage (see Insight 2.3 for information about this organization) in Manchester entitled 'A Sporting Chance – Extra Time for England's Historic Sports Venues'. The conference marked a beginning in the recognition of the role that sports buildings and locations play in England's extensive and diverse sporting heritage, with the aim of developing this into a strategy for all parties concerned and, in particular, to examine what and how developments should be funded.

English Heritage involved many other bodies in its research and planning, including the British Society of Sports Historians and Sport England. This is a theme that we shall come to recognize, as governments are increasingly keen on interested parties, both large and small, public and private sector, working together in partnership for mutual benefit.

The evidence for a growth in interest in all aspects of heritage is compelling and presented in detail later in the book, but briefly for now by the number of museums that are opening on a daily basis, the increase in heritage tourism, more and more people collecting 'memorabilia' and the unprecedented demand for food and drink that has a connection, in one or more ways, with the past. In January 2005, the Qualifications and Curriculum Authority (QCA, UK) added a study of heritage to the new GCSE History curriculum, specifically to provide students with the skills that are needed in a variety of different sectors that make up the heritage industry, something that has been happening in the USA for some time (a study of Black American history is now compulsory in the USA) and in many other countries. Indeed, one of the current paradigms in heritage is the notion of multiculturalism and how the indigenous heritage does or does not resonate with these (often minority) groups; this idea can stand alone or fall within the wider notion of heritage and identity, to which I shall return below.

The notion of globalization will also be explored later in the book as there is no doubt that this is a current trend through the worldwide convergence of consumer lifestyles and behaviour and the increasing interest in, and acceptance of, different cultures and what they have to offer. This has also caught the attention of certain theorists, some of whom argue that there has been a move to a global commoditization of heritage. The well-known marketing academic Theodore Levitt suggests that there has been a 'globalisation of ethnicity – the global growth of ethnic markets, Chinese food, Pitta bread, Country and Western music, Pizza and Jazz. Now it is the turn of African music, Thai cuisine, Aboriginal painting, and so on, to be absorbed into the world market and to become cosmopolitan specialities'.

In summary, we have established that an increasing recognition of heritage is a function of postmodernism that draws upon the sense of place and can both revalidate and revitalize a local, national or international area or something connected with it. 'There is a growing interest in the embeddedness of life-histories within the boundaries of place and with the continuities of identity and community through local memory and heritage. Postmodernity will be about a sense of identity rooted in the particularity of place' (Lowenthal, 1996b: 49).

In order to understand the indigenous consumer or those that present themselves from outside, innovative/creative techniques will need to be used to shed light on the emotions connected with heritage and the fact that heritage must be **relevant** to the individual to be effective and represent something of value.

> In the face of apparent decline and disintegration, it is not surprising that the past seems a better place ... what matters is not the past but our relationship with it. As individuals, our security and identity depend largely upon the knowledge we have of our personal and family history, the language and customs which govern our social lives rely for their meaning on a continuity between past and present. The impulse to preserve the past is part of the impulse to preserve the self ... The past is the foundation of individual and collective identity, objects from the past are the source of significance as cultural symbols.
>
> (Robins, 2004: 11)

Heritage and history

History is the main academic discipline that recalls and explains aspects of the past and aims to give a factual (based on what is known at the time) account, whereas heritage marketing (as we have established above) is usually about celebrating one or more aspects of the past, which sometimes means leaving out issues that are not appropriate for the nature of a particular type of representation or the needs of the target market; on occasion this has attracted criticism. However, historical accounts and their accuracy have also been called into question from time to time, especially when they have been scrutinized by academics from other disciplines, such as anthropology or sociology.

How a nation and its past (or aspects of it) are recalled, constructed or represented must be key areas of concern for historians, marketers and any other parties involved, in particular because, in creating for a place a temporal existence, there is responsibility in terms of appropriate interpretation and sensitivity to those to whom it belongs. The heritage marketer must *understand* the people who are connected with the entity (see the reference by Jillian de Beer, below), to do this he/she must talk to them, listen to stories and accounts, gather impressions, images, artefacts and points of view. In effect, the marketer (or an agent) becomes an **ethnographer**, which could be for a considerable period of time until accounts start repeating themselves and he/she can reasonably assume that this is as good as it is going to get (see Insight 1.2, 'The Museum in the Park', for an amplification of this point).

Marketing clearly has a role to play in bringing history and aspects of the past (heritage) to the people through appropriate targeting of consumers (starting from awareness-raising through to purchase and consumption, literal or metaphorical) and suitable physical (e.g., signage, multimedia (interactive) displays and verbally, e.g., lectures, demonstrations, audio explanations, use of 'live actors') interpretation. Consumers have never been more keen than they are today to increase their personal cultural capital, and certain age/life-stage groups have never had more disposable income and time with which to achieve this (see Chapter 2).

In the next chapter I shall be discussing how history that is taught in the education sector, in particular schools and colleges, has been very much taken up by the 'heritage industry', in particular the **built environment** sector, such as castles and stately homes, either through their own initiatives or those of organizations to which one or another might belong, for example English Heritage or a similar government initiative in other countries. There is no doubt that this is of mutual benefit, as it raises visitor numbers to the heritage site or attraction and, in turn, provides a tangible or intangible insight that might not be possible in the class or lecture room. There is much evidence to suggest that people, especially children and particularly those in their early years, are more likely to remember (and possibly better understand) something that they have seen or heard rather than an issue or concept studied from a text or paper. We shall return to this point below. The Chinese philosopher Confucius said: 'I hear and I forget, I see and I remember, I experience and I understand'. (Note: Confucius' tomb in Beijing, China is a heritage attraction.)

We have established that the notion of representing history will not be straightforward. In addition to this, many practitioners at heritage sites have to balance a multitude of factors, including tangible ones (accessibility, especially for disabled people; route; theft and vandalism; opportunities for education, perhaps a classroom, etc. – though they also have to consider the opportunity cost of using this space) and intangibles, such as which period(s) to represent and, in relation to this, which aspect(s) should be permanent and if there should be temporary ones; the appropriateness of using (modern/up-to-date) technology; and so on.

There is a danger that in being customer-responsive and providing **three levels of product** (1. **core**, for example, the heritage site or heritage product itself; 2. **actual**, for example, interpretation facilities or packaging; and 3. **augmented**, the brand or 'added-value' services such as retail/shopping and eating opportunities), the heritage marketer or manager is compartmentalizing activities, whereas what customers really want is an individual experience and to provide their own interpretative slant. Another dilemma for the heritage marketer, flexibility in the provision, as far as this is practically possible, is the key to satisfying the (ever-changing) consumer.

In short, the representation of history and heritage is problematic and the heritage marketer has additional (operational/practical) problems to deal with other than the ideological ones mentioned above. 'Try to explain London's post-war development without reference to eastern Europe, try to explain its functioning without reference to the West Indies and South Asia' (Goodey, 2002).

'Wine thrown inadvertently at a valuable canvas during wedding celebrations, the ravages of a film crew are the hushed up secrets of the heritage world in the individual battle for survival' (Millar, 1999: 17).

Heritage and identity

Earlier I touched on the fact that in dealing with the heritage consumer we need to understand the notion of **identity**. Students of marketing will have come across this notion before in terms of the way that organizations have to establish a corporate identity that should be immediately recognizable by the public or markets it serves (for example, through the use of logos and possibly slogans) and be **symbolic** of something ('cheap' deals, 'added-value', philanthropic), particularly for the purposes of competitive positioning in the marketplace. Let us consider an example in relation to consumers. In survey after survey Australians always identify 'prisons' and anything to do with prisoners and prison life as an aspect of heritage that they consider to be top priority when deciding how to spend their heritage-related leisure time. Singaporeans have gradually moved away from, but never really got over, their obsession with the colonial past of the country; it is no coincidence that the foremost heritage attraction in Singapore, both for locals and visitors, is the legacy of colonialism in the shape of the (recently re-built) Raffles Hotel. Conversely, in India there is great disdain amongst the general indigenous public for most of that which has been inherited from their imperial past. The number one heritage attraction, which is also a World Heritage Site, is the Taj Mahal, built by the Mogul leader Shah Jehan in 1632.

Therefore, another approach to the concept of heritage is to recognize that it links us as individuals and groups into broader constituencies (the local community, nation, racial or religious group, group based on sexuality) or to other 'things' such as consumer brands (we shall return to this point later in subsequent chapters) which is part of **identity** making, of **nostalgic** or **nostaphobic** remembering, of **connecting with roots and origins**. 'The experience economy extends our horizons into valuing the **emotional and spiritual assets** of communities. It builds on the concepts of understanding our brand heritage, our sense of place in relation to the natural and built environment, our sense of space in the virtual environment, our dreamscape and our storytelling for current and future generations' (de Beer, 2004: 3).

However, not everyone's heritage is necessarily represented by local and national governments or by private providers, amenity groups and associations and indeed we should look critically '. . . at the ways in which particular ideas of the "nation" are created and embedded in the exhibitionary forms of a range of cultural practices and institutions, such as tourism, museums, expositions and heritage displays' (Evans, 1999). I know that some of the 'larger' institutions in the UK such as The National Trust and English Heritage are engaging with this debate but suggest that it needs a wider airing. Another view which builds on the above is that of Tunbridge and Ashworth:

> cultural aspects of the nation [need to be understood] – the ways in which our sense of nationhood and of national identity arises from arrangements of meaning-making, from symbolic practices, what it means to be and feel English (or French, Swiss, Australian, South African, Egyptian etc.) for example, is bound up with the ways those nations and regions are made tangible through repeated and recognisable symbolic forms, narratives and communication styles – in short, the sum of cultural representations that go to make up the achievement of a national identity. Our knowledge and sense of what Englishness for example, are a function of the images and narratives that constitute it, that provide it with its identity as English, rather than say, Scottish.
>
> (Tunbridge and Ashworth, 1996: 11)

Heritage inclusivity is an issue that many national governments in the current climate are concerned to address and for which financial support is increasingly being made available. Further research therefore is needed with respect to the relationship between heritage and identity (especially a greater understanding of minority groups). I believe that this will provide powerful clues for the heritage marketer and enable him/her to target niche markets more effectively. Identity is, of course, inextricably part of **personality**, which is one-half of the equation when evaluating psychographics as a segmentation variable (the other is lifestyle and lifestyle choices).

The limited information available to date has largely concerned itself with ethnic minority groups (which can represent significant numbers in many

economies). However, much more information is needed on homosexuals, as
the power of the 'pink pound' should not be underestimated and, indeed,
there will be aspects of their heritage that could prove to be lucrative opportunities for the heritage marketer. Homosexuals are already being targeted,
usually through specialist media (as are ethnic groups), to consume particular brands, the marketers of which are keen to get them on board the **ladder
of loyalty**, although there is no reason why they should not have the same
issues as mainstream consumers in terms of their mind-set or disposition
towards a particular brand, i.e., either an inept, inert or evoked mind-set.

Judy Ling Wong, OBE (one of the foremost current writers on multiculturalism) presents a very important approach to the concept of identity
(especially in relation to our personal heritage), which is that 'who we are
and what we can achieve depends on how we see ourselves against the
enormous pressure of how others see us' (Wong, 2002).

So, to begin to achieve some understanding of the importance of identity,
students and practitioners of heritage should follow through with the following questions:

1   What do we mean when we identify aspects of heritage. Can we only
    identify a spatial definition, and if so, what are the limits of this concept?
2   When does an 'on-going' foreign socio-cultural influence become
    regarded as part of a nation's (or locality's) heritage? Does it depend on
    how long it has been there or is it through simply being physically pres-
    ent? Is it through subscribing to the ways of a culturally dominant group
    or through being someone who has obvious influence on the evolution
    of a nation's (or locality's) heritage?
3   Is heritage a fixed quantity or is it re-assessed and re-constructed for
    each period?
4   How do we value mythology that we no longer identify with? Is there a
    case for the creation of new mythology?
5   Is local heritage conceived as something that is embodied in concrete arte-
    facts within a locality or the manipulated character of the landscape? Or,
    on the contrary, is it the non-manipulated character of a landscape? Is it
    considered as being also embodied in the living memory of (local) people,
    including those who bring their heritage with them when they arrive?
6   Should a (local) heritage initiative take its inspiration from existing arte-
    facts or landscapes, or to seek to identify and celebrate meaningful her-
    itage that is invisible through the creation of new artefacts?
7   Does the significance of heritage have anything to do with how old it is?
8   Who decides what is significant and meaningful?
9   Is what we present intellectually and physically accessible to all?

In the UK, very recently and particularly following the events of 11
September 2001, 'Asians', especially the 18–25 age group, are calling into

question this umbrella term that was coined by the British in India during the Imperial era. Asians in Britain are therefore increasingly asking to be addressed according to their religious identity (Muslim, Sikh, Hindu, Jain, etc.) and not for the fact that their families were **diasporized** from the Indian sub-continent, some as much as 60 years ago. If Asians in Britain represent approximately 10 per cent of the population (i.e., about 6 million people) and the different religious groups can be quantified (and identified/profiled in other ways in terms of their wants, for example geo-demographic segmentation), this will inevitably make for more effective targeting.

One example of where people have been actively engaged in an exploration of their own identity and place in the world is by the UK's National Trust's historic houses and gardens. 'London Links' was a project devised to help achieve this, particularly for those people who would not normally consider a National Trust property relevant to their lives. The project enlisted the help of professional artists who assisted four different community groups to express their feelings and attitudes towards four alternative National Trust sites using a variety of art forms; this creative process enabled the participants to engage at a deep emotional level in terms of their cultural identity and to examine issues of social exclusion.

A specific example of this project is Ham House in London. A total of 48 children aged from 6 to 16 years, all of whom had either refugee status or were asylum seekers from a diverse range of countries such as Afghanistan, Kosovo, Croatia, Somalia, Iran and Pakistan, collaborated with professional puppeteers. 'Puppetry crosses cultural boundaries and enables children to express themselves without worrying about language. The children explored the seventeenth century formal gardens, the furniture, textiles and paintings and heard stories about the history of Ham House . . . some of which mirrored their own personal experiences' (Hetherington and Andrews, 2002).

Using a different mode of communication, in this case photography and poetry, six people who had experience of homelessness explored 'what home means' at Sutton House, another National Trust property. Once again, the aim was to enable the participants to engage and express their feelings at a deep emotional level in order to reveal their innermost attitudes, even if this meant making them feel somewhat uncomfortable at times, and to relate this to the use of the house as a squat in the 1980s – **connection, association, nostophobia** were all evident in the expressions of the participants.

In early 2004, New York City Marketing (a government department responsible for the five boroughs of New York City: Brooklyn, Staten Island, Manhattan, Queens and the Bronx) briefed the world-renowned Wolff Olins corporate identity agency to 'capture its essence and promote its identity to businesses and consumers globally' (*Marketing Magazine*, 2004). The agency was required to give the city a meaningful identity beyond its main tourist attractions such as the Statue of Liberty and Times Square, to weave together its various dimensions and to focus on what the city stands for, both for the general public (businesses, tourists) and also for its own indigenous populus, in particular to rebuild civic pride following 11 September 2001.

We shall look more closely at city heritage marketing later in the book but this idea in the context of identity has been picked up by another theorist who has taken a wider economic view and states that 'the reorganisation of the international economic order has also changed the nature and role of cities . . . stimulating global competition between cities to attract ever more mobile investors . . . there is now a renewed emphasis on territorial locations as poles of identity, community and continuity . . . [there is] the emergence of a new global – local nexus'.

I am sure that the above will lead to many interesting discussions about the complexity of the notion of heritage. In your deliberations or reflections, you might want also to consider this quotation, which brings into play marketing concepts such as segmentation, targeting and positioning and summarizes much of what has been put forward in this section. 'We have come to the end . . . of one heritage, one market, one story interpretation. Quietly permeating world discussions of heritage is the realisation that we are not conserving one heritage, for one society, with one correct story, to be enjoyed by one, paying, market' (Goodey, 2002).

In order to bring together some of the elements of this chapter and to test your understanding, please study Insight 1.2 and Case study 1.1.

Insight 1.2: The Museum in the Park, Stroud, Gloucestershire, UK – the making and marketing of a museum

For almost 100 years Stroud Museum shared a purpose-built premises with the School of Science and Art. However, by the late 1980s, visitor figures were falling; and the needs of the Museum had outgrown the building in several ways:

1 there had been a huge growth in the collections but there was not enough storage space;
2 display space was also inadequate and there were no modern exhibition cases and materials;
3 lack of conservation materials and facilities, together with inadequate security arrangements made it difficult to care for the collections properly;
4 there were no facilities for schools and adult learners – access was difficult for disabled visitors;
5 there was no parking;
6 public pressure for a new Museum was increasing.

In addition, the Museums Association had set new professional ethics and standards for museums to which a response was needed. Similarly, the

Museums and Galleries Commission had introduced new Registration for museums, which meant that they now had to meet a minimum standard to get grant aid, or host temporary exhibitions from other museums.

Stroud District Museum Service is a discretionary public service provided by means of a partnership between Stroud District Council and the Cowle Trust (a registered charity). The Council provide the management and funding for the service and the Cowle Trust are the legal guardians of the collections. Their mission statement is as follows:

Inspiring people to explore the past, understand the present and imagine the future.

The aims of the service and delivery of the mission are as follows:

1   Encouraging people to find out about the people and place of Stroud district through the Collections and services.
2   Collecting and recording evidence of the lives and achievements of the people of Stroud, its special identity and environment in a time of constant change.
3   Managing the Collections to the recognized national standards to ensure their preservation for future generations.
4   Developing knowledge and expertise.
5   Providing:
    a) a place to which people will want to return
    b) a place from which people will want to explore the local environment and the world beyond
    c) cultural opportunities that act as a catalyst for learning and enjoyment.

The Museum Service plays an important role in assisting Stroud District Council to fulfil its overriding purpose, which is to make the Stroud District a better place to live and work for everyone. Four of its six corporate aims are:

1   To ensure that high-quality services are provided that meet public needs by striving for continuous improvement by:
    • challenging the need for services
    • consulting local people and service users
    • comparison with others
    • testing whether competition would bring about improvement.
2   To help build economic prosperity by providing a high-profile visitor destination and a social and cultural resource for the district.
3   To help those in particular need and to prevent and reduce crime and disorder by providing museum services that are socially inclusive.
4   To create and expand recreational and cultural opportunities through the provision of the Museum's core displays and public programme.

Getting started

In 1992, provisional Registration was granted after a Museum Development Plan was produced – this recommended two phases of development:

- Phase 1: new, centralized storage premises with conservation facilities.
- Phase 2: new displays and education facilities at a better site.

The Mansion House

Between 1992 and 1994, several potential display sites were assessed in feasibility studies.

The Mansion House, a Grade-II listed Clothier's House dating back to the 1600s was recommended after careful consideration. The following year, a single site was secured for a new Collections Management Centre. The Collections Management Centre was paid for by Stroud District Council and through grant aid from the South West Museums Council and the Museums and Galleries Commission.

Gaining control of the collections

It took two years, from 1994 to 1995, to set up the Collections Management Centre and to organize the transferral of some of the collections to the site; some objects had to be fumigated under a giant bubble whilst others were treated in the laboratory; many smaller objects had to be packed in acid-free materials and boxes – these were then colour-coded and stored according to the category of collections: archaeology, geology and social history. Larger objects from the fine and decorative art collections were stored separately. Some objects, including part of the reserve collections, are still stored at the original location.

A customized computer database was set up to record:

- what was in the collections
- the size and condition of objects
- where objects were stored
- any information from donors about the original ownership of objects as well as when, where and how they had been made and used.

Such information was crucial in deciding whether objects were selected for display, education, handling by visitors or the reserve collections.

Funding

Funding for the Museum came from three main sources.

1   *The UK's Heritage Lottery Fund.* The decision to apply for a grant was made in 1996 and a great deal of thought and planning went into the

application. Market research evidence showed that visitors would be mainly families and schools and also disclosed what local people hoped to see and experience at the new Museum; this information was crucial for the business plan. Preliminary building and display designs were drawn up. A display briefly outlined the range of objects that visitors would be able to see. Details were given of how the Museum would meet standards set by the Museums Association and the Museums and Galleries Commission. The completed application totalled 1000 pages and filled three files – six copies had to be produced. The application was submitted in June 1996. In February 1997, £1.8 million was awarded towards a £2.5 million scheme; the contract that released lottery funding was signed in December 1997.

2   *Stroud District Council.* Matching funding has come from Stroud District Council but with substantial contributions from local and national sources.

3   *The Friends of the Museum.* 'The Friends' played a major role by organizing fund-raising events. It is an association that anyone can join.

Phase 2

Transforming the Mansion House into a museum was Phase 2 of the Museum Development Plan and there was a great deal of work to be done.

Before building work could begin, the grounds of the Mansion House were excavated by archaeologists; this took place in 1998 and the first few months of 1999. Excavation showed that there had been an Iron Age settlement nearby and also revealed the remains of post-mediaeval buildings, plans of which are kept in the Museum.

The Mansion House was a fine period building but it had its faults:

- structural defects made the building unsafe
- the roof was in poor repair and needed new leading
- ceilings were collapsing
- floors and woodwork were rotten.

Museum staff and building specialists prepared detailed specifications and designs; building work would cost £1 500 000.

Construction work began on the Mansion House and its extension in March 1999. Once the roof was on, a 'Topping Out' ceremony in August 1999 celebrated the completion of the basic structure and, by December 1999, the building work was complete.

How 'green' is the museum?

The entire Mansion House has been given new life as the Museum. Wherever possible, materials were salvaged and re-used; original slab stones from the paved area outside the Mansion House have been re-laid – some bear a quarry mark and a Roman numeral denoting the original square measurement of the stone. A circular stone, perhaps once the base of a statue, has been used in the forecourt of the entrance.

The Museum features many aspects of modern museum design. Inside, these include:

- up-to-date displays with many objects on show for the first time;
- a system that monitors the environment and controls the central heating; the relative humidity is kept between 50 per cent and 60 per cent by controlling the temperature;
- display cases that keep light levels low and protect objects from the damaging effects of light;
- a play area for pre-school children;
- a lift for disabled access;
- doorways wide enough for wheelchairs and pushchairs;
- an induction loop that amplifies sound for people with hearing aids;
- staff offices.

The extension has various amenities:

- a temporary exhibitions gallery
- an education room for adults and children
- toilets and a baby-changing room
- a shop.

Outside the Museum there are 30 faces of adults and children from the Stroud District cast in bronze; they were made to show that this Museum is for the people and the local community they represent.

Moving in

Staff moved into the new building in January 2000, although most contractors were still in the process of their work.

The colours for paints, carpets and display case fabrics were chosen according to four main criteria:

1 they recalled the colours of the famous local cloth: scarlet, blue and green;
2 they reflected some of the colours of the local landscape: creamy Cotswold stone, the warm red brick from the Severn plain, the rich russets of beech woods;
3 they were known to have been used in domestic interiors during the 1700s and 1800s;
4 they were thought suitable for the themes of the displays.

The last stage was dressing the cases and display areas with graphic panels, objects and labels.

Display themes

The themes of displays are based on what is available in the collections, which means the Museum can never tell the 'whole history' of the Stroud District. The number of objects in the Museum is approximately divided as follows:

- social history   59 per cent
- numismatics   6 per cent
- geology   17 per cent
- arts   5 per cent
- archaeology   12 per cent
- natural history   1 per cent.

The displays brief

A preliminary displays brief described the criteria for selecting objects and served as a framework for in-house, freelance and volunteer researchers and the designers. It outlined the intentions of the Museum staff, which were broadly to:

- use objects to illustrate the rich and varied history of the local landscape and its people;
- illustrate, through objects, how some aspects of social and personal life are common to all cultures and periods;
- give accurate, easily understood information, without using academic language;
- encourage and inspire children and adults to learn about their heritage;
- welcome and engage visitors.

Specifically, the aims of the Museum displays brief was to:

- develop the potential of the Mansion House and Parkland setting as an appropriate and distinctive setting for Stroud District Museum's collections without subordinating the Museum to the house; the overall concept of a Museum in the Park is integral to the interpretation of the collections;
- to provide an accessible, informative, stimulating and enjoyable environment where visitors can find out about the Museum's collections and how they relate to the heritage of the Stroud District;

- to make a positive contribution to Stroud District Council's Leisure and Tourism Marketing Strategy; visitors to the area should feel it is necessary to visit the Museum to find out about the heritage of Stroud District.

The key objectives for the Museum displays brief were to ensure the concepts and themes of the displays reflected the strengths of the collections, and specifically to:

- offer an interdisciplinary interpretation – to widen the appeal of the displays to visitors who have interests other than social history;
- provide opportunities to create object-rich displays and thereby increase public access to the collections;
- demonstrate the significance of the objects as primary sources;
- illuminate the history of the district;
- encourage visitors to relate to the objects and experiences interpreted in the displays by drawing analogies with their own experiences;
- ensure that the facilities meet the expectations and needs of the target markets:
  - local teachers and schools – displays must be capable of being used for cross-curricular National Curriculum classwork and that circulation and space around the cases allows teachers and their groups to congregate easily and comfortably
  - family groups – activities such as family quizzes should be available; handling exhibits should be possible; and there should be sufficient space around displays to enable family groups to look and discuss the displays together
  - visitor comfort – seating should be strategically placed throughout the galleries that allow groups to absorb the displays quietly (or just to relieve fatigue)
- achieve a successful combination of academic and visual interpretation. In developing the brief, the Museum Displays Brief Project Team had preliminary discussions with the Museum designers to explore how the academic content could be given appropriate but stimulating visual expression;
- use varied means of communication that are suitable for visitors of varying levels of interest and abilities, such as:
  - tiered levels of written information, distinguished by use of large and emboldened captions and text panels
  - static, but stimulating, visual images and text throughout the galleries
  - interactives: judicious use of interactives to support particular topics ranging from touching and 'doing' activities to user-friendly, touch-screen computers
  - audio-visual interpretation including feature film and sound archive relating to life in the District;

- ensure that the core displays maintain visitor interest and encourage repeat visits through having:
  - sufficient content and variety for their full import to be absorbed by successive visits
  - flexible content and layout to allow elements of the core displays to be changed during their lifetime;
- ensure that the Museum was not 'just another local history museum'.

Creating the displays

The in-house and freelance researchers selected objects for display that could be clearly and easily interpreted according to particular themes.

The experiences of local people were collected in a specially commissioned Rural History Project; this was used to enrich the displays text.

Volunteer researchers helped with primary research for text and labels. Specialist designers and contractors made the display areas and cases. Sound and video recordings, and even smells, were used to recall bygone days (**nostalgia**).

Other help

Local adults and children, including members of Stroud Access Group for Disabled People, came into the Museum to look at draft layouts of text and images; some of their suggestions were used to revise the final graphic panels – others will be used in temporary exhibitions.

The Young People's Advisory Panel helped with ideas for displays, the computer interactives and fabric colours for the cases.

The Marketing Plan

The Marketing Plan for The Museum in the Park, Stroud, is clear and ambitious but the level of activity, year on year, is subject to budgetary constraints. However, the principles of marketing are applied and follow below.

Market research

As part of the initial submission to the Heritage Lottery Fund, the Council carried out extensive market research into demand for a museum in the district. The research included surveys, focus groups and desk studies and its purpose was mainly to discover what the content of the future museum should be, together with a notion of its physical shape and space.

The Council also commissioned a report from specialist Consultants on likely target markets and visitor numbers and also conducted a random telephone poll of residents to test their views on the subject of charging entry fees – this revealed that charging for entry was acceptable to the majority of people, of all ages, in the district.

The marketing environment

Although there are several museums in Gloucestershire, The Museum in the Park had only limited competition because of its geographical location and content; no other museum catered for the whole of the district.

Indeed, the view of the curators was that the presence of other museums, showing different aspects of the county's heritage were a positive factor in encouraging overall visits.

The museums in Gloucestershire work in collaboration through the Gloucestershire Museums group (GM). GM 'promotes and enhances professional standards within the sector and increases awareness and enjoyment of museums amongst the public'; specifically, it provides:

- free training sessions for museum staff;
- a forum for sharing/communicating information about developments and initiatives involving museums both locally and nationally;
- opportunities for member museums to discuss/develop partnership and networking initiatives;
- an opportunity for a regular point of contact with Gloucestershire Tourism, for the mutual sharing of information. The objective of this is to raise the profile of Gloucestershire museums as visitor attractions. Gloucestershire Tourism assists individual museums in promoting their services and employs a press officer who assists museums in, for example, writing press releases relating to new initiatives/temporary exhibitions/events etc.

GM is grant-aided by Gloucestershire County Council and the South West Museum's Council but it is likely to become increasingly autonomous, relying on private fund-raising and grants from other sources; this will increase the scope of the group.

The presence in the county of large numbers of tourists is another positive factor. The industry is well developed in the county and marketing is mainly aimed at the cultural short-break market; Stroud District Council communicates through a high-quality brochure that is distributed through Tourist Information Centres, by direct mail and by the county marketing consortium.

The target market

The principal audiences for the Museum have been identified as families and children, although the Museum is of, and for, the whole district. The secondary target is visitors to the district and adult learners.

The current population of the district is approximately 108 000 people, of which 26 per cent are under 16 years of age.

Each year the district receives up to 2 million visitors from all forms of tourism. The main visitor attractions in the district are concentrated in two 'zones': Slimbridge/Berkley and Painswick/Prinknash. The Museum in the Park is geographically located between these two zones but visitors have been difficult to attract, for two reasons:

1   there are few opportunities to visit, and
2   visitors are mainly in the area for short breaks.

However, in spite of the potential difficulties of creating an audience beyond the locality, marketing objectives were set, in 2001, as follows.

1   To attract 16 000 visitors in the first full year of operation and maintain this number in subsequent years.
2   To attract 75 group visits in the first full year of operation and 100 in each year thereafter.
3   To achieve £40 000 income in each year at 2000 prices.
4   To ensure that the average 'satisfaction rating' is 8 out of 10, or more.
5   To achieve a return visit rate within one year of: 10 per cent primary catchment (Stroud District); 20 per cent primary school groups; 10 per cent secondary school groups.
6   To ensure that 95 per cent of residents of Stroud District are aware of the Museum.
7   To align the demographic profile of the visitors with that of the district over 5 years, making progress in each year.

The product, services, relationship marketing, corporate identity and branding

The Museum in the Park aims to reflect and interpret life in the south Cotswolds and Severn Vale, seeking to define its distinctive qualities and explain why it is what it is. It does this in a lively and diverse way, by using objects and creating a multilayered, multisensory environment in which they are interpreted; it is not a repository of things that are no longer used, but a mirror on society. The Museum is housed in an historic building that is itself an interpretable object, located in the middle of the ancient Stratford Park in Stroud.

The design of the displays and of the new elements of the building is reflective of the architectural and craft styles that characterize the district. The Museum itself becomes a part of its own story in the way in which it draws together heritage, the present and the potential of the future held in the present.

The Museum delivers its services in a number of ways and one can begin to identify aspects of **relationship marketing** in this provision:

- collecting and caring for the heritage of the Stroud District
- developing and sharing expertise
- providing a high standard of facilities and a venue for the short-/long-term display of objects from the Museum's collections and from other national and international sources
- providing an exhibition programme
- delivering a programme of educational and cultural activities
- enhancing the museum experience by providing a shop
- providing a venue for educational, cultural and social events, for example weddings.

The Museum has developed a new **corporate identity** that defines the product and embodies the values of the service in a distinct **brand**; this is in the form of a logo of a cockerel, which is an object in the Museum's collections and is used in the design of:

- corporate stationery
- staff call cards
- corporate invitations
- the Museum's general marketing leaflet
- sticky labels for children's Museum activities/competitions, etc.
- packaging for items sold in the Museum shop
- personalized items sold in the Museum shop
- packaging for food products sold at the kiosk
- staff and volunteer name badges
- displays for external notice boards at the Museum
- posters/external banners advertising exhibitions and events
- feedback systems for market research.

Implementation

Specific activities to implement the plan included the following:

- recruitment of commercial agent/consultant responsible for marketing;
- creation and presentation of external signage system;
- familiarization tours for staff of Gloucestershire Tourist Information Centres, accommodation providers, local press, registrars, potential corporate bookers, etc.;
- preparation of information about educational provision at the Museum and submission to GlosNet for inclusion in the new Education in Gloucestershire Museums website;

- creation of The Museum in the Park website, initially as a promotional tool but subsequently as an information/research/educational resources site; the Museum website was linked to both GlosNet and the 24-hour Museum websites;
- customer care procedures;
- staff training in customer care;
- provision of editorial copy for local newspapers to promote the cockerel logo;
- development of contacts with possible exhibition and event collaborators – organizers of local festivals, etc.;
- developing contacts with possible partnership organizations for education initiatives;
- identification of relevant local, regional and national 'whats on' type programmes/features/pages and attempts to have the museum's activities included;
- providing an on-going special events programme to complement the exhibition programme;
- ensuring that both Stroud District Council's Information Officer and Gloucestershire's Tourism officers are fully informed about on-going developments in the Museum's public programme; forwarding of copies of all editorials to Gloucestershire Tourism for inclusion on their website.

Monitoring and evaluation

For The Museum in the Park this is an on-going activity and specifically consists of the following:

- visitor analysis database – hour by hour record of visitor numbers, notes on weather, etc. (see data below);
- monthly review of visits and income from various sources against marketing objectives;
- regular user survey forms with qualitative and quantitative data, including record of where visitors heard of the Museum, to allow for review of information channels;
- a marketing review group within the Museum, together with corporate representatives to meet quarterly to review success of marketing against objectives, review of the objectives themselves and to create an annual marketing plan.

Museum in the Park data

By kind permission and acknowledgment: Abigail Large/Elizabeth Eliot, The Museum in the Park, Stroud, Gloucestershire, UK, 2004.

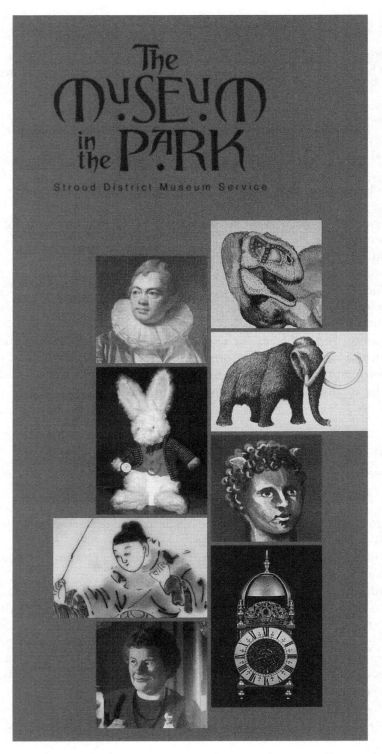

Figure 1.2 The Museum in the Park brochure. Courtesy of The Museum in the Park, Stroud, Gloucestershire.

Figure 1.3 The Museum in the Park logo. Courtesy of The Museum in the Park, Stroud, Gloucestershire.

Table 1.1 Summary of visitor numbers for financial year 2001–2002

	April–June 2001	July–Sept 2001	Oct–Dec 2001	Jan–March 2002	2001–2002 TOTALS
TOTAL NUMBER OF VISITORS	**4144**	**2975**	**2169**	**2423**	**11711**
School Groups – Number of Pupils	**450**	**255**	**184**	**382**	**1271**
School Groups – Number of Teachers	not recorded	not recorded	16	32	48
Other Groups	438	76	76	22	612
Visitors attending Museum Events	not recorded	130	131	283	544
Public Bookings	not recorded	62	61	67	190
MUSEUM VISITS	**3256**	**2452**	**1701**	**1637**	**9046**
Single Visit Ticket Sales					
Adult	1095	773	296	516	2680
Child	660	450	129	303	1542
Concession	1013	862	283	273	2431
Complimentary	24	29	707	292	1052
Season Ticket Sales					
Adult	20	22	1	0	43
Child	71	36	4	0	111
Concession	0	1	4	0	5
Family	85	27	10	2	124

Continued

Table 1.1 Summary of visitor numbers for financial year 2001–2002 (continued)

	April–June 2001	July–Sept 2001	Oct–Dec 2001	Jan–March 2002	2001–2002 TOTALS
Couple	19	14	2	0	35
FSM Adult	0	0	0	0	0
FSM Child	0	0	0	0	0
FSM Family	0	0	0	0	0
STC Adult	2	2	1	0	5
STC Concession	7	5	0	0	12
STC Family	4	7	0	0	11
STC Free	55	6	3	1	65
Season Ticket Repeat Visits					
Adult	37	35	22	39	133
Child	42	49	16	1	108
Concession	0	7	8	16	31
Family	111	103	196	170	580
Couple	11	24	19	20	74
STC				4	4
TILL COUNTER TOTALS	4403	3196	1732	1592	10 923

NB: Admission charges dropped from April 2002.

Table 1.2 2002 Calendar year summary of visitor numbers

	Totals	January	February	March	April	May	June	July	August	September	October	November	December
General	**19 434**	451	591	595	2289	1910	4672	1356	3425	1154	1516	726	749
Groups	**54**	0	0	22	0	0	0	0	11	0	21	0	0
School Groups – Pupils	**1366**	158	66	158	183	393	96	85	0	30	122	43	32
School Groups – Adults	**193**	15	4	13	15	65	20	13	0	8	24	10	6
Museum Events	**1453**	97	127	126	12	0	289	161	294	186	0	119	42
TOTAL VISITORS	**22 500**	721	788	914	2499	2368	5077	1615	3730	1378	1683	898	829

Table 1.3 2003 Calendar year summary of visitor numbers

	Totals	January	February	March	April	May	June	July	August	September	October	November	December
General	**19 827**	966	1514	1452	2303	2552	1438	2201	2825	1335	1929	1067	245
Groups	102	0	0	0	34	0	27	4	19	7	11	0	0
School Groups – Pupils	**396**	0	12	18	87	0	56	99	0	55	34	35	0
School Groups – Adults	**86**	0	4	6	20	0	11	23	0	9	8	5	0
Museum Events	**1708**	58	161	20	61	266	52	305	354	0	264	167	0
TOTAL VISITORS	**22 119**	1024	1691	1496	2505	2818	1584	2632	3198	1406	2246	1274	245
Exhibition Visitors (incl. above)	7017	448	623	927	1216	483	831	0	880	450	461	670	28
Paid	914	380	N/A	N/A	N/A	N/A	N/A	N/A	336	198	N/A	N/A	N/A
Free	6068	68	588	927	1216	483	831	N/A	544	252	461	670	28

CASE STUDY 1.1: Hidden Ireland

'Hidden Ireland' was created in 1987 to enable visitors to experience a short or long stay in private 'heritage houses' located in many different parts of Ireland. By 1999 its members had grown to 43, each of whom owns a house of architectural and historical importance. The members benefit from being included in an overall marketing strategy, a central booking facility and as a lobby to the government; they also benefit from the knowledge-base generated by Hidden Ireland regarding architectural conservation and environmental restoration, specifically in relation to historic gardens.

Hidden Ireland is now a limited company and has recently developed its market by allowing self-catering accommodation to join the network. Every place uses the history, heritage and possibly natural assets as cornerstones of their marketing strategy; although the houses in the Hidden Ireland network vary in size, most of them are set in estates or parklands with their own unique ecosystems. In some cases, for example, Bantry House, Co. Cork, the owners have been the recipients of environmental awards and financial aid from Bord Failte (Ireland's National Tourist Board) to restore the architectural and environmental heritage of the houses and their surroundings.

Hidden Ireland has established formal relations with Bord Failte and has links with 'Europe of the Traditions', a European network of heritage houses that it helped to establish.

Acknowledgment: Ireland Promotion Unit (CPPU) and University College, Cork, 2004.

Questions

1 What are the benefits to the owner of a 'heritage house' from joining a network such as Hidden Ireland?
2 On what sorts of issues could this network lobby the government?
3 Who would be in the market for a concept such as Hidden Ireland? Explain and briefly evaluate each one.

Summary

In this chapter we have established how the definition of marketing can be used in a heritage context and have explored some of the philosophical and intellectual discourses about heritage as a generic concept.

Heritage is a contentious and much debated notion in the literature but, if we distinguish it from history in that marketing efforts seek to celebrate the past rather than re-tell it, there must be room for us all, and may marketers long be challenged about their heritage provision.

The literature on marketing is clear about the centrality of the consumer and consequently understanding his or her behaviour is the key to success, whether this is to be measured in quantitative or qualitative terms. In particular, the notion of personal identity will become increasingly important as a means of understanding consumer behaviour, which will give rise to niche marketing opportunities/emerging markets. At the very least it should create a greater degree of awareness and sensitivity on the part of the heritage marketer in understanding what is appropriate in terms of the needs of the customer.

Discussion questions and activities

1   Briefly define the terms Marketing and Heritage.
2   Explain your understanding of these terms.
3   Heritage can cover any aspect of life, give some examples.
4   Look up the National Trust, government department or equivalent in your country (or another country) on the World Wide Web and briefly summarize its aims.
5   Consider some aspects of heritage in your country and discuss which of the following should take priority:
   • education
   • conservation
   • preservation
   • restoration.

Recommended reading

Amery, C. and Cruickshank, D. (1975) *The Rape of Britain*. Routledge, London.

Appandurai, A. (ed.) (1986) *The Social Life of Things: Commodities in Cultural Perspective*. Cambridge University Press, London.

Ashworth, G. (2003) *Heritage: Management, Interpretation, Identity*. Continuum Books, London.

Ashworth, G. and Howard, P. (eds) (1999) *European Heritage Planning and Management*. Intellect, Bristol.

Boniface, P. and Fowler, P. (1993) *Heritage and Tourism in the 'Global Village'*. Routledge, London.

Cohen, E. (1988) Authenticity and commoditization in tourism. *Annals of Tourism Research*, 15, 19.

Cormack, P. (1978) *Heritage in Danger*. Second edition. Quartet, London.

de Beer, J. (2004) *Community Aspiration and Authentic Expression*. de Beer Marketing and Communications, Auckland, New Zealand.

Dibb, S. and Simkin, L. *et al.* (2002) *Marketing Concepts, Techniques and Strategies*. Houghton Mifflin, London.

Edensor, T. (1997) National identity and the politics of memory: remembering Bruce and Wallace in symbolic space. *Environment and Planning: Society and Space*, 29, 23.

Evans, J. (1999) Nation and representation. In Evans, J. and Boswell, D. (eds) *Representing the Nation: A Reader: Histories, Heritage and Museums*. Routledge, London.

Goodey, B. (2002) Re-visioning the past for the future. *Interpretation Journal*, 7(2).

Herbert, D.T. (ed.) (1995) *Heritage, Tourism and Society*. Pinter, London.

Hetherington, L. and Andrews, P. (2002) Connecting people through place. *Interpretation Journal*, 7(2).

Hobsbawm, E. (1983) *The Invention of Tradition*. Cambridge University Press, London.

Kirshenblatt-Gimblett, B. (1998) *Destination Culture: Tourism, Museums and Heritage*. University of California Press, Berkeley CA.

Lowenthal, D. (1996a) *The Heritage Crusade and Spoils of History*. Viking, London.

Lowenthal, D. (1996b) *The Past is a Foreign Country*. Cambridge University Press, London.

MacInnes, L. and Wickham-Jones, C. (eds) (1992) *All Natural Things: Archaeology and the Green Debate*. Oxbow Books, London.

Millar, S. (1999) Co-ordination, co-operation and collaboration: operations management – the neglected heritage profession. *Interpretation Journal*, 4(3).

Prentice, R. (1993) *Tourism and Heritage Attractions*. Routledge, London.

Robins, K. (2004) In Boswell, D. and Evans, J. (eds) *Tradition and Translation, National Culture in its Global Context in Representing the Nation: A Reader*. Routledge, London.

Samuel, R. (1989) *Patriotism: the Making and Unmaking of British National Identity. Volume 1*. Routledge, London.

Swain, H. (ed.) (1993) *Rescuing the Historic Environment – Archaeology, the Green Movement and Conservation Strategy for the British Landscape*. Routledge, London.

Tunbridge, J.E. and Ashworth, G.E. (1996) *Dissonant Heritage: The Management of the Past as a Resource in Conflict*. Wiley, London.

Wong, J.L. (2002) Who we are. *Interpretation Journal*, 7(2).

Chapter 2

Environmental factors

Social factors

In every country social factors change over time. This creates dynamism in the market – ever-moving goal posts on which the heritage marketer must keep a watchful eye. For example, in the recent change-over from one Millennium to the next, in the UK and USA there was an almost instantaneous explosion of 'Bollywood' culture, which up to that point in time had largely been the preserve of the Asian community. Films, musicals, increased variety and availability of ethnic foods were just some of the changes seen in the market that have continued for approximately five years. However, there is clear evidence that consumers are keen to be challenged by a different culture and therefore, especially in the UK, the current demand is for all things Thai and, soon, Vietnamese (the latter food culture has been the mainstay of ethnic 'eating out' in France for many years).

Other areas of popular culture in which aspects of heritage have played a part are music, literature, television dramas and art. For example, classical music has come to the mass markets of the world in the shape of Nigel Kennedy, a British violinist, Bond, an all female quartet and, most recently, Il Divo, a band of four male opera singers from various European countries. Although Kennedy plays mostly in the classical style, his 'youth' and *avant-garde* looks and dress sense made him more accessible to audiences that previously might not have considered listening to this type of music. Similarly, the latter two bands are also relatively young but have changed the dynamics of classical music and opera, respectively, to make it more 'easy listening' than would otherwise be the case – their CDs have sold in millions.

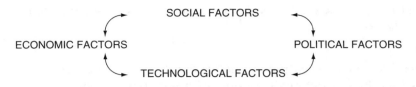

Figure 2.1 The main environmental factors that impact on heritage marketing.

In terms of literature, the 'classic' novels are as popular today as they have always been and contemporary writers who reflect aspects of the heritage of their country are read all over the world. For example, authors such as J.K. Rowling with the *Harry Potter* books that reveal life in a British boarding school (albeit one that largely teaches witchcraft!); Isabel Allende who reflects on aspects of South American heritage; and also travel writers who might be based in a country for a short while but are able to examine its heritage and provide us with (often amusing) accounts, such as the books by William Dalrymple who writes mainly on India.

'Period costume dramas' are watched by global audiences and continue to sell for many years after they have been shown on network television or at the cinema, through Video and DVD packs available both in retail outlets and online – many producers have advocated that it is the retail sales that enable production costs to be recovered. Costume dramas such as *Gone with the Wind*, and others made specifically for television such as Jane Austen's *Pride and Prejudice* and Thackeray's *Vanity Fair*, have been successful because they offer us an intimate view of the relationships between people at all levels in society, especially at a time when the levels were more pronounced (or perhaps less exposed by the media) than they are today. The demand for voyeurism is at an all-time high, based on fact or fiction. All of these examples illustrate heritage marketing in practice.

Further to this, there is an increasing desire by consumers in many countries to live in the countryside, either that of their own country or of other nations. The aspiration to live in a 'period property' has been a trend in many European countries for several years and looks as if it will continue as consumers perceive this to be one of the factors in their **quality of life index**. Both of these psychograpic factors and other segmentation variables will be discussed more fully in the next chapter.

Heritage gains popularity

All at once heritage is everywhere . . . in the news, in the movies, in the marketplace . . . in everything . . . it is the chief focus of patriotism and a prime lure of tourism. One can barely move without bumping into a heritage site. Every legacy is cherished. From ethnic roots to history theme parks, Hollywood to

> the Holocaust, the whole world is busy lauding . . . or lamenting . . . some past,
> be it fact or fiction.
>
> (Lowenthal, 1996)

Lowenthal's view, even though he was writing almost a decade ago, confirms that there is definitely an upward trend, both in people appreciating that heritage is important at one level and, at another, that significant strides are being made not to lose aspects of the past (through redevelopment, theft and vandalism) by a variety of different stakeholder groups, some profit-motivated, others not.

In the previous chapter we began to establish that there is a growing appetite around the world for many different aspects of heritage. With increased national and local government backing, there has never been a better time to engage in heritage marketing, both for quantitative and qualitative reasons, in order to generate a surplus or to make a profit. However, compared with most sectors of an economy, in general the heritage sector in most countries remains underfunded, especially museums and in particular salaries for employees who work in museums. There is also a shortage of craftspeople skilled in conservation and restoration, which will compound the problems of the built heritage sector in the future.

But what is the evidence of increasing consumer demand for aspects of heritage, indigenous or otherwise?

A statement made in a press release from the UK's National Trust on 26 November 2003 states that '. . . heritage is as popular as ever, with growing support, increasing visitor numbers [and that] . . . by involving people in caring for their heritage, they take more pride in their local area'. In a press release dated 12 February 2004, Fiona Reynolds, the Trust's Director-General, stated 'The public demand for heritage and for a well maintained and diverse natural environment is enormous'. Despite the esteem and respect with which national trusts around the world are held, this statement alone is not evidence enough.

In 2000, the UK government under the auspices of the Secretary of State for Culture, Media and Sport (the government department largely responsible for the heritage of England, Wales and Northern Ireland, which is largely administered by English Heritage) and the Secretary of State for the Environment, Transport and the Regions, created an 'Historic Environment Steering Group' (there were 20 members from diverse backgrounds) chaired by Sir Neil Cossons (who was also the Chair of English Heritage at the time), in order to lead a review of policies relating to the historic environment of England.

The result was a publication entitled *Power of Place: The Future of the Historic Environment* (2000). The research and consultation process was both wide-ranging (in terms of aspects of heritage considered and respondent profiles) and extensive. MORI (the market research agency) were used for the qualitative aspects of investigation, namely to determine peoples' attitudes to the historic environment and of the value they place upon it. Five main messages were advocated as a result of the findings:

1 Most people place a high value on the historic environment. 87 per cent think it is right that there should be public funding to preserve it. 85 per cent think it is important in the regeneration of towns and cities. 77 per cent disagree that too much is preserved. It is seen as a major contributor to the quality of life.
2 Because people care about their environment, they want to be involved in decisions affecting it, and, in a multicultural society, everybody's heritage needs to be recognized.
3 The historic environment is seen by most people as a totality. They value places, not just a series of individual sites and buildings; what people care about is the whole of their environment – this has implications for the way we identify and value significance.
4 Everyone has a part to play in caring for the historic environment. Central and local government are critical; so too are amenity societies, community groups, owners, developers, professionals in the field, schools and universities – more will be achieved if we work together in partnership.
5 Everything rests on sound knowledge and understanding. Good history is history that is based on thorough research and is tested and refined through open debate; it accommodates multiple narratives and takes account of the values people place on their surroundings.

MORI's survey of 3000 people in England, which was part of the research process, presented the following conclusions:

- 98 per cent think that all schoolchildren should be given the opportunity to find out about England's historic environment (this is discussed more fully in Chapter 3);
- 96 per cent think that the historic environment is important to teach them about the past (see examples in the next chapter);
- 88 per cent think that it is important in creating jobs and boosting the economy (the regeneration or multiplier effects);
- 87 per cent think that it is right that there should be public funding to preserve it;
- 85 per cent think that it is important in promoting regeneration in towns and cities;
- 77 per cent disagree that we preserve too much;
- 76 per cent think that their own lives are richer for having the opportunity to visit or see it;
- 75 per cent think that the best of our post-war building should be preserved, rising to 95 per cent of the 16–24 age group.

There are many additional points made in the publication but, for the purposes of this book and as generic principles that can be used in any country context as food for thought, the following are most relevant.

- Like people, places have to evolve, react and grow – there must be a balance in the need to care for the historic environment with the need for change. 'Redevelopments which are inspired by the identity of an area can capture a uniqueness which draws people long after the fizz of new buildings has passed' (Wilkie, 2000).
- We need to understand better the character of places and the value and significance people ascribe to them.
- Heritage organizations must work more in partnership. The National Trust, the Council for British Archaeology, the Civic Trust, Save, the national amenity societies and their local counterparts have done much to build public consciousness of the issues as well as providing an unrivalled source of specialist knowledge and detailed local scrutiny. The Heritage Lottery Fund has made substantial new resources available, promoted a wider view of heritage and placed a new emphasis on education and improved access.
- The historic environment is an irreplaceable asset representing the investment of skills and resources over centuries. It gives places a unique competitive advantage; it generates jobs; it attracts people to live in an area, businesses to invest and tourists to visit.
- Conservation-led regeneration encourages private-sector investment.
- Most historic buildings are fully capable of economic use. Listing (see below) often adds to the value of private houses. In 1998 the investment return on listed office property was 11.9 per cent compared with 11.4 per cent for unlisted property. The **intangible value** of using well-loved buildings that add character to an area is difficult to measure but is recognized by individuals and businesses.
- Historic landscape confers economic advantage – it stimulates tourism and enables farm diversification. The Countryside Agency's 'Eat The View' campaign is using the quality of the rural environment to support farmers' markets (see Chapter 3) and create **additional marketing opportunities** such as 'Made in the High Weald'.
- Conservation and regular building and maintenance create long-term, sustainable jobs. Pound for pound, repair and maintenance of heritage buildings create more employment than new-build.
- Tourism can be a great catalyst for regeneration in both countryside and urban areas; historic buildings and landscapes have been saved by adapting them creatively and sympathetically for tourism.
- Regeneration budgets are set to grow by an average of 15 per cent per year. Regeneration can provide the basis for the **regional branding** of agricultural produce and manufactured goods.

- English Heritage and the Commission for Architecture and the Built Environment (CABE) must work closely together to ensure that the benefits of both old and new are fully respected and integrated in all significant new development schemes.
- People are interested in heritage but many feel powerless and excluded. The historical contribution of their group in society is not celebrated; their personal heritage does not appear to be taken into account by those who take decisions – if the barriers to involvement can be overcome, the historic environment has the potential to strengthen the sense of community and provide a solid base for neighbourhood renewal; this is the power of place.
- Priority should be given to schools – this will establish long-term foundation and lifelong interest. This captive audience's attitudes can be shaped for life.
- Museums, libraries and archives are central to any initiative to introduce people to the historic environment. Archaeological collections are essential to interpret sites and field monuments. Social history collections explain how buildings were used. Rural life museums hold tools that help explain the history of the countryside. Some museums and galleries are housed in historic buildings and, in some cases, a whole historic entity – a building in its landscape with its content – is managed as a museum.
- Other people find themselves excluded from enjoying aspects of heritage as a result of disabilities; this covers access to information as well as intellectual and physical access to historic properties. English Heritage has developed best practice in the difficult area of reconciling the needs of people with disabilities with alteration to historic fabric. The Disability Rights Commission expects that, with the Disability Rights Act, 2004, best practice in considering the needs of people with disabilities will become normal practice.

Finally, the Steering Committee presented a number of recommendations for the heritage industry, which included the following.

1 Find out what people value about their heritage and why, and take this into account in assessing significance.
2 Create an electronic network of information about the historic environment accessible to professional and public alike, linked to 'Culture Online' (an initiative of the Department for Culture, Media and Sport).
3 Develop local 'heritage links' (see Insight 4.6 'The King Harry Maritime Trail') bringing together non-governmental organizations, agencies and local government.
4 Ensure that heritage professionals have the skills and training to involve people in decisions, think creatively and find solutions to problems.

5   Owners of heritage attractions should provide facilities and educational material to encourage visits by schools and community groups (see Chapter 4 for a full discussion and examples of good practice).

Following on from *Power of Place* (2000) and a subsequent publication *A Force for Our Future* (2001) the UK Government has recently published a consultation paper entitled *Protecting our Historic Environment: Making the System Work Better*, which has the overall aim of setting out a vision for the historic environment and, specifically, the need to review heritage designations and protection schemes as they are considered to be too onerous, too complex and too inflexible and also lack the capacity to cope with the number of buildings or monuments that ought to be listed. The paper is part of a wider review into how England's historic buildings and monuments should be statutorily protected. The proposals have implications for all areas connected with the historic environment and include:

1   listed buildings
2   conservation areas
3   scheduled monuments
4   registered parks and gardens
5   registered battlefields
6   World Heritage Sites.

Insight 2.1 gives a detailed account of the National Trust which has been largely responsible (together with English Heritage, see the section on political factors) for the acquisition, preservation/restoration and marketing of different aspects of heritage, mainly buildings, monuments and landscapes. In many ways it is a model organization and many countries around the world have used it to create their own systems of heritage preservation and funding. The details below will continue to provide evidence of the case for the rising interest in many aspects of heritage, in particular the built environment and natural landscapes.

Insight 2.1: The National Trust, UK

In 2004, the National Trust became Europe's largest conservation organization with over 3.3 million members. Membership increased by 20 per cent between 2001 and 2003 and the Trust is now a larger organization than all the UK political parties and the Church of England combined. On average, in 2003, three new members joined the National Trust every two minutes. A total of 12.7 million people visited National Trust pay-for-entry sites; this latter statistic is of significance to marketers as it is often argued that the public will not visit heritage or historical sites (for example museums, etc.) if entry charges are levied (we shall return to this underpricing consideration later in the book).

The National Trust was founded in 1895 by three Victorian philanthropists. They set up the Trust out of concern over the impact of uncontrolled development and industrialization, so that it would act as a guardian for the nation in the acquisition and protection of threatened coastline, countryside and buildings. The Trust owns over 248 000 ha of countryside in England, Wales and Northern Ireland (there is a separate National Trust for Scotland), over 600 miles of coastline and more than 200 buildings and gardens, most of which are held indefinitely, securing their long-term future.

The National Trust is a registered charity and independent of the British government, relying mainly on the help of volunteers and donations from the public. It has developed into a large organization, employing a range of salaried specialists (including marketing) as well as contracting out some of its unique needs for restoration and preservation of buildings, monuments, gardens and so on.

From its humble origins and as a result of its growth both in membership volume and revenue through subscriptions, site entry charges and income earned from the sale of other goods and services, for example through their mail-order catalogue (collectively known as National Trust Enterprises) and donations, there is no doubt that the Trust has become a powerful force in the UK and is using this to protect, preserve and enhance a range of projects, mainly for public use. It continuously lobbies government departments and agencies and has partnered its government-funded counterpart, English Heritage (see below).

Year End membership figures:

1983	1.1 million
1984	1.5 million
1991	2.1 million
1995	2.3 million
1999	2.5 million
2003	3.1 million

Income from membership, admission and legacies increased as follows:

	2001/2002	2002/2003
Membership	£66.8m	£75.6m
Admission fees	£8.5m	£10.7m
Legacies	£39.0m	£45.1m

The contribution from National Trust Enterprises increased from £10.4m to £11.5m over the same period.

The track record of the National Trust in raising revenue for heritage projects has undoubtedly been very successful and currently the organization is turning its attention towards some of the more finer aspects of marketing in order to '. . . build a more user-friendly image with advertising that high-lights some of the unique stories involving its properties and gardens. The 1.5 million press, outdoor and radio initiative is intended to draw in 12 million visitors by presenting its sites as appealing and relevant options for a day out' (Tylee, 2003).

The objective of this marketing communications campaign is to sustain the interest of regular visitors but also to **leverage** the brand and promote it to people who have not visited National Trust (NT) sites. Clearly there is money to be made and the NT is going for a slice of consumer leisure-time spend. Other ways in which the NT has marketed its brand are with the following types of appeal (NT press release, 9 September 2003):

> In addition to membership, you can help the National Trust in its ongoing conservation work in many ways:
>
> - By visiting the many houses and gardens, coast and countryside properties, and spending money in our shops, tea-rooms and restaurants nationwide
> - By donating to our appeals such as the Neptune Coastline Campaign, the Lake District Appeal or other NT projects of special significance to you
> - By becoming a Patron or Benefactor, which would mean you would be invited to a programme of special, private events
> - By buying raffle tickets, by staying in one of 300 beautiful NT holiday cottages or by buying tickets to our extensive range of concerts and events
> - By volunteering to help on a range of tasks from room stewarding to participating in a Working Holiday
> - By making provision for the National Trust in your Will as a lasting gift. Every sum, no matter how small, is welcomed and not a single penny of any legacy gift is ever spent on administration. Choose, too, where you want your money to be spent – on a place or property that has special significance to you.

The National Trust is also capable of extending its message beyond national boundaries, in particular for special projects. For example, in 2002, the Trust launched an unprecedented appeal to raise approximately £8.2 million in order to purchase a property near Bristol, UK called Tyntesfield. The Trust considered this building and its contents to be of considerable historical and architectural importance and wanted it intact, eventually for enjoyment by the public. The Tyntesfield campaign gained international recognition through representation in the media and **specific target marketing** by the Trust, both in the UK and overseas. More than 12 000 public donations were received from countries such as America, Canada, Australia and

New Zealand and many other organizations also responded to the campaign. On the strength of this, in September 2003, the National Trust won the 'Fundraising Campaign of the Year Award'.

National Trust properties and other assets are often featured on television programmes and they have exploited links with other (intangible) aspects of heritage, such as 'nostalgia' (we shall be returning to this concept), most recently through the acquisition of Sindy Dolls and their presentation at museums with the aim of '. . . helping visitors to recall childhood memories' (Alex Youel, Head of Customer Services, the National Trust, 2004).

Insight 2.2: National trusts or equivalent in other countries

Further 'national trusts' and a synopsis of each are presented below.

- The National Trust of Australia has as its strapline 'Inspiring Australians to conserve our heritage for the future' and identifies itself as a non-profit, non-governmental organization supported by its members. It seems to support almost every aspect of Australian heritage, from art, literature and historical buildings through to animal conservation, antiques and other collectables.
- The equivalent in the USA is known as the National Trust for Historic Preservation, which is 'a privately funded non-profit organization that provides leadership, education and advocacy to save America's diverse historic places and revitalise our communities'. It is interesting that they have in their mission statement a link between heritage and regeneration but perhaps not surprising, given the capitalist nature of this economy(!). The website highlights a wide range of activities including preservation (for which tax breaks are available), study tours and the recent acquisition of a twentieth-century house that will become a museum.
- The Indian National Trust for Art and Cultural Heritage (INTACH) is a nationwide, non-profit organization founded in 1984 with the aim of protecting and conserving India's natural and cultural heritage. I think it is probably fair to say that India's natural and cultural heritage, individually, let alone combined, is far 'greater' than all its magnificent buildings and artistic treasures, of which it does have a great many.
- Jersey has a heritage trust whose mission is to care for and promote wide access to all aspects of the island's heritage. The Trust was founded in 1981 and is an independent organization but which receives an annual subsidy from the States of Jersey in order to help with costs. The Trust is very keen to support scientific and technological research as the trustees believe that this helps to create a better understanding of the contribution that heritage preservation makes to society by emphasizing issues such as heritage value, cultural tourism, cultural identity, quality of life,

urban planning, maintenance and whole life costs, economic competi-
tiveness and wealth creation.

- The Heritage Council of Ireland was founded out of the Heritage Act,
  1995. The role of the Council is to propose policies and priorities for the
  identification, protection, preservation and enhancement of the
  national heritage. They define the national heritage to include monuments, archaeological objects, heritage objects such as art and industrial
  works, documents and genealogical records, architectural heritage,
  flora, fauna, wildlife habitats, landscapes, seascapes, wrecks, geology,
  heritage gardens, parks and inland waterways. The Council regards its
  main task to be the promotion of interest, education, knowledge and
  pride in the national heritage. The Council was funded from the
  National Lottery's Heritage Fund, which has enabled them to support
  many projects: 171 between 1992 and 1995, including:
  - the industrial archaeological interpretation project at Foxford
    Woollen Mills
  - the conservation of the State's geological collection by the Geological
    Survey of Ireland
  - a stone axe project
  - the establishment of a Field Study Laboratory at Millstreet County
    Park by the Irish Peatland Conservation Council.

Political factors

There is no doubt that the economic value of heritage cannot be underestimated (see below) and this has not escaped the notice of governments
around the world.

An article in *The Times* newspaper (London) in October 2004 confirmed a
number of the issues that we have established above and that will be further
amplified in this section, notably that more people than ever are interested
in heritage sectors. When asked about visiting museums (in a survey by
MORI), only 19 per cent said that there was nothing for them, compared
with 41 per cent five years ago.

In the UK and several other countries, lottery funding has helped to grow
the heritage industry (especially heritage tourism), which in export terms is
estimated to be worth billions of pounds.

Although financial support might wax and wane, the heritage industry
now seems to have the support of all political parties and therefore some
continuity and stability is likely, even if the colour of governments might
change. Substantial financial support from the government is in most countries, of course, closely linked to the funds generated through the lottery and
there is some evidence to suggest that the public contribution through lottery ticket sales is beginning to slow down.

The UK has established a sophisticated system of governmental support for the heritage industry, which is best explained by Insight 2.3.

Insight 2.3: The UK's Department for Culture, Media and Sport and English Heritage

English Heritage (which is considered in detail below) was created by (what is now known as) the UK Government's Department for Culture, Media and Sport. This Department also has responsibility for three other significant bodies connected with Heritage, namely Historic Royal Palaces, The Royal Parks Agency and The Heritage Lottery Fund.

The Department clearly establishes **the link between heritage, conservation, sustainability and education**, which may of course be the cause of tensions and dilemmas as various stakeholders attempt to execute them; issues to which marketers must be able to respond – we shall consider this point through various further insights.

The Department is responsible for creating and upholding policies for the following:

- alcohol and entertainment
- architecture and design
- arts
- broadcasting
- creative industries
- cultural property ('The Department is responsible for protecting cultural objects of outstanding quality for the whole nation ... cultural property policy aims to improve access for all by permitting and encouraging the highest quality works of art to remain and be displayed in the UK.' Website: http://www.culture.gov.uk, 2004)
- education and social policy
- gambling and racing
- the historic environment ('The Department's involvement with this sector covers responsibility for the identification, conservation and enhancement of the historic built environment in England. This includes listing and scheduling of historic buildings and ancient monuments, protection of conservation areas, management of the DCMS historic buildings estate together with State ceremonial duties. DCMS also carries out European and International work on the historic environment including the selection and arrangements for care of World Heritage Sites under the World Heritage Convention.' Website: http://www.culture.gov.uk, 2004).

In 2001 the Department published *The Historic Environment: A Force For Our Future*, a policy document in which they set themselves five specific tasks:

1   providing leadership
2   realizing educational potential
3   including and involving people
4   protecting and sustaining the historic environment, and
5   optimizing its economic potential
   • libraries and communities
   • museums and galleries
   • national lottery
   • public appointments
   • sport
   • tourism.

The website contains many fascinating facts and figures, including the fact that in England there are approximately 500 000 listed (see end of chapter) buildings, 17 700 scheduled monuments and 8500 conservation areas. The UK currently has 20 World Heritage Sites and Lottery funding for heritage projects was around £300 million during the year 2000.

Culture Online is the UK government's £13 million Internet initiative with the specific aim to reach audiences who seem to be inaccessible to much of the heritage sector. It is in its second phase and, in this round in particular, has developed a series of city guides that profile the heritage highlights of each area, together with an electronic archive of recollections of the Second World War.

The aim of the World War Two Remembered concept is to give senior citizens an opportunity to record their own experiences of the War. The BBC and Age Concern have been allied to this event and will run workshops introducing people to the Internet and enabling them to add stories to the BBC People's War website, under the overall auspices of the museums, libraries and archives councils, in four regions. (The Museums, Libraries and Archives Council (MLA) is the national development agency working for and on behalf of museums, libraries and archives, advising government on policy and priorities for the sector. Archives are at the heart of recorded heritage. The records they contain, from the Doomsday Book onwards, span an unbroken chain of over 1000 years of knowledge and information. 'A nation without archives is a nation without memory' (MLA, 2004)).

The city guides are an extension of the *24 Hour Museum* site that was launched in 1999 and includes detailed information, updated weekly, about museums, galleries and heritage attractions in ten English cities, with contributions from local people, museum staff and community organizations.

The *24 Hour Museum* is the UK's National Virtual Museum providing a national guide to 3000 different heritage places; its audience has doubled year-on-year. In 2000 the website attracted 2 million visitors who, between them, accessed nearly 8 million pages; currently, this medium attracts over

240 000 visitors a month who spend on average 10 minutes per session viewing the content. In a recent survey, over 85 per cent of respondents replied that using the *24 Hour Museum* had made them more likely to visit a museum or gallery.

The site has also adopted the concept of 'trails', which they have found a useful way of presenting information to new audiences, linking museums by theme or location. Recent trails have covered subjects as diverse as football, fashion, trench warfare and the literary heritage of Tolkein.

Show Me was launched in November 2003 with the aim of encouraging children aged 4–11 years to enjoy, explore and engage with museum and gallery collections, both online and on site. The content has been designed and organized so that it relates to the National Curriculum.

The website has games, interactive activities, stories, exhibitions and ideas for doing things offline. There is also an interactive map to help children find museums and exhibitions near them. Within three months of its launch the site achieved 30 000 visitors per month.

A Manifesto for Museums: Building Outstanding Museums for the 21st Century (MLA, 2004) is a recently published document that incorporates the findings of a series of major reports commissioned by the UK's national museum sector and the results of a number of baseline studies and research reports commissioned by the MLA. The overall aim of the document is to quantify the contribution that this part of the heritage sector makes to the economy and as a means of lobbying for increased funding. In particular, they identify the government's initiative entitled 'Renaissance in the Regions' as clearly demonstrating the benefits that can be reaped by society through having access to high-quality museum services that are relevant, inspiring and accessible.

The 'Renaissance in the Regions' programme, led by the MLA, brings together selected museums into 'regional hubs' as part of a national framework that includes Regional Agencies, national museums, Designated Collections and other key partners. It is transforming the way in which museums work with each other and the way audiences use them (for a further example of a similar concept from The Netherlands, see Chapter 3). The evidence is compelling:

1   The 2500 museums in the UK receive more than 100 million visits each year; more than to all the country's live sporting events combined.
2   Investment in museums pays: the three regional hubs that were funded in the first phase of the programme saw visits increase by 7 per cent.
3   37 per cent of UK adult residents, over 17 million people, visit museums and galleries at least once a year; this is one of the highest proportions in Europe.
4   50 per cent of school-age children visit museums and galleries at least once a year.

5   Museum visitors come from diverse backgrounds, with proportionate levels of participation by most ethnic groups in comparison with their population sizes.
6   Research shows high satisfaction levels with museums, rising from 73 per cent in 2000 to 80 per cent in 2002 – one of the few increases in public satisfaction across all public services in that period.
7   The UK's museums are custodians of over 170 million objects and natural specimens.
8   National museums are responsible for over a million educational sessions per year and expect to host and inspire 1.72 million in 2004.
9   A quarter of all museum visits are made by children.

A recent survey of visitors to regional hub museums conducted as part of 'Renaissance in the Regions' revealed the following:

1   Museums have been effective at inspiring curiosity among their visitors (86 per cent positive response) and in imparting new knowledge and understanding (83 per cent).
2   Two-thirds of a sample of over 15 000 visitors said that they felt inspired by their visit, whilst three in five said that their visit had 'moved' them.
3   More than nine in ten visitors agreed that regional hub museums are places where their children can learn things they do not in the classroom and that museums and galleries play a vital role in helping to preserve our heritage.
4   Four in five visitors also agreed that regional museums help them to understand more about their local area and its people.

The economic impact of museums

1   Using Treasury formulae, the economic impact of the UK's national museums is in the region of £2 billion.
2   National museums had an overall turnover of £715 million in 2003/2004; this is comparable with the box office takings of the whole theatre sector in the UK.
3   Regional museum turnover is estimated at £875 million in 2003/2004.
4   Spending generated by visitors to national museums is estimated to be at least £565 million.
5   The UK museum sector as a whole employs over 40 000 people.
6   In 2001/2002 national museums sponsored by the Department of Culture, Media and Sport generated £220 million towards their running costs from sponsorship, grants, special exhibitions, donations and trading.
7   It is estimated that regional museums generate in excess of £250 million.

Figure 2.2 A local (UK) heritage provider. Wiltshire Heritage Museum, Gallery and Library. Courtesy of Wiltshire Archaeological and Natural History Society and Wiltshire County Council and Kennet District Council.

8   In the Southwest region it has been estimated that museums and galleries support £51 million of Gross Value Added (GVA) to economic activity; if replicated across the UK, this would amount to £800 million GVA.

Museums as key partners in travel and tourism

Museums are major attractions for both domestic and international tourism.

1   Of the top five tourist attractions in the UK four are museums.
2   Foreign visitors cite museums and galleries as being amongst the prime reasons for a visit to the UK.
3   Overseas tourists make a quarter of visits to museums.
4   Overseas visitors to the national museums in 2003/2004 are estimated to spend at least £320 million in connection with their visit to a particular museum or gallery.
5   48 per cent of frequent (at least once a year) visitors to museums say that they go to museums when they are on holiday or short break in the UK – that is over 8 million adults every year seeing and using museums as part of the domestic tourist industry.

Museums and regeneration

Museums make important contributions to urban, economic and social regeneration. The manifesto documents gives many examples, below are a few.

• To mark the first anniversary of Tate Modern in 2001, the McKinsey consultancy evaluated the impact of the gallery in the light of figures for the first year. In only one year Tate Modern had become the third most visited tourist attraction in Britain and the anchor attraction on the South Bank, drawing attention and people to a previously undiscovered and undeveloped part of London; it has generated £100 million worth of economic activity and 3000 new jobs.
• In Sheffield the £15 million Millennium Galleries are seen as the cornerstone of a larger £120 million regeneration of the Heart of the City project. City centre office rental values have increased with quality retail operations looking to invest in the city centre.
• Manchester Art Gallery has helped transform the city and its future. Of Manchester Art Gallery's visitors 11 per cent are from overseas, compared with 2 per cent five years ago; four times as many people visit the Gallery as did five years ago and 44 per cent of them are under the age of 25 years.
• In Bristol, ambitious plans for a revitalized Museum of Bristol are a key component of the city's aspirations for cultural regeneration and are

proving to be a powerful focus for attracting inward investment to create new facilities, services and jobs.

Museums as civic and community spaces

From art museums to science centres, museums are gathering places for people to meet and spend time with families and friends.

In a recent survey of over 15 000 visitors to regional hub museums, 76 per cent of visitors agreed that the museum/gallery is an appealing (safe, welcoming and congenial) place and this is true for people from all walks of life – 25 per cent of visitors to hub museums are from socio-economic groups C2, D and E (this is an interesting piece of evidence in favour of the 'Renaissance in the Regions' programme as hitherto the majority of visitors to museums, as we shall see in the next chapter, have tended to have an A, B, C1 socio-economic profile, excluding the schools market).

A recent MORI GB Omnibus Survey (February 2004) reported that 82 per cent of respondents felt it was important that their local town or city has a museum or art gallery.

A new generation of cultural spaces that is more open, transparent and accessible, both to the visitor and to the surrounding communities, has emerged. These include the National Waterfront Museum in Swansea, National Galleries of Scotland's Playfair project in Edinburgh and the Great Court at the British Museum.

Museums as catalysts for creativity

Museums act as catalysts for individual creativity and inspiration. For example, from fashion students to established designers, the Victoria and Albert Museum in London occupies a unique position as a source of stimulation and research – an initiative that many museums have incorporated into their programmes, permanent and temporary for a range of target markets. For example, the Bristol Museum and Art Gallery has used its South Asian textile collection to work with women from the local South Asian community, with events such as embroidery and henna sessions.

The Royal Albert Memorial Museum in Exeter presented an innovative exhibition, 'Love, Labour and Loss', about British livestock farming to encourage regeneration after the outbreak of foot and mouth disease and to promote southwest regional cultural heritage.

Museums as centres of research and innovation

Museums have proved themselves as key resources for industry. The National Gallery's collaboration with Hewlett Packard and Tate's work on transport technology (since utilized in many other sectors) are only two examples.

The Natural History Museum makes contributions on a global scale to medical and environmental research. Its Biomedical Sciences Group is a world-leader in research into diseases such as river blindness, malaria, schistosomiasis and leishmaniasis.

Museums also encourage debate and intellectual development. For example, the Science Museum's Antenna Gallery and Dana Centre at the Wellcome-Wolfson Building enables visitors to reach their own conclusions about such issues as MMR (the combined mumps, measles and rubella vaccine) and genetic engineering. Also, through the Turner Prize, there has been a significant raising of awareness and discussion amongst all section of society on 'art'.

Museums as agents for social change and promoting intercultural understanding

Museums act as leading agents in the nation's move towards social and ethnic inclusion. Initiatives such as the Bradford-based National Museum of Photography, Film and Television's Youth TV Project and the Tate's Karrot fashion project are two examples of the lasting impact these programmes have made on people's lives.

Through an MLA/MA (Museums Association) programme called Diversify, young people from ethnic minorities were sponsored to take up museum studies courses and placed in hub museums for work experience.

Acknowledgment: The Directors of the National Museums, The Chairman of MLA, The Chairman of AIM (The Association of Independent Museums), The Convenors of GLLAM (The Group for Large Local Authority Museums), The President of the Museums Association, The Chief Executive of the Regional Agencies (2004) in *A Manifesto for Museums: Building Outstanding Museums for the 21st Century*.

English Heritage

The aims and policies of English Heritage are much the same as for the National Trust (and indeed they will often partner each other in joint projects of heritage conservation, restoration, etc.). They want to make sure that the historic environment of England is properly maintained and, through its presentation, enable people to understand and appreciate all that is on offer. In addition, they explicitly state that '. . . the historic environment is a fundamental tool for **regeneration** . . .', a matter to which we shall return later.

In a MORI Poll for English Heritage, conducted in 2000, entitled, 'What Does "Heritage" Mean To You?', the findings revealed the following:

- 98 per cent of people think that the historic environment is vital to educate children and adults about England's past, this was defined to include history and national identity.

- 51 per cent of the population visited a historic attraction in 1999 compared with 50 per cent visiting the cinema and 17 per cent attending a football match.
- More than half said that they were as interested in learning about other people's cultures as learning about their own.
- 46 per cent think that Black and 45 per cent think that Asian heritage is not adequately represented.

The poll concluded that everyone has a very personal view of what represents their heritage and that the majority of the public value both nationally important attractions and key elements of their own localities. The public also seemed to associate visiting heritage sites and attractions as an important educational opportunity. Professor Robert M. Worcester, Chairman of MORI, added 'While the nation cares passionately for its heritage, "the heritage" as it is currently perceived seems to lack relevance to a significant minority of the public, particularly those in ethnic minority groups. It also faces keen competition from other leisure interests which have multiplied as a result of the benefice of the Lottery [see below]'. We have discussed the first point in the previous chapter and will look at the substitutability aspects in the section Economic Factors below and in subsequent chapters.

In 2003, English Heritage published a document entitled *Heritage Counts* based on another MORI poll, which revealed that 92 per cent of people in the UK thought it important to retain historic features when regenerating towns and cities and 90 per cent understood this to mean their locality as well as castles and stately homes, etc. 82 per cent thought heritage could be fun.

Other significant data to emerge from this publication are as follows:

1   More than half (52 per cent) of people in a nationwide poll in 2003 had visited a historic park or garden in the last twelve months and 46 per cent had visited a historic building.
2   41 per cent of respondents said that they would be interested in taking their family to a museum or historic site.
3   Over one-third (36 per cent) said that they would like to find out more about the local history of their area, while 32 per cent said that they were interested in tracing their family tree.
4   Heritage organizations need to communicate better to a diverse range of audiences. Young people and people from ethnic minorities are less able to give a spontaneous response to the question 'what do you understand by the term heritage?'.
5   Cost is frequently a barrier to participation. Around 43 per cent of all respondents to the survey said that cheaper entry would encourage them to visit historic sites more often, while 29 per cent said that more special events would encourage them to go.

6   Transport, better information and parking were mentioned by more than one in three participants. Adults on lower incomes would be encouraged by better transport (40 per cent), a warmer welcome (27 per cent) and better facilities for disabled people (29 per cent). Many of the poorest households do not own a car, pointing to the need for better public transport links.

7   There were an estimated 3 million school visits to historic attractions in 2002. More could be achieved with better transport facilities and opportunities for schools.

8   A conservative estimate suggests that volunteers contribute the equivalent of at least £25 million a year to the heritage as a result of their unpaid work. Volunteers make up 64 per cent of the workforce in historic houses open to the public.

9   England has an active heritage volunteer workforce of at least 157 000 individuals, who give their time and energy to over 107 national voluntary bodies and associations.

The *myheritage* website invites the public to contact English Heritage and tell them about any aspect of the environment that is significant to the individual or group in terms of their cultural heritage and that may be supported through part or full funding. Latterly, English Heritage has been keen to include more of the UK's multicultural society in its work and one example of how this has manifest itself is through the creation of a national Anglo-Sikh Heritage Trail. 'The project highlights 150 years of Anglo-Sikh history at key sites around the UK. From Spring 2004 it will bring that heritage to a wider audience and new generations through its website' (website: www.english-heritage.org.uk, 2004).

Heritage Trails are an innovative way of presenting either similar aspects of a heritage issue or linking different ones together. Insight 1.1 in the previous chapter gives several examples and further ones will be explored in Chapter 4.

English Heritage undertakes a number of marketing initiatives including membership recruitment drives through **direct marketing**; on-site recruitment of members; off-site recruitment campaigns; membership **sales promotions**; a historic attractions map; a handbook, which is their main **publication** and features all the sites; *Heritage Today* magazine; and other ongoing direct marketing activities. However, in an article published in *Marketing Magazine* (2003), Tania Mason suggests that 'English Heritage is to focus its marketing on its most profitable properties . . . and to communicate the breadth of English Heritage's offer, emphasising that it not only operates properties, but also advises the government on property preservation and gives grants to other organisations that work to preserve England's heritage'. In order to achieve these objectives, the marketing department has been restructured into three groups: online communications, regional marketing and marketing and membership services.

The marketing strategy is developed through a process of consultation with regional departments and is presented in the form of an annual marketing plan, with specific goals for income generation, visitor numbers, raising awareness and understanding amongst customer groups, existing and potential, customer service and the encouragement of longer-term commitment through progression up the **ladder of involvement**, which is presented below.

The 'ladder of involvement' represents a framework for marketing communications, programmes and activity to increase the involvement and commitment to the organization at various levels. The general public is encouraged to proceed up the ladder by firstly becoming admission-paying visitors and then to become more committed by attending events, concerts and taking out membership.

The English Heritage ladder of involvement:
Total public
School/education sector
Admission-paying visitor
Repeat visitor
Merchandise
Concerts
Special events
Mail order purchaser
Membership recruit
Direct debitor
Covenantor
Long-term member
Donor
Volunteer
Legator
Sponsor
Corporate

From this ladder of loyalty we can begin to appreciate the target markets that English Heritage seek to attract. These include domestic holiday makers and overseas visitors, existing members, new members and the school and corporate markets.

Publicity programmes are put in place to **raise awareness**, convey better understanding of the role of English Heritage and to **attract people** to their sites as visitors, members or supporters. Programmes of interpretation, publications, events, concerts, education and customer care are all designed and promoted to both enhance understanding and create satisfaction through entertainment.

English Heritage works closely with all the UK's major tourism organizations, including the British Tourist Authority (BTA) (where they cooperate in

BTA promotions such as the 'Great British Heritage Pass', which enables visitors from overseas to maximize their exposure to the heritage of England by gaining free admission to English Heritage and other heritage attractions); the English Tourist Board (ETB) with whom they were active partners in ETB national promotions such as Henry VIII (1991) and Industrial Heritage (1993); and with Regional Tourist Boards. As well as partnering the National Trust, as mentioned earlier, they also work closely with other bodies such as the Historic Houses Association and are an active member of the Association of Leading Visitor Attractions (ALVA) whose members account for approximately 30 per cent of all visits to attractions.

One of their greatest marketing initiatives and successes in terms of raising the awareness of built heritage are the **Heritage Open Days**. Heritage Open Days were established in 1994 as England's contribution to European Heritage Days, in which 47 countries now participate and many organizations such as the National Trust and private participants will (metaphorically speaking) throw open their doors, free of charge, for visitors.

Heritage Open Days regularly attract an audience of 800 000 visitors and there is an opportunity to see some properties that might not otherwise open to the public.

Finally, the National Monuments Record (NMR) is English Heritage's public archive; a resource that provides information on the architecture and archaeology of England and that can be consulted either in person at the EH headquarters or through the enquiry service.

Insight 2.4: The Heritage Lottery Fund, UK

The Heritage Lottery Fund was set up in 1993 and offered funds to support a wide range of projects involving the local, regional and national heritage of the UK; this was an additional responsibility for the trustees of the National Memorial Fund, which was created by parliament in 1980. The trustees are guided by experts on heritage matters and operate within the legislative framework but produce independent policies and make their own decisions – they are therefore officially known as a 'non-departmental public body', although the Secretary of State for Culture, Media and Sport accepts overall responsibility for the way in which this body works.

The aims of the Heritage Lottery Fund are to distribute funds raised through national lottery ticket sales for all aspects of heritage in the UK and award both capital grants (for equipment and/or building projects) and time-limited activity grants.

During the period 2002–2007 they have the following main goals:

1   to involve a greater number of people in decisions about heritage;
2   to conserve and enhance the UK's diverse heritage;
3   to enable education, access and enjoyment of heritage for everyone.

On their website they make clear that education about and access to heritage are top priorities that can be achieved in many ways, categorized as:

- *physical*, the enjoyment of buildings or artefacts, including disabled access and a consideration of the needs of young children;
- *cultural*, for example support for 'local communities' in their celebration of religious or spiritual events;
- *sensory*, interpretation of heritage that improves access, such as through better signage or multimedia activities in, for example, museums;
- *intellectual*, responsiveness to different levels of need.

'Heritage' includes many different things that have been, and can be passed on from one generation to another. Among these are:

- countryside, parks and gardens (. . . to protect and open up their countryside, parks and gardens and to make vital contributions to nature conservation, . . . especially where this is at risk);
- objects and sites that are linked to our industrial, transport and maritime history (. . . to help communities buy, repair, conserve and restore things and places relating to this heritage);
- records such as local history archives, photographic collections or spoken history records (. . . [we want] to make sure that these are properly conserved and better housed and presented);
- historic buildings (. . . to save buildings at risk or find appropriate new uses for old buildings . . . we fund sites of local value as well as those of outstanding national importance . . . [which may] contribute to the regeneration of deprived areas);
- museum and gallery collections (. . . to help people enjoy and get more from their museums, galleries and other important collections).

The website also identifies other aspects of heritage that are being supported, including canals and waterways, arts buildings and language heritage.

Heritage includes people as well as places, and so funding also covers cultural and local traditions. 'Projects that care for and protect heritage are at the core of our work . . . [and these activities] can stimulate regeneration in both urban and rural environments.' Website: http://www.hlf.org.uk

An indication of the level of support offered is that, in 2002, £5.2 million in grants was awarded to 49 non-national museums and galleries, under the government's Designated Museum Challenge Fund.

One recent example of an organization to benefit from the Heritage Lottery Fund is London's Transport Museum, which embarked (Summer 2004) on an extensive building and redisplay project, having received a grant of £9.47 million. The total cost of the project is £18 million, the remainder of which has come from Transport for London and the Friends of London's Transport Museum; a further £3 million is to be raised from industry, trusts and foundations and the new museum is expected to open in 2006. The London Transport Museum has the world's finest urban transport collection, which provides an insight into the unique 'story' of London and its people. The project will enable the museum to put more artefacts from its collections on display; renew the current exhibitions and enhance control of light and ventilation; rearrange interpretation; create a new lecture theatre, shop and café area and improve educational facilities.

Restoration

In 2003, a unique BBC television series was presented at prime time and was called *Restoration*, presented by Griff Rhys-Jones. Based on the success of the first series, a second began in May 2004.

The aim of the television programme was to highlight the plight of several buildings, some of which were completely derelict but which contribute to the heritage of either England, Scotland, Wales or Northern Ireland. At the end of each show, a 'winner' was declared based on the telephone votes cast by the public, with each vote having a small financial value (effectively a donation by the voters). The eventual winner of the first series was the Victorian swimming baths in Manchester, which had been closed to the public for some time and is now undergoing restoration as a result of the funds generated by the series. The Heritage Lottery Fund offered £3 million towards the 'Restoration Fund' and the amount raised by the public was approximately £350 000.

The television programmes reflected the mood of the UK population at the time (and which I believe continues to grow) and was definitely a success in terms of raising awareness of the state of some of the UK's national buildings, evident through the numerous follow-up articles in the media and references made on the programmes themselves.

The *Restoration* website (http://www.bbc.co.uk/history/programmes/restoration/heritage) lists many UK organizations that are involved in protecting and/or enhancing buildings around the UK.

Listed buildings

Buildings are listed in the UK by the Secretary of State for Culture, Media and Sport if they are of special architectural or historical importance and because they identify our heritage; they are included in a national register of such buildings – the term 'building' can also include other structures such as walls, bridges and milestones.

The listing process gives such structures more protection than might otherwise be the case and gives local authorities the tools to monitor changes that could take place by requiring applications specific to these buildings; any alterations proposed must be done in a manner that will respect the building and not cause damage to its historic structure.

Buildings eligible for listing are selected against a set of national criteria (which changes over time) and application is made to the Department of Culture, Media and Sport, which is advised by the government agency, English Heritage (see above).

Broadly, listed buildings include:

- all buildings built before 1700, which survive in their original state;
- most buildings built between 1700 and 1840;
- buildings of 'definite quality' built between 1840 and 1914;
- very 'outstanding' buildings built after 1939.

In the choice of buildings, attention is paid to their special value in architectural terms or planning reasons or because they illustrate a period of economic history (examples include schools, hospitals, railway stations, industrial buildings, etc.), technological innovation or virtuosity, association with well-known characters or events (English Heritage's Blue Plaque scheme commemorates places associated with famous people from the past, such as a building in which they were born or lived) and group value, such as squares and terraces in towns or cities.

There are three categories of listing:

Grade 1   denotes buildings of exceptional interest (only about 2 per cent of all listed buildings are Grade 1);

Grade 2*   are particularly important buildings and more than special interest (about 4 per cent of all buildings are Grade 2* listed);

Grade 2   are buildings of special interest that need protection to preserve them.

Buildings are listed in their entirety, i.e., this includes their interiors, exteriors and anything that might be attached to the building.

Local authorities deal with planning applications in relation to listed buildings, which gives them an opportunity to monitor possible changes. They have various statutory powers to help them ensure that listed buildings are kept in a good state of repair and, indeed, can take action to secure repairs from owners if it becomes evident that a heritage building is being allowed to deteriorate.

Specifically, local authorities can apply Section 54 of the Planning (Listed Buildings and Conservations Areas) Act 1990 in order to carry out necessary repairs for the preservation of a listed building and Section 55 gives them the power to recover the expenses from the owner.

Under Section 48 of the Act, local authorities can serve a Repairs Notice to owners and if the work is not carried out they can proceed under Section 47 and issue an SOS, which is advised to English Heritage.

The Royal Institute of Chartered Surveyors in the UK have recently added to the debate regarding the preservation of local heritage with the following points:

1   . . . there should be the establishment of 'heritage champions' in combination with 'champions for the historic environment'. The heritage champion can provide a useful contribution to the process of matching appropriate uses to buildings. In fulfilling this role the heritage champion should conduct an overview of local occupancy patterns to identify opportunities for avoiding the redundancy of heritage properties and sites.

2   The role of the public sector in generating, promoting and maintaining skills at all levels in the conservation sector is the key to the maintenance of the entire heritage environment. Regular inspections are only one facet of proactive property management. Functions related to lease covenants, insurance renewals, service charge management, routine fire precautions (to name a few) also need to be planned and co-ordinated . . . [and] should be promoted as part of the planned maintenance arrangements for heritage assets.

3   We acknowledge that there are sometimes benefits in selling historic buildings on the open market in order to secure investment in repair and restoration. English Heritage might also wish to consider the possibility that local authorities will have conflicting interests as both an enforcer of repair for listed buildings and an owner of listed buildings. In order to avoid conflict in the disposal of historic property we would suggest that, where a change of use is inevitable, the necessary consents should be put substantially in place prior to disposal. This should ensure that the property does not become redundant.

4   There is a clear case for a planning brief or conservation statement in the disposal of historic buildings and sites. However, we believe that conservation plans should be produced for any historic building and not just 'large and complex' buildings or sites. We would suggest that many of the smallest buildings are of considerable historical interest and value.

Economic factors

Macro- and micro-economic factors are always closely linked and especially in the context of marketing and pricing initiatives (or not to price at all, as this will be more effective in stimulating demand – we shall be returning to this latter point in Chapter 3 because in the heritage tourism sector, as we saw briefly under political factors, museums that do not charge for entry have seen an unprecedented increase in visitor numbers, particularly in the UK). Therefore, the intricacies of demand and supply analysis (micro-economic factors) will not be discussed here but macro-economic factors, in particular the causal relationship between investment in heritage, especially that of the built environment and the resultant multiplier effect on that local economic area, are discussed below.

Regeneration/adding economic value through heritage provision, investment and marketing

In the sections above, we already have some evidence from the findings of the Historic Environment Steering Group, English Heritage and the National Trust that confirm that regeneration of towns and cities leverages the economic value of these places *and* is capable of **changing perceptions** of them; therefore investment, restoration and preservation should be supported and on-going.

What further evidence do we have of this causal link?

In the UK, English Heritage funding is often the first-generation funding to be offered and it usually stimulates additional funding from other sources, public and private.

In 2002 English Heritage published a document entitled *Heritage Dividend: Measuring the Results of Heritage Regeneration from 1999–2002*. The document set out the regeneration impact of heritage funding through Conservation Area Partnership Schemes (CAPS) and Heritage Economic Regeneration Schemes (HERS – launched in 1999, this scheme is run in partnership with local authorities and encourages investment from public and private sources) from April 1999 to October 2002.

The main conclusion of the report is that heritage funding makes a highly significant contribution to the regeneration and sustainable development of communities across England. 'By investing in the physical fabric of towns and villages – the buildings and the public spaces between them – we "pump prime" wider regeneration initiatives and, together, improve business confidence, give pride to local communities and strengthen the sense of place which makes the historic environment so popular' (English Heritage, 2002).

Specifically, the investigations discovered that £10 000 of heritage investment levers £46 000 match-funding from private sector and public sources and this delivers, on average:

- 41 m^2 of improved commercial floorspace, plus
- 103 m^2 of environmental improvements, plus
- 1 new job, plus
- 1 safeguarded job, plus
- 1 improved home.

A variety of heritage initiatives were supported, across England, including the following.

1   The aim of supporting the historic port of Bideford in Devon was to help restore the shops and boost the local economy. All of the town's commercial activities, including shopping, banking and restaurants, are located within a conservation area that for years had been blighted by empty property. The centre has suffered commercial decline in the face of competition from large centres, out-of-town developments and changing consumer demands. Shoppers' and visitors' perceptions of the town were prejudiced by the dilapidated appearance of these buildings and there was a real danger of the spiral of decline accelerating to such an extent that the town's commercial prosperity would be irretrievably damaged in the long run. The HERS in Bideford was funded by £92 376 of English Heritage grant, which levered an additional £267 302 of public- and private-sector funding; together these investments have improved 20 buildings, 910 m² of commercial floorspace and 33 homes – as a consequence, 30 new jobs have been created.

2   The village of Cromford in Derbyshire is often referred to as the cradle of the industrial revolution and is part of the Derwent Valley Mills World Heritage Site, designated in 2001. The restoration of the old mill complex and canal wharf is being carried out by the Arkwright Society (named after the inventor Richard Arkwright who built the world's first successful water-powered cotton spinning mill), which purchased the site in 1979. The mill is open every day and attracts visitors from all over the world; it has a visitors' centre, shops and café and plans have been in progress to create an exhibition with working machinery, meeting rooms for schools and other educational groups together with a library and study centre. Prior to English Heritage funding, the village of Cromford suffered neglect, unsympathetic alterations to the built heritage and environmental problems as a result of the nature and extent of traffic nearby. Heritage funding for this scheme (which was a combination of funding for repairs and maintenance to period homes in the village as well as an environmental enhancement project) totalled £245 651 and was further supplemented by £311 686 of partnership funding; this total investment delivered improvements to 55 buildings, including 38 private homes.

3   The support for Gravesend in Kent helped to build confidence in under-valued heritage at this historic Thames riverside port. Gravesend's economy was traditionally based on industries such as cement and paper manufacture and, with the river, through a variety of shipping-related activities. As these industries declined, so did the area's economic well-being; the town further fell victim to two new major shopping centres sited on major motor arterial routes, Lakeside and Bluewater. The detri-

mental consequences for Gravesend were many, including deterioration of many significant historic buildings, which in turn had 'knock-on' effects on the visual amenity and living and working environments. Heritage funding for this scheme (a major part of which was to refurbish the Town Pier) totalled £897 818 and was supported by a further £4 668 110 of funding from partner organizations. The investment delivered improvements to 24 homes, 3396 m² of commercial floorspace and 5789 m² of public space.

4   A large number of farm buildings in the Peak District National park have suffered from falling roofs or are listed buildings at risk, which are either redundant or unusable – these buildings become a blight on an area and create a disincentive for owners to invest in their own nearby properties. The HERS in the Peak Villages was funded by £67 918 of English Heritage grant and levered an additional £39 741 from the private sector, together with £50 544 from the public domain. The investments have improved 15 buildings and safeguarded 23 jobs.

5   The funding for St John's Church in Hoxton, London, created new uses for a late Georgian church and became a catalyst for uplifting a local community. Hoxton is one of the most deprived areas in the country, at the heart of which is St John the Baptist church, a Grade 2 building designed by Francis Edwards in 1824 and set in an island churchyard surrounded by the original cast-iron railings. By 1996, the church was in a very poor condition, with leaking roof, no heating and a declining congregation. English Heritage provided £515 000 for repairs and maintenance, which has generated £2 million for regeneration of the locality.

In summary, the case studies featured in *Heritage Dividend* (English Heritage, 2002) all have a common theme, which is that the impact of heritage grant programmes can change local perceptions and create a context for people to work together and initiate new opportunities for local service delivery.

Interpretation is the process of communicating to people the significance of a place or object so that they enjoy it more, understand their heritage and environment better and develop a positive attitude to conservation.

The mission of the Association of Heritage Interpretation is to encourage excellence in the presentation and management of natural and cultural environments. Specifically:

1   the Association provides a forum for discussion and exchange of ideas on the interpretation of heritage, both urban and rural;
2   it disseminates knowledge of interpretive philosophy, principles and techniques;
3   it promotes the role of interpretation and its value among those involved with recreation management, conservation, education, tourism and

public relations in national and local government, charitable bodies and private organizations. (Acknowledgment: The Association of Heritage Interpretation (2004) http://www.heritage-interpretation.org.uk)

The Conservation Register is a national database of conservation-restoration practices meeting specified criteria. It has been established for over ten years and is a physical and online resource for both members of the public and those working in the heritage sector.

The UK Institute for Conservation is the professional body for those who care for the country's cultural objects and heritage collections. Its purpose is to benefit the public and the quality of care of the nation's heritage. Its members are conservators and restorers both working in public institutions such as museums and galleries and also in the private sector.

Other key organizations concerned with UK heritage

In order to assist farmers, landowners, individuals, organizations and local communities making environment and conservation improvements, there are a number of grants available. These are administered by various organizations, all working to help enhance the UK's landscape, cultural heritage and its biodiversity. Listed below are some of the organizations involved.

- The England Rural Development Programme (ERDP) is a seven-year programme (2000–2006) that provides funding for land- or project-based schemes that conserve and improve the environment. The programme includes a large number of schemes that can be taken advantage of in the Area of Outstanding National Beauty (AONB) designation, including the Rural Enterprise Scheme and Vocational Training Scheme – see http://www.defra.gov.uk.
- Countryside Stewardship is a scheme that offers payments to farmers and land managers to improve the natural beauty and diversity of the countryside, enhance, restore and recreate targeted landscapes, their wildlife habitats and historical features and to improve public access. The ten-year agreements also allow capital payments for various conservation works to contribute directly towards the landscape, history, wildlife and access of rural areas. Funding is available for a wide range of options, including old orchards, field margins, arable reversion to grass and historic parks. Additional payments are given where access to the public is provided. The scheme is administered by DEFRA.
- Environmentally Sensitive Areas is another agri-environmental scheme funded through ERDP. It encourages farmers and landowners to conserve and enhance areas of the countryside where the landscape, wildlife or historic interest is of national importance, by encouraging farming practices that are beneficial to the environment.

- The Organic Farming Scheme is designed to encourage farmers using conventional farming methods to convert their systems to organic production. This provides gains in terms of soil health and fertility, benefits for biodiversity and many other advantages for the historic landscape.
- The Woodland Grant Scheme (WGS) run by the Forestry Commission gives grants to create new woodland and for the management of existing woodlands. It includes opportunities for planting native species, allowing public access and community involvement and linking new woods to existing woodlands.
- The Processing and Marketing Grants Scheme (PMG) is a grant scheme to enable investment in processing and marketing facilities for primary agricultural products, excluding forestry and fisheries products.
- The Rural Enterprise Scheme (RES) provides assistance for projects that help to develop a more sustainable, diversified and enterprising rural economy and communities. Its coverage is wide-ranging but the main aim is to help farmers adapt to changing markets and develop new business opportunities. RES also has a broader role in supporting the adaptation and development of the rural economy, community, heritage and the environment. The scheme covers nine measures under which funding can be applied for, including support for activities involving the marketing of quality agricultural products, diversification both into alternative agricultural activity as well as out of agriculture, and encouragement for tourism and craft activities. There is no fixed rate of funding; instead, there are three bands of aid, depending on the extent of any commercial return of the project.
- Countryside Grant Assistance is funding offered by The Countryside Agency to local authorities and voluntary conservation organizations for schemes that enhance, conserve or improve natural features and that contribute to the public's enjoyment of the countryside. A maximum of 50 per cent of project costs is normally available.
- The Wildlife Enhancement Scheme is a grant scheme targeted at landowners who farm Sites of Special Scientific Interest. Grant awards are offered for positive management work and include capital payments (for example, hedge restoration) and grants for on-going works.
- The Traditional Breeds Incentive Scheme provides area-based financial assistance to farmers to support grazing by traditional cattle, sheep and pony breeds to achieve favourable conditions on a range of special sites, including land within or adjoining Sites of Special Scientific Interest, land designated as a Special Protection Area or a Special Area of Conservation, or a Wetland of International Importance under the Ramsar Convention.
- Rural development agencies have various funding streams available. The broad areas of interest are: IT and technology, training and skills development, local produce, tourism, business and inward investment and rural and urban regeneration/renaissance.

- The Heritage Lottery Fund's 'Your Heritage Fund' offers grants of between £5000 and £50 000 for projects that will conserve and enhance heritage and, specifically, to encourage communities to identify, look after and celebrate their heritage. Projects could include building repairs and conservation work, buying land or buildings important in terms of local heritage and making it easier for people to appreciate heritage.
- The Local Heritage Initiative (LHI) is a ten-year scheme devised and administered by the Countryside Agency on behalf of the Heritage Lottery Fund. It aims to help local groups investigate, explain and care for their local landscape, landmarks, traditions and culture. Standard grants are between £3000 and £25 000 to cover 60 per cent of project costs.
- The Association of Independent Museums:
  - lobbies on behalf of independent museums and is a powerful voice at national level in the museum sector;
  - is a self-help organization founded by independently funded museums which have led the revolution in museum presentation and management over the last 25 years. Many groups are keen to share in AIM's approach to museums, the heritage and associated activities;
  - provides a thriving network of information and advice for a wide variety and extensive number of organizations, large and small, all linked by a commitment to the preservation and interpretation of historic material.
- The International Council of Museums (ICOM) was founded in 1946 and is the leading international organization for museums and museum professionals. It is committed to the conservation, continuation and communication to society of the world's natural and cultural heritage, present and future, tangible and intangible. ICOM has 17 000 members across 140 countries and maintains formal relations with UNESCO. ICOM UK is one of 113 National Committees of ICOM around the world.
- The Forestry Commission cares for some 950 Scheduled Ancient Monuments (SAMs). These range from bothies to battlefields, cairns to castles, lodges to lumps and standing stones to slate mines, plus many others; the list of unscheduled sites numbers thousands. The corporate plan of the Forestry Commission states that they will '. . . embrace the contribution made by the FC woodlands to the landscape of Great Britain and [will] safeguard the built heritage'.

Technological factors

Advances in technology have undoubtedly benefited the heritage industry in many ways, from the quality of colour print for advertising purposes to innovations in information technology which have made available multi-media and interactive displays that can be used in any number of alternative ways and for a variety of different purposes. Some illustrative examples are given below.

New technology for heritage marketing

Firstly, heritage providers have found that new technologies can help them to reach new audiences. For example, teenagers and young adults find visual and interactive media particularly engaging. Virtual tours (many museums are considering or have adopted this concept) can reach those with physical disabilities or cultural constraints that inhibit them from accessing public places, and these can also be used for distance learning. Virtual tours can present artworks and objects in three dimensions, which can go some way towards attempting to represent their physical context and experience. One example of this is the British Museum's website, which has audio excerpts from the family tour combined with images of the objects in order to provide information and education.

Visitors with hearing impediments to heritage sites could be/are offered hand-held computers that allow them to see a sign language interpretation and/or written explanations. The Tate Modern in London opened the world's first British Sign Language Guide in October 2003; at the Great Blacks in Wax Museum, Baltimore, USA an American Sign Language Guide has been implemented; and at the International Spy Museum in Washington, USA a hand-held captioning solution has been developed for visitors with hearing problems.

In a similar vein, audio tours offer access for visually impaired visitors and foreigners. A touch tour of The Holocaust Gallery at The Imperial War Museum in London includes recreations of objects that partially sighted visitors can touch while listening to descriptions. The museum also offers a tailor-made audio tour of this exhibition to those with mild learning difficulties.

The experience of visitors to heritage sites and attractions need not necessarily involve technology; hearts and minds can be won through the **non-tangible experience**. However, this must be designed to cater for all levels of understanding and taste and incorporate the overarching philosophy that we are establishing in relation to marketing heritage, i.e., it must be capable of **educating, informing and entertaining**.

The recently opened Prisoners of the Tower exhibition at HM Tower of London engages the visitor with the experiences of prisoners held in the Tower from 1100 to 1941. The design (by design consultancy Holmes Wood) utilized the unique atmosphere and architecture of the Tower and leads the visitor on the prisoner's journey through their sentence.

In short, the examples above offer only a minor insight into this developing area which the heritage industry is increasingly adopting in order to enhance their product offering.

We have come to the end of our analysis of environmental factors and how they impact on heritage marketing. Now consider Case study 2.1.

CASE STUDY 2.1: The Dean Heritage Centre: Museum of the Forest – Gateway to the Magical Forest of Dean, Gloucestershire, UK

The Royal Forest of Dean in rural Gloucestershire, UK is an ancient woodland that has been in existence since time immemorial. Villages in the area have been home to many famous Britons and are reputed to have inspired others, including J.R.R. Tolkein (*The Lord of the Rings* Trilogy and other publications), Samuel Pepys (sixteenth-century London 'diarist'), Wordsworth (poet), Dennis Potter (novelist and playwright) and J.K. Rowling (the *Harry Potter* books) who lived nearby for much of her childhood.

The Dean Heritage Museum trust is a charity that runs the Dean Heritage Centre with the mission of 'safeguarding the heritage and culture of the Forest of Dean for the enjoyment and education of the local community and visitors to the area . . . [it] tells the story of the Forest of Dean from the earliest times up to present, a chance to take a fresh look at the past . . . [with] easier access and better facilities' (Dean Heritage leaflet, 2004). The centre is supported by a number of local and national institutions, including the Forest of Dean District Council, The Countryside Agency, the South West of England Regional Development Agency and the Heritage Lottery Fund.

However, the Dean Heritage Centre is not just a museum in the sense of a closed or open-air building/set-up and neither is it a 'heritage trail', a heritage marketing concept that is becoming fashionable in order to increase visitor numbers, both in and out of 'season'. The centre does have a museum, but it also has a library, gallery, cottage, woodland walks and demonstrations of traditional skills that are held in the woods, as well as 'added-value' services, which most visitors expect; notably in this case, a children's play area, café and shop; the latter two will almost certainly be important for generating revenue.

The museum offers visitors the opportunity to learn about the Forest of Dean, its people and the important part it has played throughout history as a Royal Forest and an iron- and coal-producing area. Artefacts, including many which have not been seen by the public before, are on display in the many galleries and offer insights into the landscape, the local industry and local history.

'The Gage Library' houses the most complete collection of published books on the Forest of Dean and a new research room allows a 'behind the scenes' view of the museum.

'The Gallery' offers a changing programme of exhibitions from local artists throughout the year and is a permanent home to two local craftsmen.

'Hidden in the Woods' is a concept promoted by the centre to demonstrate the traditional skills of the Forest, notably charcoal burning, woodturning, hurdle making and cider production; rural skills courses are available throughout the summer period.

'The Cottage' is a reconstruction of the home of a forester in 1900 and in the garden the curators have started to grow historic varieties of vegetable, as well as keeping a 'Gloucester Old Spot' pig.

Acknowledgment: Dean Heritage Centre, Gloucestershire, UK, 2004.

Questions

1 Who do you think might have wanted and initiated a 'heritage centre' in the Royal Forest of Dean in rural Gloucestershire?
2 Who do you think are the target markets for such a facility?
3 What aspects of the heritage of the Forest of Dean are on offer at the centre?
4 How do you think this centre is promoted, locally and nationally?
5 How do you think this centre measures its 'success', quantitatively and qualitatively?

Summary

The aim of this chapter has been to look at the significance of environmental factors for heritage marketing. I have also presented the application of several marketing principles, in particular aspects of target marketing, use of the Attention, Interest, Desire, Action (AIDA) principle and relationship marketing (English Heritage's 'ladder of loyalty').

Leveraging heritage undoubtedly **creates value**, which generates a **multiplier-effect** that in turn creates the further demand for goods and services from the buying public, businesses and local and national governments. Job creation is stimulated as a result and this produces additional incomes that create even more demand.

The UK, internationally speaking, has a sophisticated system of supporting heritage, from the government agency English Heritage and the Heritage Lottery Fund to non-government charitable organizations such as the National Trust, National Trust for Scotland, CADW (Wales) and Bord Failte (Northern Ireland), as well as thousands of local, national and regional organizations. Most of these perceive the need to link one or more of the following in the context of heritage provision and marketing: education (including creating an awareness of heritage issues), conservation, preservation and restoration.

Politicians and other interested parties worldwide are also acutely aware that aspects of heritage are in danger of being 'loved to death' and therefore the right balance must be struck between conservation/preservation and public access; those that work professionally in heritage marketing and management must deal on a day-to-day basis with differing public needs, attitudes and expectations, a challenge fraught with tensions.

While the public will remain interested in the concept of heritage generally, and specifically in aspects that are relevant to the individual or group, this notion is set to have an even wider meaning through the passage of time. In particular, the cultural heritage of certain sections of society will become more popular, such as the 'Bollywood' craze (Asian cultural heritage) in the UK; the culture of other decades such as the 1960s and 1970s, the celebration of which have been instrumental in keeping open UK 'holiday camps' beyond the summer season; popular culture such as film, TV, music and dance are increasingly being drawn into a celebration of heritage; food and drink, too, are gaining prominence (Parma Ham has been officially recognized by an EU Directive as a food with a unique heritage). Together with brands such as BMW, the VW Golf and Cadbury, they are all busy leveraging the past for future benefit – and services are not excluded. Finally, 'oral' history will increasingly be used as an imaginative and effective way of interpreting and presenting aspects of heritage at sites and attractions.

Discussion question

Richard Kennedy, in an article entitled 'Who is culture's keeper?', published in *Foreign Policy* (November/October, 2002) asks

> . . . what types of culture should be preserved and who should make those decisions: the marketplace?, governments?, communities?, professional artists and curators? Traditionally, wealthy patrons and governments made many of the determinants of taste . . . supporting cultural institutions such as theatres and museums with the conviction that culture needs encouragement to survive the forces of free trade . . . [latterly], large corporations to small communities are exerting their influence in the cultural world. Tax strapped governments are concerned about how to compete with these new forces while trying to support national culture.

Discuss.

Recommended reading

Church, J. (1997) *Social Trends 27*. The Stationery Office, London.
Department of Culture, Media and Sport (2003) *Heritage Counts*. DCMS, London.
Department of the Environment (2000) *Power of Place: The Future of the Historic Environment*. London.
Department of the Environment (2001) *A Force for Our Future*. London.
Dibb, S. and Simin, L. (2004) *Marketing Concepts, Techniques and Frameworks*. Houghton-Mifflin, London.

Economic Intelligence Unit (1997) The seniors' travel market. *Travel and Tourism Analyst*, 5, 15.

English Heritage (2002) *Heritage Dividend: Measuring the Results of Heritage Regeneration from 1999–2002*. Department of Culture, Media and Sport, London.

Hooper-Greenhill, E. (ed.) (1999) *The Educational Role of the Museum*. Second edition. Routledge, London.

Kennedy, R. (2002) Who is culture's keeper? *Foreign Policy*, November/October.

Lowenthal, D. (1996) *The Heritage Crusade and Spoils of History*. Viking, London.

MacCannell, D. (1996) *The Tourist: A New Theory of the Leisure Class*. Shocken, London.

Mason, T. (2003) English Heritage focuses on most profitable sites. *Marketing Magazine*, June.

Moore, K. (2000) *Museum Management*. Second edition. Routledge, London.

Museums, Libraries and Archives Council (2004) *A Manifesto for Museums: Building Outstanding Museums for the 21st Century*. MLA, London.

Tribe, J. (1999) *The Economics of Leisure and Tourism*. Butterworth-Heinemann, Oxford.

Tylee, J. (2003) BHO's National Trust debut work aims to bring its properties to life. *Campaign*, April, p. 19.

Wilkie, K. (2000) *Indignation*. Available at www.kimwilkie.com/pages/issues/iss_indign.html.

Wilson, I. (2003) *The Economics of Leisure*. Heinemann, Oxford.

Chapter 3

Market segmentation and target marketing in the heritage industry

Every weekend she [Precious Ramotswe] travelled up to Mochudi on one of the cousin's husband's buses and visited her father. He would be waiting outside the house, sitting on his stool, and she would curtsey before him, in the old way, and clap her hands.

Then they would eat together, sitting in the shade of the lean-to verandah, which he had erected to the side of the house. She would tell him about the week's activity in the bus office and he would take in every detail, asking for names, which he would link into elaborate genealogies. Everybody was related in some way; there was nobody who could not be fitted into the far-flung corners of family.

(McCall Smith, 1998: 11)

In the previous two chapters, particularly in Insight 1.2 ('The Museum in the Park'), we have touched on some of the principles of market segmentation, targeting and positioning, which is a critical area in the early stages of mar-

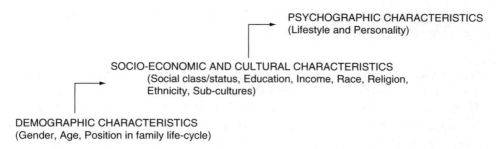

Figure 3.1 The three steps of segmentation variables to better understand consumer markets.

keting planning, analysis and decision-making. We shall now take a closer look at segmentation variables as applied to heritage marketing.

Market segmentation – a definition

Market segmentation is the process of dividing a total market (or sub-market) using the principles identified above in order to create one or more homogeneous groups or segments that can then be targeted effectively, based on the accessibility of these customers and the resources of the organization.

Segmentation research began in 1956 and, just like many principles in marketing, emerged from the academic discipline of economics. Segmentation is the key that unlocks the door to a group of consumers for an organization; it must then be backed by appropriate targeting (choice and combination of media channels to use, packaging, timing of launch, etc.) and the wider issue of positioning the organization in the marketplace as either a cost-leader or differentiator.

Almost everyone is in the market for one or more aspects of heritage, directly or indirectly, whether this is gained personally, locally, nationally or internationally. At the very least, the vast majority of people around the world will be exposed at some point in their lives or throughout their lifetime, either through an educational link or tourism (or perhaps just stories and rituals that are 'handed down'), to something from the past – no one can really get away from the past.

Research into segmentation and its application for organizations has advanced considerably over the years. At a recent conference in the UK, I was impressed by one of the foremost researchers on strategic marketing, Lyndon Simkin, and his thoughts on segmentation as a systematic process for identifying homogeneous groups that could be targeted.

A six-stage sequence . . . is able to move [a student/practitioner of market segmentation] from a sector-view or product group-based customer classification towards a true market segmentation scheme. At the heart of the process is the buying proforma.

(Simkin, 2004)

The 'buying proforma' was created by Dibb and Simkin *et al.* in 1996 to assist marketers in developing a complete understanding of their customers during the process of creating a marketing plan. Broadly speaking, it enables a systematic analysis of customers' buying decision-making processes together with the influencing factors that impact on this, the distinct needs of customers and the profile and characteristics of the customers in a sector or segment.

Simkin describes each of these stages as follows:

Stage 1 requires a description of the current customer classification scheme used, whether this is by sector, product groups, geographic territories, geo-demographics, sales volumes or values, etc.

Stage 2 requires (preferably) a cross-functional team to address the buying proforma for each existing customer group or sector.

Stage 3 allows for extensive debate on customer profile characteristics and key customer values.

Stage 4 at this stage current customer types need to be (continued to be) split until there is agreement amongst the cross-functional team.

Stage 5 warrants a thorough examination of the buying decision-making processes of the agreed set of customer types and the influencing factors in order to make sure that there are clear distinctions between them.

Stage 6 is the final part of the process and requires the team to identify common traits across the proformas that have now been established for the different customer types.

Organizations that are in the business of heritage marketing will usually address all the well-known market segmentation variables in some detail (Figure 3.1), whether or not they adopt the approach advocated above, and these are used in conjunction with the consumer decision-making model – this is how we will approach segmentation for heritage, consumer behaviour and targeting.

During the last 10–15 years psychographics has become very significant in terms of understanding consumer behaviour and is central to heritage marketing. We have already established in the previous chapters that consumers are interested in a **symbolic** relationship with heritage, i.e., for individuals and groups aspects of heritage must be relevant and meaningful; they are looking for this to be represented/embodied in their personal identity, national identity or something tangible, i.e., a product (which could be a heritage attraction or a food or drink – the two product groups/sectors that will be the focus for our attention and which will be discussed more fully in the following two chapters) or brand.

Marketers should therefore aim to engender a **symbiotic relationship** with a homogeneous group of heritage consumers in order to create a lucrative opportunity, which need not necessarily be measured in quantitative value terms, as discussed previously (also see the examples from the section on marketing heritage education, below). One key element of symbiosis, or the route to it, is **emotion**, one aspect of which is nostalgia: '. . . the generating of an emotional response is the guiding light towards the successful engagement of people . . . and emotionality has been the touchstone for projects across the world. However, with so many attractions on offer vying for the public's attention, simply trying to create an emotional response in the audience is not enough any more' (Hole, 2004: 16). (The use of the term 'nostalgia' can be traced back to seventeenth-century Greece where it described the concept of 'returning home'. Nostalgia, therefore, is about 'longing' for the past, remembering/reminiscing about it and doing so with a positive frame of mind (as the converse is nostophobia). In order to trigger this emotion the heritage marketer must offer relevant (to the individual or group) **physical or symbolic experiences** in the present – something that museums generally 'do' well – see Insight 1.2, The Museum in the Park.)

Ray Hole therefore suggests that anyone involved in the business of heritage must address a combination of biology, psychology and instinct in planning and marketing a heritage product, service or brand, which reinforces my previous theoretical arguments regarding the sovereignty of the consumer.

We have established the importance of recognizing that new segments and sub-segments emerge from time to time and that there should be a system in place to access this information, together with the fact that marketing plans may need to be changed or modified to accommodate macro and micro changes in the marketplace. Constant monitoring and evaluation of segmentation bases are highly important (daily) activities for the heritage marketer and the research methods by which data are collected must also be kept under review. Wedel and Kamakura (2000) state that '[marketers should] . . . develop models that integrate measurement segmentation, one-to-one marketing, targeting and positioning. This will lead to decisions based directly on managerial objectives and enable empirical validation of segmentation in different conditions' (Wedel and Kamakura, 2000: 23).

In summary, in the heritage industry it is fast becoming recognized that heritage attractions and brands, in particular those that want repeat business (most of them do), must address the needs of their visitors/customers and that this focus should be a (on-going) priority from which the rest (targeting, interpretation, resource management, etc.) will follow. Heritage attractions or other heritage consumer brands must appeal to the **aspirations, needs and motivations** of prospective and regular customers.

Heritage is an ideal and nostalgia, which is often closely related to the celebration of heritage, is a **positive aspirational emotion**. These aspects of heritage are wanted by all types of consumers, and this makes them ideal for marketing.

Market and marketing research

The aspirations of prospective customers (or other customers: existing ones, lapsed ones, etc.) should be identified through the processes of market and marketing research, which can be either primary or secondary research (or both), qualitative and quantitative, using an inductive or deductive approach (or both).

Customers can be researched and reached using a variety of techniques (depending on time/cost factors and information required) including, telephone, email, direct mail, face-to-face, observation (ethnographic research) and experimentation.

The aim should be to track changes in consumer profiles and attitudes over time. The information gained can be used to demonstrate the value of the heritage product, evidence that is increasingly being called for by all types of stakeholders.

A survey, part of which is usually a questionnaire, should maximize the opportunity (a respondent can usually only be engaged for a maximum of 30 minutes and may need an incentive to respond in the first place, such as a free drink in the café or an associated gift item) to solicit relevant information for current and future strategic marketing planning.

The questionnaire should be divided up as follows:

- 10 per cent of the questions should be related to the demographic and socio-economic characteristics of the respondent, as follows:
  1 gender
  2 age
  3 nationality
  4 ethnicity
  5 education
  6 address or postcode;

- 60 per cent of the questions should be on consumer behaviour. The example below is about a heritage visitor attraction:
  1 Did the visit take place alone or in a group?
  2 What was the duration of the visit?
  3 How did he/she travel to the venue?
  4 Is this a first or repeat visit?
  5 Reasons for the visit.

6   How much did the individual spend on the visit?
7   What sources of information were used to plan the visit?

- the final 30 per cent of questions should deal with what the visitor thinks about the heritage venue (using the same example):
  1   customer service
  2   the content at the venue
  3   interpretation
  4   ticket price (if appropriate)
  5   accessibility
  6   parking
  7   signage
  8   the shop
  9   the eating area(s)/refreshments available
  10   suitability for children and other groups
  11   special events.

Insight 3.1: Museum Monitor: a Netherlands market research initiative

In 2003, museums in The Netherlands created an innovative initiative to understand from each other the factors that contribute to the visit of an individual or group to a Dutch museum. This nationwide visitor research project would enable each museum to compare their relative performance continuously in terms of visitors' perceptions of the experience at the museum. Although there are costs associated with joining this consortium and individual museums have to carry out their own surveys, the results are analysed by a professional market research agency and evidence provided to individual museums from which marketing strategy, design of exhibits, presentation and interpretation of all aspects of the museum can be created and implemented. It has proven to be extremely useful feedback.

The first round of information gathering took place from 1 January to 31 December 2003. The sample consisted of 8100 visitors to 32 museums. The findings were as follows.

Profile – the main visitors to Dutch museums in terms of demographics (gender and age group) are predominantly female and usually over 50 years old (the 'grey' market). In terms of socio-economic characteristics they tend to be 'well-educated'. This confirms a consumer profile of museum visitors that is found in almost every country.

Further important consumer profiling facts also emerged:

- approximately 40 per cent visit a museum three times a year and 35 per cent visit six times or more;
- 50 per cent plus of the visitors are visiting for the first time and 20 per cent repeat their visit within a year;

- 'young' people and ethnic minority groups are under-represented among the visiting consumers;
- 40 per cent of visitors live in the region of the museum, 50 per cent in The Netherlands and 10 per cent are from other countries, mainly Germany or Belgium;
- the average length of a visit is 1 hour and 15 minutes for 'small' museums and 2 hours for 'larger' establishments;
- the vast majority of visitors arrive by car, then public transport and finally bicycles;
- the main reason for visiting archaeological or historical museums is 'information gathering'; museums of natural history scored highly as a 'nice way to spend leisure time' and 56 per cent of the respondents stated that they visit art museums for 'inspiration' and 'peace and quiet' (22 per cent). 60 per cent of visitors will see the entire exhibition/collection, 32 per cent visit for the purposes of a temporary exhibition and less than 10 per cent of visitors mentioned a museum's programme of events as the main purpose for their visit;
- museums in The Netherlands scored an 8 on a scale of 0–10 for 'friendliness', 'general atmosphere', the collections and accessibility by car, as well as information given by front-of-house staff. Large museums score better than small museums in terms of accessibility, shops and eating areas/cafés but smaller museums scored more highly on general customer care;
- approximately 7 per cent of visitors to all museums taking part in the survey found information about the collection and exhibitions, signs, shops and cafés unsatisfactory;
- the perception of a reasonable ticket price is £2.30 (€3.40) for smaller museums to £3.70 (€5.5) for larger museums. Respondents thought that children's tickets should be £1.10 (€1.70) in small museums and £1.70 (€2.60) in the larger ones and that extra facilities such as guided tours and lectures should be charge at between £1.70 (€2.50) and £1.20 (€1.85). (Acknowledgment: *Museum Practice Magazine*, Summer 2004.)

Demographic characteristics

The *gender* profile for almost all aspects of heritage tends to have a slight female bias, which must be a function of psychographic factors. That is, women are not necessarily more intrigued by aspects of the past or symbols of them (such as art, music or literature) but are more likely to spend their time and money on this than men, or at least to take the lead in the **decision-making process** when selecting a short or long break where historical architecture or another aspect of the cultural heritage of that country (such as food, for example a visit to a heritage food festival or a literature event and so on) might be high on the sightseeing agenda.

Age characteristics are very significant in respect of all sectors of the heritage industry. Notably (as mentioned above in Insight 3.1) the 'grey' market, which has increased substantially both in volume and value terms in the developed West, has contributed greatly to the engagement with many aspects of heritage, in particular heritage tourism but also the greater consumption of food and drink with a heritage connection. Simply speaking, people in this demographic group tend to be 'empty nesters' (position in **family life-cycle**) who have the greatest amount of wealth and leisure time in which to spend it (relative to other positions in the family life-cycle). In terms of psychographics, this group usually find it self-rewarding to 'discover' or experience aspects of the past and not necessarily those with which they have a direct personal connection – this therefore is a prime target market that can usually be 'easily' identified for targeting purposes through databases such as ACORN and Experian's (direct-marketing agency) MOSAIC. Both of these databases have to be paid for; however, it is also useful to the heritage marketer or student of heritage marketing to register with The Future Foundation (http://www.futurefoundation.com), as they will often release cutting-edge research shortly after they have achieved a return, which can be acquired for nothing.

Let us look briefly at two tables that amplify the fact that the majority of heritage consumers are in the 25+ age groups in most developed countries. Table 3.1 deals with the UK market, Table 3.2 with the US market.

The following facts by Datamonitor, reported in an article in *The Times*, July 2004, illustrate the significance of the over-50s (grey) market in the UK.

Table 3.1 Trends and projections in UK population, by age group, 1999–2008

Age group	1999 (000s)	Per cent	2003 (000s)	Per cent	2008 (000s, projected)	Per cent
0–4	3600	6.2	3337	5.7	3394	5.6
5–9	3855	6.6	3635	6.1	3377	5.6
15–19	3601	6.6	3832	6.4	3392	6.5
20–24	3418	5.8	3697	6.2	4000	6.6
25–34	8697	14.9	8086	13.6	7629	12.6
35–44	8464	14.5	9061	15.2	9054	15.0
45–54	7723	13.2	7607	12.8	8134	13.5
55–64	6026	10.3	6752	11.3	7305	12.0
65+	9266	15.8	9501	16.0	9948	16.5
Total	**58 481**	**100**	**59 427**	**100**	**60 392**	**100**

Source: Mintel.

Table 3.2 Trends in US population, by age group, 1995–2000

	1995 (000s)	Per cent	1999 (000s)	Per cent	2000 (000s)	Per cent
0–4	19 532	7.6	18 853	7.4	18 865	6.9
5–9	19 096	7.2	18 062	7.3	19 781	7.2
15–19	18 203	7.1	17 765	6.9	19 897	7.2
20–24	17 982	7.7	19 135	6.8	18 518	6.7
25–29	18 905	8.5	21 236	7.2	17 861	6.5
30–34	21 825	8.8	21 912	8.3	19 580	7.1
35–39	22 296	8.0	19 982	8.5	22 276	8.1
40–44	20 259	7.1	17 795	7.7	22 618	8.2
45–49	17 458	5.5	13 824	6.6	19 901	7.2
50–54	13 642	4.6	11 370	5.2	17 265	6.3
55–59	11 086	4.2	10 474	4.2	13 324	4.8
60–64	10 046	4.3	10 619	3.8	10 677	3.9
65–69	9926	4.0	10 077	3.8	9436	2.4
70–74	8831	3.2	8023	3.4	8753	3.2
Total	**269 820**	**87.8**	**219 127**	**87.1**	**238 752**	**85.7**

Source: Mintel.

1 In 2003, empty nesters (those with no children or dependants living at home) spent £38.4 billion on consumer goods – a figure set to rise to £46 billion in the next five years.

2 By 2008 there will be 8.5 million consumers in the category of 'early empty nesters' and their annual disposable income per head will have increased by 8.5 per cent to £17 872 compared with £14 382 on the Continent.

3 'Late empty nesters' (those whose children who return to the family home after an initial departure) are poorer. There are 9.5 million in this group and the average disposable income is £10 800, which is still higher than their European counterparts whose average is £10 019.

4 Visitors to heritage attractions and sites are highly likely to have completed a level of education beyond schooling, with many having post-graduate qualifications. The proportion of heritage visitors with a higher education qualification is almost double the European Union average, which means that these visitors are likely to be more educated than the population as a whole.

5 Visitors with this type of educational profile are therefore also likely to have high-status occupational roles; indeed the surveys found that 60 per cent were in managerial or professional positions. In short, visitors to her-

itage sites and attractions are almost certainly 'white collar' workers with less than 20 per cent of customers in manual or unskilled jobs. The consumption of heritage is seen by these individuals as an important element in their identity formation and projection.

6   The emerging profile of heritage visitors described above, where there is a dominant group of white collar and 'older' profile customers, means that the average income of this group is also relatively 'high'. The European Association for Tourism and Leisure Education (ATLAS) found that over one-third of heritage consumers has a household income of over €40 000 per year, which is significantly higher than the European average.

7   The heritage visitor is likely to enjoy the benefits of an attraction whilst on a 'short break', rather than as an exclusive (long) vacation. In the ATLAS studies, a large proportion of the tourists interviewed were on a touring holiday (30 per cent) or a city break (10 per cent) with the vast majority residing in the area for less than three days and with a tendency to stay in hotels (because of their disposable income) rather than in other types of accommodation.

8   Heritage consumers tend to travel with a partner or family, rarely alone. The benefits sought are new experiences and the opportunity to learn new things, in particular to be able to imagine and possibly 'see' how things were in the past – a mix of entertainment and education, which has come to be known as 'edutainment'.

9   However, the heritage site or attraction itself is rarely the motivator for making a trip but is seen as 'added value' to an area that travel consumers might wish to visit – clearly much needs to be done in order to stimulate this demand when visitors are in an area which has a heritage site(s).

The demographic characteristics of adult visitors to castles, folk parks, museums and galleries are on the whole 'younger' than visitors to historic houses. Another important fact is that repeat visits to most heritage sites are comparatively rare, compared with visits to, for example, 'roller-coaster' theme parks or 'seaside' resorts, although visits to heritage sites rank highly amongst this overall market. However, visits to cultural heritage festivals (such as literature, food and music) are more likely to have repeat visits.

The length of time visitors spend at sites is related to the type of site and the extent to which it is 'developed' in terms of interpretation and visitor facilities. Seasonality is a factor and, as we shall establish in the next chapter, creates a **product life-cycle** for these sites that they are keen to extend, in particular from September through into the autumn and possibly the winter months.

Although the concept of seasonality is well documented in terms of tourism, a relatively new and under-researched area of segmentation is

chronographic segmentation, which is segmentation of consumers based on an understanding of their temporal preferences (i.e., timing/time) for the consumption of certain goods and services. Price discrimination, which is usually based on matching time differences and consumer characteristics, is well documented in the literature and widely practiced but there is room for more refinement of this approach, which might lead to greater product/service satisfaction, enhanced profitability and competitive advantage.

Several other important age groups include schoolchildren, who are important for the built environment and possibly also other aspects of heritage depending on what they are studying: art, artefacts and curios from indigenous and other cultures, music, food and drink, literature, etc.; 'young' adults, who have fuelled the 'short-break' market in many countries (see Table 3.3), aided by low-cost airlines and the frequency and flexibility that they offer for travel; and 'middle-aged' women (the 'yummy-mummy' market), which has created a gradually increased demand for short visits (day, weekend) to 'spas', which are usually located in historical buildings, an important factor in choice of venue for this market.

National and international target markets

Visit London (http://www.visitlondon.com) is a website aimed at communicating with a national and international market for visitors to London. The key target markets (segmented by country) it identifies are as follows:

Table 3.3 An insight into the 'Top 10' 'short breaks' destinations

Ranking (2003)	Destination	Previous year's ranking (2002)
1	Paris	1
2	Amsterdam	2
3	New York	3
4	Barcelona	5
5	Prague	7
6	Dublin	6
7	Rome	4
8	Venice	8
9	Brussels	9
10	Bruges	–

Source: American Express Travel's annual short breaks survey, *Travel and Trade Gazette* (2003).

- *USA* – in this market *Visit London* is trying to attract **Baby Boomers**, aged 40–55 years, who live in large cities such as New York, Chicago, San Francisco and Washington, have a family income in excess of US$70 000 and '. . . who appreciate the heritage, culture and shopping experiences of London'.
- *France* – the key target market in France is **Young Independents**, aged 18–25 years, who reside in large conurbations and are likely to take short city breaks. Another target market here is **DINKS** (Double Income No Kids), aged 25–35 years, with an interest in culture, nightlife and shopping.
- *Germany* – from this country the aim is to attract **Young Urban Professionals**, aged 25–35 years, who are likely to take 'out of season' city breaks; also both DINKS and **Empty Nesters**, aged 35–55 years, living in large cities and interested in heritage, culture, shopping and restaurants.
- *Ireland* – once again, a prime target market is DINKS, aged 20–35 years, living in main cities, able and willing to take low-season city breaks and want museums and historical sites together with restaurants and nightlife.
- *Spain* – a key target group are DINKS, aged 25–44 years, living in the largest/most populated cities such as Madrid and Barcelona, who are interested in city/short breaks and looking, in particular, to discover something of the London **way of life** (its heritage), together; more specifically, shopping, art galleries, museums, events, musicals, trendy restaurants and clubs (in other literature they may be referred to as 'culture vultures').

From time to time *Visit London* runs 'sectoral' communications campaigns, heavy on advertising, particularly in the print media, although leaflets may be sent to travel agents and agencies used for **door drops** in various parts of Europe. Examples include 'sectors' such as 'Royal London' (this was significantly the case at the time of the Golden Jubilee in 2002), 'Eating' and 'Shopping'.

Insight 3.2: London – ten facts and figures

Clearly many consumers are interested in coming to London because of its heritage (or aspects of it). Some of London's heritage can be described using the following data and information:

1　London is the UK's most populated city, with 7.19 million residents (2001 data).
2　London is 'young' and vibrant, 47 per cent of its population is aged 16–44 years.

3   London is 'diverse' in terms of its population; over 200 languages are spoken in London.

4   London is an international business centre with over 25 per cent of the world's largest companies having their European headquarters based there.

5   Almost one-third of London's geographical area is 'green' space or parks, many of which are Royal Parks – this is more than any other city of its size, in the world.

6   London has 6000 restaurants and 5000 pubs and bars, and (in 2001) 20 000 licensed taxis (to get you home!).

7   There are 151 historic buildings and ancient monuments and 33 historic gardens; it has three world heritage sites: HM Tower of London, Maritime Greenwich and Westminster Abbey.

8   London has over 200 museums, 500 cinema screens, 108 music halls, 1500 drama groups, 600 dance troupes and five symphony orchestras.

9   In terms of sport and sporting heritage, there are 95 golf courses, 50 athletics tracks, 2000 tennis courts, seven ice rinks, 546 swimming pools, 37 rowing clubs, 12 professional soccer teams, two county cricket clubs and six race courses, all within an hour of London.

10 In 2002, 28 million people visited for at least one night.

Acknowledgment: *Visit London* website http://www.visitlondon.com (2004).

Socio-economic and cultural characteristics

What about the JICNARS social-class/status categories?

ABC1s, sometimes heavily influenced by their children ('reverse socialization') are also a prime target market for many aspects of heritage because of their relative levels of education and income (compared to the C2s, Ds and E groups), in particular at a local level for visits to museums. In many surveys they have revealed that their reasons for visiting are to become more **culturally aware** of their locality or of something that has been made locally accessible to them (for example, the wish to learn from a temporary or 'travelling' exhibition), as part of a self-education process. This group, irrespective of ethnic origin, more often than not, places a high value on education generally (see Case studies 3.1 and 3.2 on Brighton Pavilion and Warwick Castle, below).

We have studied some of these points in the previous chapter under social and political factors but, in addition, it is worth noting that in recent research carried out by MORI in the UK (which can be extrapolated to most other countries), it was found that after schools and libraries, parents view museums as the most important places for educating their children and some of the most trustworthy sources of information, more highly valued than books, radio, newspapers and the Internet.

1 80 per cent of parents believe that museums are a very important resource for educating their children.
2 85 per cent of parents believe visits to museums should be part of the National Curriculum.
3 National museums are responsible for over 1 million educational sessions per year and expect to host and inspire 1.72 million this year.
4 Children make one-quarter of all museum visits.

What further evidence do we have of socio-economic groups and their level of cultural capital?

In 2001, Mintel, in conjunction with the Target Group Index (TGI), carried out an extensive survey of marketing to AB adults in the UK in order to discover the extent of their knowledge and culture. Table 3.4 below identifies

Table 3.4 Interest in the arts, as watched on television, by stage of life-cycle

'Art' form	Pre-family (%)	Family (%)	Empty nesters (%)	Post-family (%)
Opera:				
Men	8	7	15	15
Women	9	7	15	29
Ballet:				
Men	5	5	7	19
Women	13	13	22	38
Contemporary dance:				
Men	4	5	8	8
Women	7	14	16	15
Classical music, concerts:				
Men	10	16	27	43
Women	17	17	29	46
Jazz performances:				
Men	11	14	16	17
Women	9	11	16	14
Popular/rock concerts:				
Men	58	58	51	11
Women	60	52	45	9

Source: Premier TGI, BRMB 1999, 2000/Mintel.

Table 3.5 Interest in the arts, as read about in newspapers, by stage of life-cycle

'Art' form	Pre-family (%)	Family (%)	Empty nesters (%)	Post-family (%)
Theatre – musicals:				
Men	18	15	22	26
Women	36	32	35	37
Theatre – plays:				
Men	26	19	29	30
Women	38	34	42	43
Opera:				
Men	5	4	9	13
Women	12	5	14	18
Ballet:				
Men	4	3	5	7
Women	16	8	16	20
Contemporary dance:				
Men	3	3	5	2
Women	8	7	10	7
Classical music, concerts:				
Men	11	9	15	21
Women	12	8	21	27
Jazz performances:				
Men	13	9	10	10
Women	6	7	9	8
Popular/rock concerts:				
Men	52	38	33	5
Women	47	35	28	6
Art galleries/exhibitions:				
Men	33	22	29	30
Women	30	30	36	36
Museums:				
Men	29	30	33	32
Women	36	34	34	36

Source: Premier TGI, BRMB 1999, 2000/Mintel.

their interest in the arts, as watched on television, and Table 3.5, as read about in newspapers and magazines.

Table 3.6 refers to AB men and Table 3.7 to AB women. These tables determine their purchase of different types of paperback books.

Table 3.6 Choice of book by AB men

Book type	Pre-family (%)	Family (%)	Empty nesters (%)	Post-family (%)
Fiction	63	61	60	43
Travel	29	19	24	15
Reference	23	23	26	22
Biography	21	20	23	17
Sport	16	14	11	9
Cookery	11	9	10	6
Home/garden	9	10	10	10
Health	6	5	4	5
Children's	5	32	3	7
Other non-fiction	37	24	29	25

Source: Premier TGI, BRMB 1999, 2000/Mintel.

Table 3.7 Choice of book by AB women

Book type	Pre-family (%)	Family (%)	Empty nesters (%)	Post-family (%)
Fiction	80	70	74	56
Travel	27	17	25	13
Reference	24	19	23	20
Biography	23	23	18	12
Sport	3	4	5	1
Cookery	21	23	22	14
Home/garden	11	14	16	14
Health	12	12	11	7
Children's	15	57	16	19
Other non-fiction	21	26	26	19

Source: Premier TGI, BRMB 1999, 2000/Mintel.

Tables 3.4–3.7 confirm the female bias in terms of all aspects of cultural heritage, except Jazz performances, and the extent to which the alternatives are patronized (through the media of television viewing and newspaper/magazine reading) by AB adults, namely that there is more interest in popular/rock concerts amongst all adults regardless of gender than for any other type of culture investigated in this survey. In terms of books, the 'take up' amongst both genders declines steadily through the life-cycle stages and, with the exception of travel, there is a female bias again in all types of books.

'Heritage tourism' (which is covered much more extensively in the next chapter) and 'arts tourism' are often either lumped together or the terms are used interchangeably, often under the more generic category of 'cultural tourism'. However, research by the European Cultural Tourism Research Project (begun in 1991 and has conducted two major surveys, in 1992 and 1997) run by ATLAS concludes that there are major differences between the two and that a recognition of these is crucial for both understanding the different segments and targeting them appropriately.

In short, heritage attractions tend to be more easily accessible and attract a much broader target market than arts-based attractions, the latter requiring a much greater level of 'cultural capital' from the visitor than is the case for most heritage attractions.

The surveys also revealed clear differences in visitor profiles, for example:

1   Heritage attractions also tend to have a much broader appeal as far as tourists are concerned. Over one-third of tourists visiting heritage sites surveyed in Europe came from outside Europe, compared with 15 per cent of tourists visiting other cultural attractions. Local residents accounted for only 16 per cent of visitors to heritage sites.
2   Visitors to heritage sites tended to have an 'older' profile than visitors to other sites. Over 40 per cent of heritage visitors were aged 50 years or over, compared with 25 per cent of visitors to other cultural sites. The surveys have advocated that there is a definite 'growth' in nostalgia, which has fuelled the demand for visits to heritage sites and attractions and, without doubt, contributed to the increased demand for specific heritage tourism.

In terms of socio-cultural characteristics such as race, religion and ethnicity or sub-cultures such as those which are sexuality based, it is clear that little has been achieved in addressing the aspirations of these target markets, particularly in European countries (there have been many more advances in the USA). However, this is high on political agendas as we saw in the previous chapter, particularly in countries such as England, France, The Netherlands and Germany. For example, there are very few museums (let alone anything else) around the world dedicated to the religious and spiritual heritage of very large international populations such as Jews, Hindus, Muslims and Catholics. All of these groups have been persecuted over the centuries and although there may be historical documentation to account for this, it is usually too 'highbrow' to be accessible, even to niche markets – they have stories (and many, many other aspects of heritage) which are not just worth telling but must have a wider audience and, as we have seen above, the customers are of exactly the right type, ready and willing. At a more 'local' level, although there may have been significant changes in local government policy in many countries to allow for the building of temples, synagogues and mosques (Belfast is about to have its own purpose-built mosque) and to encourage the celebration of cultural heritage aspects such as food, dance and music, much, much more can be done. In the UK alone there are approximately 7 million Asians and, even though increasingly they do not want to be recognized as a singular group, there are important similarities between them that would enable them to be a target market (for all sorts of identity-connected goods and services); this also applies to the current generation, which still, on the whole, has a personal connection with roots and origins. There is a danger that the identity of subsequent generations will become subsumed into the more 'general' indigenous culture and that diversity will, itself, be remembered nostalgically.

Psychographic characteristics

We have overlapped with psychographics several times in analysing the segmentation variables above but now we must go back to a specific target market briefly mentioned above, the 'Yummy Mummy' market. This is a relatively new way of psychographically profiling women from ABC1 socio-economic backgrounds and who tend to be in the mid-40s age group. In terms of position in the family life-cycle, they are usually 'Full-nest 1 or 2' and, with respect to the consumer decision-making model, take responsibility for organizing family holidays but are also in the market for some personal luxury/quality time. This target market has proven to be very lucrative for the 'spa' entrepreneurs in particular (most facilities are based at heritage sites/hotels), both in the UK and other parts of Europe such as The Netherlands, Belgium, Hungary and some Scandinavian countries where 'traditional'/period buildings and landscapes are often used to house the latest in health and beauty provision; they are always **premium priced** leisure options (see Insight 3.3).

The business to business **(B2B)** market, which is also a significant target market for these types of venues will be discussed more fully later in the chapter.

Insight 3.3: Grand Heritage Hotel: Cliveden, Buckinghamshire, UK

Cliveden is a hotel in the Buckinghamshire countryside that comes under several **umbrella brands** of hotels, notably the Grand Heritage collection, which is international. This particular brand targets the general public, especially ABC1's, the 'grey' and 'yummy mummy' markets, business/corporate market, the Wedding and other social occasion market and 'club' members.

> **Pleasure, frolic or extravagant diversion was all that he laid to heart.**
> (The Second Duke of Buckingham, 1666)

Cliveden House is Britain's only AA five red-starred hotel. It was formerly a stately home and is now owned by The National Trust; it is set in 376 acres of landscaped grounds and parklands on chalk cliffs that gave the estate its name.

The House was built in 1666 and, since then, three Dukes, an Earl, the Astors and Frederick, Prince of Wales have all owned and lived at Cliveden. Because of its proximity to Windsor, Queen Victoria visited no less that eight times – she was not amused when in 1893 it was bought by William Waldorf Astor, America's richest citizen, who gave it to his son and daughter-in-law in 1905. It became famous for its social events, which included guests such as Charlie Chaplin, Winston Churchill, President Roosevelt and George Bernard Shaw. It is a remarkable stately home of astonishing grandeur and with many stories to tell. Edwin Lee, butler to the Astors from 1912 to 1960, recalled that in its Edwardian heyday 'Dinners for between 50 and 60 were very frequent and probably two or three balls for anything up to 500 or 600 would be given in a season'. Stephen Ward and Christine Keeler were staying in Spring Cottage in the grounds of the hotel when they set off the infamous Profumo scandal. Harold Macmillan, another frequent guest, when told that the house was eventually to become a hotel remarked, '. . . My dear boy, it always has been'.

Cliveden was originally conceived as a hunting lodge by the 2nd Duke of Buckingham where he could entertain his friends and mistress. His legacy is still evident in the range of activities on offer, including golf, fishing, shooting, archery, horse-riding and a flotilla of vintage launches in the Cliveden Boathouse; there are more 'up-to-date' facilities for tennis, squash, health (The Cliveden Spa) and fitness also available.

Cliveden has earned a place in history through every century of its existence, for example, the first performance of *Rule Britannia* by Thomas Arne was staged at Cliveden and, when the main building was burnt down in 1850, it was the architect Charles Barry, famous for creating the Houses of Parliament in London, who was commissioned to redesign the present house.

Cliveden is widely acknowledged as one of the world's great hotels, much aided by the fact that it is only a 20 minute drive from London's Heathrow Airport and only 40 minutes from central London.

Food and drink are a major part of the Cliveden experience and for both short stay and business target markets. There are various options on offer, including:

1   the Terrace Dining Room, which has views down the Parterre to the river Thames;
2   Waldo's, Cliveden's Michelin-starred restaurant, which has also won many other awards and accolades under the direction of the Executive Head Chef;
3   the French Dining Room has a unique décor and history originating from the Chateau d'Asniere, together with, reputedly, the finest French Rococo décor outside France;
4   the Cellar Dining Room, which was once the cellar of the house but restored by the Astor family; and
5   the Macmillan Dining Room.

Cliveden also targets the Wedding, day-trip and leisure markets, notably for the latter with 'The Cliveden Spa', providing a range of treatments from aromatherapy and Reiki massage to reflexology, all administered by professional therapists.

Finally, 'The Cliveden Club' offers members a complete programme of social events throughout the year, including a winter season of soirees, the annual Club Ball, visits to European cities, champagne and gourmet dinners, guest-speaker lunches and informal themed dinners. Additionally, the Club Room offers additional private meeting and dining areas.

The Grand Heritage guide, which includes 'The Distinguished Hotels Group', lists 145 'exclusive' heritage hotels in its portfolio. However, Cliveden is also part of another umbrella brand of 'select' heritage hotels that includes The Royal Crescent Hotel in Bath and Thornbury Castle, Gloucestershire.

The Royal Crescent Hotel occupies two central buildings in one of the most well-known landmarks in Bath, the Royal Crescent. Both the hotel and the Crescent are Grade 1 listed and were built by John Wood the Younger in the eighteenth century; the setting and architecture of the buildings remain unchanged. The Hotel targets the same markets as identified in the Cliveden example but the type of service differs slightly; for example, the whole ambience is less ostentatious, bedrooms are called 'Bedchambers' to reflect the period of history in which the hotel was built and personal touches such as a decanter of sherry and 'real fires' are provided in guests rooms.

Thornbury Castle was built by Edward Stafford, the third Duke of Buckingham who received a royal licence to build this 'fortified manor'/castle-palace in 1510; although work started the following year, it came to a halt in 1521 when the Duke was executed on grounds of treason. However, the building was finished and today it looks much the same as it did in the sixteenth century, with displays of coats of arms, intricate oriel windows, arrow loops and ornate carved ceilings.

Acknowledgment: Grand Heritage Hotels Guide, 2004 and website http://www. distinguishedhotels.com 2004.

Other changing/emerging lifestyle patterns

In the previous chapter, under social factors, we acknowledged that the heritage marketer must stay abreast of any changes, locally, nationally or internationally, which might give rise to opportunities. There are hundreds of examples that could be cited as the industry is vast, although the heritage marketer will usually be located within a particular sector, which makes the task somewhat more manageable. In the following two chapters this theme will be carried forward and many examples of heritage tourism and food and drink connected to the identity or heritage of regions and countries, localities and specific individuals will be given. However, there are a few general trends, particularly in the developed West, in terms of the current psyche of consumers that have great relevance for heritage marketing and are worth considering here.

In recent years, in the UK, there has been a growth in the demand for consumer foods that are sourced from as close to their origin as possible and have perhaps been grown or produced using 'traditional methods'. Increasingly, these have become available outside normal shopping environments (supermarkets) and notably at places such as 'Farmers Markets', which are often held in the 'open-air'. The reason for the exponential growth of such markets is because they are reminiscent of how shopping was transacted in the past – nostalgia again. In many parts of the world, of course, this is still the norm and consumers are looking to capture some of the enjoyment they have **experienced** on holidays in exactly those types of places – they now want it on their own doorstep. Local producers have risen only too happily (and profitably) to the challenge. There is a clear causal relationship here between a mass market (unusual for the heritage industry), nostalgia, experience and willing support for local enterprise that has benefited all parties concerned.

In many countries, especially Europe and the USA, for many years – and in particular with the growth in home ownership – there has been an unprecedented demand for 'period' homes. There are numerous examples of dwellings (**vernacular** and otherwise) that have been converted out of buildings with a history, many of which were originally designed for an entirely different use than living accommodation; examples include churches, schools, storage warehouses and windmills. This, too, is a function of changing lifestyles but also the perception amongst property consumers that these buildings (or converted units in them) offer unique living opportunities, exclusivity and overall a quality of life that is perhaps not achievable in more conventional dwellings. These types of property are sought after by a complete range of socio-economic groups and do not attract a particular age profile, although they do tend to be premium-priced options and often built by construction companies that have a **premium position** in the marketplace (see Insight 3.4).

In the previous chapter we saw that there is widespread recognition of the built environment as a tangible manifestation of local history and as a key determinant of the character and identity of a place. Investment from public- and private-sector sources in the re-use of historic buildings to enable consumption by new businesses and homes can only help to reinforce local identity and foster civic pride.

> In a context of increasing globalisation and the standardisation of high street multiples, it is the built form that gives an area uniqueness, character and distinctiveness.
>
> (English Heritage, 2002)

The increase in single-person households and an ageing population (demographic factors) are creating pressure for new homes on almost all urban locations. Heritage funding (as we saw in the previous chapter under economic factors), where it is matched or enhanced by contributions from other sectors, will create a positive multiplier-effect that can go some way (perhaps a long way) to regenerating a locality and also conserving parts of the built heritage that might otherwise be destroyed.

Insight 3.4: Framewood Manor, Ribston Hall and Priday's Mill

Framewood Manor in Buckinghamshire dates back to 1905 when it was built for The Lord Mayor of London but it has also been an independent school for girls, Halidon House School. Sixteen years ago it was converted into separate apartments for the AB socio-economic groups – these are highly premium-priced living options, partly because of the land values in this part of the country and also because of its proximity to London, which is reached by road or rail in approximately 30 minutes. The developer also provided a range of additional facilities for residents, including indoor and outdoor heated swimming pools, two tennis courts, spa area with steam room, solarium, Jacuzzi and a fully equipped gym; these are in addition to the beautiful landscaped grounds (over 6 acres) with extensive trees, shrubs and flowers, beyond which is the natural woodland.

Ribston Hall in Gloucestershire was originally a hotel called 'The Spa Hotel', built to accommodate visitors to the (then) fashionable Gloucester Spa, which was on the opposite side of the road. From 1860, Ribston Hall became a college for young ladies and later a College of Art. In 2003, the largely derelict building was sold by Gloucester City Council to Parkstone Homes (developer) who converted it into various types of living accommodation, from four-bedroom town houses to one-bedroom apartments, with communal landscaping, car parking, and shared corridors and lobbies. The developer has tried to preserve the history of Ribston Hall by maintaining and repairing existing features and overall by being sympathetic in their restoration techniques; they have paid particular attention to the restoration of the stucco external walling, which was decorated in a Greek Revival pattern. The prices charged for the units of accommodation are considerably lower than for Framewood Manor and reflect land values, local labour costs (for the building and restoration) and what customers are prepared to pay for similar types of housing in this locality, in this part of the country.

Gloucester Docks form the northern terminal of the Gloucester and Sharpness Canal; this Canal originates at Sharpness where it joins the River Severn, north of the Severn Bridge, and stretches some 12.5 miles up to the city of Gloucester. The Docks (wet and dry) have been in existence since before Victorian times but were particularly vibrant during that period because of international trade and the extensive use of waterways in Britain for the movement of goods. The Docks are home to many large warehouses (known as 'Mills') which were used for the storage of goods awaiting shipment to other locations; they have fallen into decline over many years but have recently been given 'licence' by the Council to private firms to turn them into business and living accommodation. Priday's Mill Homes Ltd was the first developer to contribute to the regeneration of this inland port. Priday's Mill, one of the warehouses, was built in 1850 for Priday Metford and Company Ltd, flour merchants, and has been transformed into 40 one- and two-bedroom luxury apartments. The units are of a 'higher specification' than those at Ribston Hall and, whereas the target market for the latter is largely local, the aim with Priday's Mill is to attract a more national profile of client, in particular young, urban professionals who might want to make a base/home in Gloucester but spend much of their time away on business.

Acknowledgments: Hamptons Estate Agents, Lane Fox Estate Agents, 2004.

One further heritage market that continues to grow is that for automobile heritage. This market caters for general car enthusiasts but also those who are interested in the heritage of branded cars, such as the UK's 'Morgan' car, BMW in Germany, Volvo and Saab in Sweden, or other 'vintage' cars. Once again, these are always premium-priced brands and there are often very long waiting lists for new models, such as is the case for Morgans. Morgan cars are modelled on 'old' or 'traditional' styles, i.e., the type that the company used to make. They have to be specially ordered from the firm itself – this can be explored further in Chapter 6, together with a consideration of some companies who use their heritage actively in many marketing initiatives.

The business to business/corporate target market

The **business to business** (B2B) market, in particular for 'corporate events' such as exhibitions, parties and conferences, has become (and continues to grow, corporate budgets allowing) a significant consumer of heritage products. In particular, **heritage venues** such as period properties are popular for hosting events, although modern-day state-of-the art technology and possibly health and fitness and other sporting facilities might also be required. A combination of the 'old' (for example, a period building) and 'new' (up-to-date facilities) is becoming a growth area and is primarily being taken on board by hotel chains and individual private providers (see Case study 4.1, 'A new era for spas in the UK' in the next chapter).

Insight 3.5: One Birdcage Walk, London

One Birdcage Walk is a 'corporate events' location in the heart of London between the Houses of Parliament and Buckingham Palace. There are eleven different meeting rooms that can accommodate from 12 to 200 delegates and full catering facilities are available to suit the clients' needs, from a simple buffet to a complete 'silver service' dinner. The venue also has an extensive collection of audio-visual technology and, of course, the **atmosphere** and **ambience** of a unique, architecturally significant historical building in one of the oldest built environments in the world: London.

One Birdcage Walk was originally the site of James I's aviary, which his grandson, Charles II, extended. Birdcage Walk was created as part of the post-restoration remodelling of St James's Park; up until 1828 only the Hereditary Grand Falconer (the Duke of St Albans) and the Royal Family could drive down it.

The building is regarded as one of the finest examples of traditional architecture in Westminster. The interiors and function rooms are styled to reflect Birdcage Walk's heritage and its strong engineering tradition; the accommodation is situated between the graceful eighteenth-century houses of Queen Anne's Gate to the East and the Wellington Barracks to the West. Birdcage Walk is surrounded by notable landmarks including Westminster Abbey, Buckingham Palace and the Houses of Parliament.

Acknowledgment: One Birdcage Walk, London, 2004.

There are hundreds of different venues which have literally 'opened their doors' (see Case study 3.3, 'The Admirable Crichton, Events and Parties Organizers, London, UK') to the corporate market, many of which are block-booked years in advance of the event taking place. They are chosen because of the immediate existence of a **WOW factor**, which is offered by the **uniqueness** of the interior and exterior of their heritage buildings and landscapes. This factor can be very difficult to create in a different way.

In Scotland, historic sites such as Edinburgh and Stirling Castles, Castle Fraser and Haddon House in Aberdeenshire are amongst the most popular choice of **heritage venue** for the business to business market. Edinburgh Castle can accommodate 120 seated delegates or 1000 standing, and Stirling Castle can accommodate 700 for a corporate reception and up to 300 for a full-service dinner. If space is at a premium relative to the required number of guests, temporary structures can be set up alongside to provide the additional space.

In May 2003, Zygo Events devised structures for the Antiques and Audacity exhibition at Arundel Castle, UK. The 2040 m² 'Premier Pavilion' provided an exhibition area, dining area, reception and toilets and there were additional storage and kitchen facilities. Challenges for these organizers included operating through restricted access (because of the width of the castle gates) and ensuring that there was no damage to the castle grounds – scaffolding up to 4-m high was required in setting up the structure.

Temporary structures such as marquees create capacity and flexibility, which may be important if, for example, the venue is also open to the public. The corporate hospitality can continue in the unique environment but without necessarily encroaching on the enjoyment of other consumers.

Glasgow's Corinthian building, which in the past has been the Union Bank of Scotland and the city's High Court, has a domed main bar, restaurant, cocktail lounge, late-night piano bar, nightclub and two floors of meeting and event spaces. South of Glasgow is another popular heritage venue, Floors Castle, home of the 10th Duke of Roxburge. It offers 22 bedrooms, space for up to 150 delegates for a reception or 80 seated and a range of **heritage sporting facilities** including clay-pigeon shooting and fly fishing.

Several Scottish Museums are also looking increasingly at offering their heritage venues and unique collections for the corporate market. The National Museums of Scotland, in six different locations including the Royal Museum and the National War Museum of Scotland, offer all the dining facilities required by this target market, in addition to a rolling programme of temporary exhibitions. This means that even if the same venue is re-used, the chances are that there will be something different to view on offer.

In 2001, expenditure by delegates at conferences, corporate events and incentive programmes in Scotland amounted to £888 million, almost a quarter of total tourism spend. Edinburgh is now ranked among the top ten business locations in the world, while Glasgow is the fastest-growing business destination in Europe ... within ten years, if not before, Scotland will be recognised by meeting and event planners and the wider business community throughout the world for its great venues, great service and great value for money ... Scotland offers the chance to combine business and pleasure ... it's unique because it blends tradition with modernity ... it's also easily accessible (mainly because of frequent and 'low cost' flights) yet, once here, you feel you've escaped into a totally new environment; organisers are increasingly aware that it takes only one hour to get to Edinburgh (from London) while I can take that long to get to the M25.

(Packman, 2003)

Unique Venues of London (UVL) has 54 venues that are primarily used for the corporate events market and represent £25 million in turnover for the company. Recent 'acquisitions' include Tate Britain, which has greatly increased the overall business for the firm because of its ability as a venue to provide reception/dining facilities and private viewings of the art. A further addition has been Tower Bridge, which immediately on its acquisition generated 70 enquiries that, more importantly for UVL, were from events organizers that attend trade fairs to seek out venues that they do not. On the other side of London in Westminster, the Cabinet War Rooms have also been added to the list of venues, as they have been recently restored and areas of the site hidden since the Second World War have been uncovered – a restored generator room has proved popular for firms who are launching a new product – and in general the 'secret history' of the location inspires and interests people.

The overall business to business/corporate target market can be segmented according to **needs, size (volume of guests and value, i.e., spend per head) and also match with sector/profession**. For example, the Tudor Hall at the Honourable Society of Lincoln's Inn was used by the American Bar Association who wanted an 'associated' but distinctly British venue for its recent meeting. The Dulwich Picture Gallery is often used for fashion shows because of its long, slender geometry and Shakespeare's Globe Theatre on the South Bank in London (a reconstruction of the original building that was located nearby in the 1500s) is often requested by organizers for events that have a literary or theatrical association.

French cosmetics firm Clarins held a three-day corporate event for its London sales staff at Sadler's Wells, a seventeenth-century theatre that has recently been redeveloped (at a cost of £50 million) into a multipurpose venue. The Sadler's Wells 'red', which stands out throughout the theatre, worked well with Clarins' own brand colour and the stage was used for a 'Moulin Rouge'-style theme.

Ironbridge Gorge Museum in Shropshire, a UNESCO World Heritage Site (see Chapter 4 for more details on both the museum and World Heritage Sites in general) has also undergone a redevelopment. £7 million has been

spent on transforming the engineering floors of the former cast iron manufacturing facility at Coalbrookdale into the 'Engine Shop', which can hold
banquets for up to 400 delegates. The venue recently played host to the
Organisation of World Heritage Cities (which includes the 198 UN World
Heritage Sites) for a regional (northwest Europe) meeting. Norway's city of
Bergen director of heritage management (Siri Myrvoll) summed up the
essence of the meeting: 'The Victorian village came to life in a wonderful
way and the evening was a perfect end to a successful meeting at an **inspirational** venue' (*EventsSolutions Magazine*, 2003).

The National Coal Mining Museum, which is situated between
Huddersfield and Wakefield, offers all the facilities required for a corporate
event, together with mining-**themed** adventure days. These take place 140 m
underground and are designed to improve communication and problem-
solving skills.

> The themed party has been around since Egyptian times ... today, theming has
> become de rigeur for corporate and private events.
>
> (Hoare, 2003)

The main aim of 'theming' is to make the event more **memorable** than
another and to allow delegates the chance to express some of their own indi-
viduality (and use their **imagination**): imagination is always more powerful
than the creativity of a graphic artist. For example, a few years ago, Arena
Events hired disused warehouses in London's Docklands in order to produce a Christmas Fun Fair, the most attractive part of which was the stun-
ning wood and paintwork of an ancient tobacco warehouse. 'By using
lighting, dramatic natural greenery and fairground stalls, the warehouse
was transformed into an atmospheric party venue. In the harsh reality of
daylight, the venue still resembled a disused warehouse but at night it came
alive' (Hoare, 2003).

When Arena used the Commonwealth Institute for the first time the
museum still had a large collection of artefacts that could not be disguised or
removed; these were involved in an overall theme that became 'Christmas in
the Lost Kingdoms'. On another occasion, the same venue was transformed
into an ocean-going liner, the SS Viceroy of India, by creating a ship's bridge
and producing a moving sky that, together, gave the impression of being on
board a ship.

Once a theme has been selected, it is important to follow it through from
the invitation to the reception, catering event staff, entertainers and even
gifts or other promotional items/'give-aways'. This **reinforces the message**
and the event should remain uppermost in the mind of the guests.

The Royal Museum in Scotland was used by United International Pictures
for the film premiere party for *The Thomas Crown Affair*. They wanted this
location because it was considered by the organizers to be unusual and
combined character with culture.

Another target business market is **film and television producers** (and advertising agencies that brief Directors) who frequently use heritage buildings and houses, either as backdrops or indeed the whole building (interiors included) as locations for the filming of their project. They might also choose to use a heritage venue for **PR** (as in the case of the party for the premiere of *The Thomas Crown Affair*). For example, Knebworth House in Hertfordshire, UK has been used in many films, advertisements, television programmes and music videos, including *Inspector Morse* and the Gene Wilder (American comedian) films/'spoofs'.

Knebworth House, because of its extensive outside space and unique backdrop (the House itself), has accommodated many rock concerts, which attract in excess of 15 000 people. The revenue from these types of events helps towards the maintenance and repair of such large and old heritage venues.

The demand for large venues is likely to grow in the next few years, in particular for music concerts as artists will look to live events as major revenue generators in the light of falling sales of CDs etc., largely a result of the downloading of music from the Internet.

The schools market

We mentioned this target market under demographic factors briefly, above. In many countries there are significant links between the teaching of history and the national curriculum. Heritage sites, either the physical sites themselves and/or the educational facilities they might provide, are increasingly being targeted by teachers (and *vice versa*) in order to provide a practical dimension to the subject or topic being studied. The majority of heritage organizations, such as the National Trust in the UK, Historic Scotland and English Heritage, claim education as a primary role for their sites in the heritage sector.

'English Heritage Education' has produced an extensive range of resources to support formal qualifications and also for other, more general use in schools and colleges, in the UK. These include fact sheets on 120 sites, publications on management and customer care, videos on interpretation and arranging events and other subjects, and 12 case studies on major sites providing a range of information. They also offer free educational group visits to 400 different historic sites that include opportunities to go 'behind the scenes' and talk to curators, which the general public may not be able to do.

Local councils in conjunction with schools, and sometimes schools themselves perhaps in association with local businesses, engage in local heritage initiatives for the purposes of education. One recent example of this is a project by Bonneville Primary School in London to explore and raise awareness of the Edwardian Heritage of the school buildings as well as local Edwardian plant varieties, as many of these were originally imported from overseas, interestingly from countries that reflect the multicultural profile

Figure 3.2 A 'flyer' to describe another unique heritage venue for the corporate market. It is also targeted at the general public as a museum. Courtesy of the Cabinet War Rooms, London.

of that locality. The scheme was initiated by the Friends Association of Bonneville, the local community and Learning Through Landscapes '. . . pupils of the school will research material on intercultural links of the Edwardian era in terms of plants, buildings and music and the results of the research will be a musical performance, multimedia presentations and pamphlets. Other project inputs will include the restoration of an Edwardian steeple in the grounds and the establishment of a garden to act as a "vehicle" for showing the process of producing fruit and vegetables in Edwardian times' (Countryside Agency, 2004).

Historic Scotland is the Scottish Government body that '. . . safeguards the [Scottish] nation's built heritage and promotes its understanding and enjoyment on behalf of Scottish Ministers' (website: http://www.historic-scotland. gov.uk 2004). Historic Scotland is responsible for 300 properties and keeps the listed buildings schedule as well as the record of ancient monuments. The education arm of Historic Scotland is impressive in its aims and achievements, and is a reflection of the high value the country places on education and the overall quality of learning that Scotland offers its pupils.

> Education is an important aspect of Historic Scotland's work and we encourage learners of all ages to explore Scotland's fascinating built heritage. Whether it's history or conservation you're interested in, our specialist Education teams can help.
>
> (website http://www.historic-scotland.gov.uk 2004)

The Education Unit of Historic Scotland provides a range of exclusive resources for schools, including free visits, themed tours, costumed role-play and story-telling activities. Approximately 60 000 pupils visit their sites and engage with the activities each year; two examples follow.

In March 2004, at Fort George, in collaboration with the Highland Regimental Museum, the education unit offered pupils the chance to 'meet a soldier' from the First World War and the Second World War (this was targeted primarily at 6–7-year-olds) to find out what life was like in a fort during the wars; special resource packs were developed for visits from schools. During the same month, in collaboration with the National Trust for Scotland, Historic Scotland's education unit offered pupils the opportunity to take part in a joint visit to both Fort George and Culloden on the theme of Jacobites. 'Live' interpreters were used to recount the battle and its aftermath – the activity was followed up by a performance from the specialist theatre group, Meanbh-Chuileag.

The 'Technical Conservation Research Education' unit of Historic Scotland

> works closely with conservation professionals and practitioners to develop a range of training and education initiatives including:
>
> • development of Scottish Vocational Qualifications in conservation;
> • EU projects and contracts: Leonardo, Jeunesse et Patrimoine;

- establishment of the Scottish Conservation Forum in Training and Education;
- short courses and workshops to improve conservator's skills;
- Internships and Fellowships working alongside experienced Scottish conservation professionals.

Website: http://www.historic-scotland.gov.uk 2004)

Specifically for the schools market, for use across the curriculum in the classroom and to complement visits, they have packs and posters and specialist publications, which include the following:

- *Heraldry in Scotland*
- *Skara Brae: A Study of Early Settlers*
- *Investigating Scotland's Burghs*
- *Castles in Scotland*
- *Investigating Scotland's Schools*
- *Siege Engines*

A final demonstration of their commitment to heritage education for the schools market is in the recent dedicated appointment of an education officer on-site at the Queen Anne Building at Edinburgh Castle, in order to coordinate activates with teachers. The Queen Anne Building at Edinburgh Castle is a £3.5 million refurbishment and conversion, which now has an education suite and activity space, specifically for use by schools.

The National Trust pioneered the concept of **Guardianship Schemes** approximately ten years ago. The aim is to link local schools with National Trust properties and staff in a joint programme of **conservation and environmental education**. Guardianships occur across England, Wales and Northern Ireland and, more recently, the private sector has been encouraged for involvement/sponsorship. This has been taken up by a number of organizations, including the Norwich Union Insurance Group.

One further recent initiative by the National Trust has been to offer a series of lectures in London by 'leading' figures on a range of different subjects, all of which are connected to the concept of heritage. Examples from the 2004 series include:

- Sir William Proby talking about his 350-year-old family home, Elton Hall;
- Thomas Pakenham's (historian/explorer/author) lecture on 'Remarkable Trees' and the legends surrounding them;
- Sir Simon Jenkins sharing his passion for architecture, which has been advocated in a book, entitled *England's Thousand Best Houses* (2003);
- Lawrence Llewellyn-Bowen on his view of changes in interior design through the decades.

In the private sector, Shakespeare's Globe Theatre has embarked on a wide range of initiatives in order to promote the better understanding of this literary heritage and the learning of the works of William Shakespeare. For the schools market, they have developed specific resources in relation to Key Stage 2 (7–11 years), Key Stage 3 (11–14 years), Key Stage 4/GCSE, A/As level, International schools' qualifications and for those with special educational needs (SEN). Specifically for university students, there are series of lectures, workshops, seminars, rallies and short courses, and for postgraduates/scholars of English and Drama there are MA courses and modules, together with a special 'Globe research seminar' in Early Modern Drama which is part of their unique 'ReadNotDead' season. Resources for students also include an online reference library, internships and work placements and an on-going programme of 'themed' events for the general public, which in Spring 2004 was centred on the relationship between Shakespeare and Islam.

Teachers also have dedicated resources available through the Globe's education programme including distance-learning materials and a virtual tour of the Globe Theatre. For the local community there are periodic projects under the marketing initiative of 'Our Theatre' and which have been taking place since 1997.

Adult education

In terms of heritage the **adult education market** tends to be dominated by the two major organizations in the UK, English Heritage (they offer a complete range of crafts and traditional skills courses) and the National Trust.

Heritage Education For All is one example of specific provision for this target market, which is supported by the Heritage Lottery Fund. The aim is to offer adults accessible courses and activities that take place at National Trust properties and which can range from demonstrations of ancient cookery to woodland tours, practical art, archaeology, and appreciating parks and gardens. In order to make these activities accessible to all adults, consideration is given to supporting people through the availability of induction loops, sign language interpreters, tactile diagrams and audio-guides, together with specific travel arrangements should this be necessary.

The parents/guardians for school's market: public and independent/private schools

The UK has a very long heritage of private (fee-paying) schools, the vast majority of which are housed in period buildings and often have either horticulturally or other naturally significant landscapes, not least because many are in rural areas. Many are also associated with religious foundations as often they were originally set up for religious instruction and, ironically, generally to educate the poor.

Public or independent schools (as they are now commonly known) are more often than not international, i.e., they have pupils from many parts of the world and compete locally, nationally and internationally for their clients (parents/guardians and students) as there are many established schools both at home and abroad. This sector is set to expand with increasing interest being shown by commercial/investment organizations, particularly in high-density urban areas such as London where presently demand for schools outstrips supply. However, generally, most of these schools are in a **competitive market**.

The **symbolic** characteristics of public schools sought by parents are **quality**, both in terms of the education itself (limited numbers of pupils in classes, usually below the state average) but also of the **environment** (period buildings, landscaped gardens, sporting facilities) in which this takes place, upholding of 'traditions' which also adds to the general knowledge/learning experience of pupils, and **exclusivity** which this heritage environment is capable of providing and for which people are prepared to pay premium prices. Schools in this sector are usually charitable foundations and therefore are allowed to make a profit or surplus; however, the condition of this status is that all profit be spent on school-related activities or facilities.

The marketing activities of most public and independent schools include the use of traditional and non-traditional media, including the following.

- 'Open Days' with tours of the school – these are usually scheduled several times a year and will often coincide with critical decision-making times for parents in terms of the educational provision for their children or with fund-raising events – this is classic personal selling.
- School Prospectus – a generic tool that can be sent out at any time of year and usually has a supplement listing the current fees and any additional information that is subject to change.
- Other publications – one or more sent out to pupils and parents (current and possibly prospective) in order to inform of events and activities that have taken place, in particular 'extra-curricular' activities, awards received and ceremonies undertaken.
- Personal selling – by means of a meeting with the Head of the School or other Senior Personnel, and through the termly or yearly 'letter from the Head'.
- PR – notably through press releases to the media, often local but sometimes national, with 'newsworthy' stories that are cost advantageous and communicate with current and prospective target markets. They also generally raise the awareness of the positive aspects of the school amongst the general public.
- Advertising – in local or possibly national print media, on local radio and, depending on the existing profile of the school, specialist media

may also be used, for example related to a specific aspect of the school, such as a religious affiliation or the school's location.

- Websites – most have a range of interactions available for site visitors from 'virtual tours' to requests for brochures and up-to-date information of issues/activities in relation to the school.
- Corporate livery – notably the school's unique 'coat of arms' (and perhaps the school motto) which is usually used on all communications, from letterheads to prospectus(es).
- School uniform – the style and (combination of) colours will usually be representative of the corporate livery or the distinctiveness of the school.
- Setting up an alumni – to create a relationship marketing strategy, feedback from past pupils will often be used to 'enhance' the school and be promoted in the school's range of communications' activities.

Public schools are also increasingly hiring or leasing their facilities for use by the business to business market – companies who are looking for a heritage site that is unique and distinct but capable of meeting their needs and perhaps conveniently located (see the section above on business to business target markets). One example is Bearwood College, a private school which has its own theatre (useful for presentations, for example), landscaped private grounds with enough space for a marquee, parking, a proscenium arch (unique architectural feature) and good acoustics.

Insight 3.6: The King's School, Gloucester, UK

Cathedral schools are part of our heritage.

(Robertson, 1974)

King's School (like many public/independent schools) has a legacy of traditions and rituals, famous (or perhaps infamous, in some cases!) past pupils and many other facets that make it unique and give it an identity.

The reasons parents choose King's are many. The following have been amongst the most commonly used phrases during my terms:

- ambience of Cathedral setting
- Christian ethos
- musical heritage
- a sense of history
- a sense of community
- a friendly, family atmosphere.
  (Mr Peter Lacey, Headmaster, The King's School, Gloucester, 2004)

The King's School was founded in the reign of Henry VIII and was originally called the College School (although it has been argued that there was a school on the site as far back as 1072); this was kept separate from the Choir School. The school was set up for the sons of 'gentlemen' and citizens in order that they learn grammar, whilst choristers had to learn 'trades' when they were not required to sing in the Cathedral or Choir School. It was not until the end of the seventeenth century that choristers entered the school and only in 1854 did they do so at the insistence of the Dean and Chapter of the Cathedral. Gloucester Cathedral (as it is now known) was in fact spiritually and physically the Benedictine Abbey of St Peter but subsequently became Cathedral Church of the Holy and Indivisible Trinity. As an abbey it had trained monks and as a Cathedral it became an education centre for scholars and choristers.

The changes, physical and otherwise, that have taken place at the school are too numerous to mention, except for two: in 1972 girls were admitted as Sixth Form students for the first time and throughout the school from 1985; and in the mid-1980s the school was invited to join one of two international umbrella brands for private schools, the Head Masters Conference (HMC). The other is for schools with only female pupils and is known as the GSA (the Girls Schools Association).

By kind permission of Mr Peter Lacey, Headmaster, The King's School, Gloucester, 2004 and acknowledgment: David Robertson, *The King's School, Gloucester*, 1974.

Other (direct and indirect) target markets

In the previous chapter we established that many different types of people and businesses will have an interest in issues to do with heritage provision, management and marketing, and at times these may conflict, which presents a challenge for all concerned.

Conflicts and tensions aside, there is no doubt that investment in heritage, as evident through the quantitative and qualitative returns presented by English Heritage in their publication *Heritage Dividend* (2002; see previous chapter) levers many benefits for (nearly all?) parties.

However, this view is not restricted to English Heritage, as Frank McAveety MSP, the Scottish Minister for Tourism, Culture and Sport told the Scottish Parliament in March 2004. 'The historic environment is crucial to Scotland's economy . . .', but more significantly he made the point that **many other businesses** are affected by investment in heritage. For example, £1.5 billion is spent in the construction industry on the maintenance and conservation repair of historic buildings, monuments and townscapes in Scotland alone; this concept is known as the multiplier-effect, as explained in Chapter 1.

Looking after our historic buildings and places pays dividends – it results in a high quality and distinctive environment where people want to live and work . . . Independent research has shown that listed buildings have higher capital

and rental income values than their non-listed counterparts. People are prepared to pay a **heritage premium** – they value quality and a sense of place.
(Historic Scotland Press Office, March 2004)

Since 1991 Historic Scotland has paid over £100 million in grants to support
the regeneration of old buildings, which has created a further £200 million
in value (from investors, rents, raising of property values, etc.), some of
which has in turn been used to support professional and craft skills and, in
particular, the use of traditional materials in reconstruction work. Another
important factor for the Scottish Parliament is that through this regeneration
they have been able to satisfy social goals and justice, for example, the former St Francis' Friary in the Gorbals has been converted into a community
centre and social housing; former jute mills in Dundee have been turned
into housing.

The speech by Frank McAveety concluded: 'Our historic environment . . .
with its rich heritage of historic buildings, conservation areas, monuments,
archaeology, gardens and landscapes – is a major part of our diverse cultural
life at national and local level. The precious achievements of the past are in
every part of Scotland and are as much a part of our cultural heritage as the
performing and decorative arts. But they are also part of a thriving and
modern Scottish economy' (Historic Scotland Press Office, March 2004).

Once again we can see links between various issues in heritage marketing,
education, commercial enterprise, regeneration, job creation, public perception and involvement, and so on; there are usually many stakeholders in
respect of any heritage marketing initiative.

One illustration of this point is London's bid to stage the 2012 Olympic
Games, which apart from being an honour in terms of this unique historical
event, should have the additional aim of improving the overall image of
London amongst various target markets, including business to business
(although the Games will need to be a 'success' in order to win this positive
perception). The bid has since been successful.

The Royal Horticultural Halls in London are not designated to be
involved with the Games, should they take place, but the Managing
Director nevertheless believes that hosting them would focus so much
attention on the city that there would be positive benefits for many sectors
of the market. 'Visitors to London would not only focus on the host venues but would hold conferences, dinners and dances at other venues.
I think it would have an impact before, during and after' (Dee, 2004).
Heritage venues are always sought-after locations, as we have already
established above. Together with the fact that there will be 'spin-offs' for
many other industries: caterers, hoteliers, media, florists, cleaners, additional police officers and/or 'overtime', etc., as well as additional government and private investment in for example transport and other
infrastructural needs, it can be seen that the Olympics will be good for
almost every industry.

Target marketing

Heritage marketers are increasingly making use of a wide variety of marketing methods for target marketing, in particular with respect to the use of **marketing communications**.

Marketing communications are critical in the early stages of a product launch in order to raise awareness; they then have a role to play in relation to the other aspects of the **AIDA principle**: creating an interest, stimulating desire or decision and initiating action. In short, media campaigns should consist of five main steps:

1   planning and research (as explained above);
2   creative thinking;
3   marketing communications;
4   developing media contacts; and
5   evaluating the results.

Specifically in terms of marketing communications, heritage marketers can use public relations (PR) for considerable effect. PR is effectively 'free', as the marketer presents a press release to the media (these can also be displayed on a website for other target markets, in particular the consumer public) and awaits its publication. The aim should be to send it to editors of publications/broadcasts that will communicate with the desired target market(s) and is a very useful way to at least create awareness on a modest budget.

The use of PR is briefly discussed in Insight 1.2 on 'The Museum in the Park' and there is no doubt that it is used by the heritage sector, in particular museums, as a cost-effective way of raising or maintaining a profile, local, national or international, and 'advertising' something specific that is to take place.

The first step in planning and presenting an effective press release is to think about the **unique selling points** (USPs) of the event and the key message(s) to be conveyed. It is very important to think about which points (from a list already drawn up) are likely to interest an editor of a publication and the readership or viewing/listening audience (which may differ from one to another). The 'story' must also reach the right person at the right time, as editors will assess each incoming piece in terms of its newsworthiness, for which heritage marketers can plan on a yearly schedule.

The starting point for producing a piece of editorial/press release should be a brainstorm with colleagues, if possible. The result will be a variety of different ideas and angles on the same issue that will create food for thought. For example, rather than commenting on an exhibition or event in its own right, it may be more appropriate to adopt an angle, perhaps one that dovetails with another newsworthy item of the time or something that is seasonally (for example, Christmas) or perennially popular.

The process of drafting a press release is as follows:

1   the first paragraph must cover the five W's of the story ('who, what, why, where and when');
2   each paragraph should be concise and easy to understand, with a simple, uncluttered layout;
3   the language should be straightforward, factual and lively;
4   no jargon should be used as the editor/audience may be unfamiliar with 'industry speak';
5   the message must be clearly tailored to the target audience/readership;
6   the words 'Press release' must appear at the top of the first page;
7   all contact details and any appropriate background information must be included at the end of the press release as 'notes to editors';
8   the press release should occupy a maximum one side of A4 and only exceed this in exceptional circumstances, otherwise you run the risk of having the press release cut down substantially and its essence may be lost;
9   images should be used where appropriate and in the right combination with words. Remember: 'a picture speaks a thousand words'.

Finally, follow up a press release with a telephone call to the editor within a few days. This personal element to your approach might invite additional questions and also offer the opportunity of a further pitch.

The lead times for various types of media (i.e., the length of time a piece is required before publication) are as follows:

Newspapers and magazines:
1   weekend newspaper supplements: three to four months
2   national newspapers (dailies and weekends): three to six weeks
3   weekend listings, including previews in listings: four weeks
4   consumer and lifestyle magazines (monthly): four to six months
5   specialist (monthly) magazines: four months.

Television:
1   national television (full-length programme): six to twelve months
2   national television (magazine programme): three to six weeks
3   national television (news): one to two weeks
4   local television (magazine programme): three to six weeks
5   local television (news): one to two weeks.

Radio:
1   radio (specialist shows): two months
2   radio (news): two weeks.

One example of the use of PR by a national organization that devolves down to specific museums involved with the campaign is 'The Big Draw'.

'The Big Draw' is part of the Campaign for Drawing that was launched in the UK in 2000 (the centenary of the death of John Ruskin) by the Guild of St George, a trust to support artisans founded by Ruskin. John Ruskin was a Victorian artist and writer who believed strongly that drawing could be used to educate and develop the intellect of individuals; but his aim was not to teach people how to draw, rather it was to teach them how to see. The Campaign for Drawing works in partnership with the Esmee Fairburn Foundation, the Heritage Lottery Fund and the Department for Education and Skills.

The overall aim of 'The Big Draw' (which takes place in October of each year) is to get more people drawing in museums and, indirectly, to get people to visit their local or a national museum that perhaps otherwise they may not. The Big Draw has proved to be very useful in helping museums attract visitors and retain them, if only in terms of this special event (99 per cent of participants return in the subsequent year). It has also helped partner organizations. This initiative has also attracted funding for museums from local government and private organizations.

Apart from press releases, there are many other types of marketing communications that can be used.

Newsletters or other regular means of communication can be targeted at members or 'friends' of the organization. This vehicle can also be used to cross-reference with (additional) information elsewhere, for example on a website, and is a useful way of generating an (on-going) interest in issues.

Events such as press conferences, advanced briefings with selected members of the media, parties and launch ceremonies can all be used to create additional interest and media coverage, either of an organization or of something specific to which attention should be drawn.

Advertising can take any number of different forms and should be chosen for its appropriateness in terms of what the organization expects of the target market(s) and how it fits into the lifestyle of targeted audiences, as well as considerations of cost and timescale – wherever possible, if the organization has a website, its URL address should be offered.

A number of different media options can be used simultaneously, either for the same target market (perhaps to reinforce the message) or for different ones. For example, for certain target audiences, organizations such as the Science Museum and Natural History Museum are using 'specialogues' through **direct marketing** initiatives and **online shopping** opportunities. This has the advantages of raising the awareness of consumers of the heritage provision. They may not be in the market to actually visit but they may be interested in goods and services that are 'associated' with these heritage institutions. This concept is also known as perceptual franchising, i.e. 'lending' or transferring the status/credibility of an organization on to other (previously unrelated) goods and services in order to create a further marketing opportunity.

Three possible media options are:

1 Media Partners are sometimes sought, as the relationship can be of mutual benefit. For example, some heritage institutions offer their facilities (such as 'behind-the-scenes' tours) and other benefits (such as free tickets) in return for the creative services of a variety of different companies.

2 On-site advertising can have the benefit of creating interest, desire and action. Any part of the site is capable of being used, from the reception area inside to areas outside. Admission tickets (if applicable) can be used for cross-advertising with media partners or to draw attention to, for example, the website, perhaps with a special user name and password for early or restricted access, i.e. before public release.

3 Websites must be both useful and pleasurable to use, which may encourage repeat visits. It is important to link popular sites with that of the organization and add links from the organization's website to others with both similar themes and quality of content; examples include local councils, regional organizations (public and private), national and possibly international ones. The website needs to be favourably indexed with search engines and directories – the evidence on Internet use is that, increasingly, web surfers will visit search engines, portals or community sites each month and will frequently return to favourite sites. In order to make online advertising of an organization's website effective, it needs to have a compelling message to drive traffic to the site.

Once a market has been segmented and the target audience made aware of the product offering, the expectation is that they will want to visit a site or acquire the product or brand.

In the context of heritage site visits, it is usually important to offer a focal point and this has hitherto tended to be in the shape of a 'visitor centre'. 'Visitor centres aim to provide services and facilities for activities that take place in and around them and the building needs to be designed around these activities. As well as being an attraction for visitors and tourists, it might well serve as a focus for local community activities. In addition to visitor services a centre may perform administrative and maintenance functions for a site' (Atkinson, 2004: 4). Visitor centres normally offer a range of services and facilities including an information point that might be 'manned', toilets, catering areas, exhibitions (permanent, temporary or both), space for educational groups to meet, trails, walks and tours, and possibly other facilities too. In considering whether to build a visitor centre, there are many factors to take into account, including:

1 *capital costs* – including building costs, interior fittings, creation of car parking spaces, landscaping;

2   *operating costs* – otherwise known as 'running costs', which include staff costs, maintenance and repair costs, direct costs ('overheads') and indirect costs such as heating and lighting;
3   *income* – that which can be gained from admission charges (if appropriate), subsidies or grants, sales revenue from a shop/café, etc.

The costs and income should be part of an on-going review into the viability of the centre.

With or without a visitor centre, many heritage organizations use **signs and displays** to offer guidance and interpretation in and around heritage sites. Specifically, the following are extensively used:

panels – these are signs that provide information on the site and its facilities, orientation and interpretation. The main aim of panels is to enhance the visit by providing concise but accessible information on the site and any additional information as appropriate, such as on the area, flora and fauna, wildlife, etc.;

lecterns – these are particularly suited for use in car parks, at viewpoints and locations requiring large amounts of orientation or interpretation;

mile posts – these are plank-sized posts containing A4-size interpretative panels;

fence posts – these are trailhead-sized posts suitable for small amounts of interpretive material;

signal posts – these are fencing-grade posts with a pivoting arm in the body of the post which contains small interpretive panels;

sacksigns – are ballast-filled waterproof 'socks' pre-printed with interpretive message(s); these are particularly useful where discrete or non-invasive wayside signage is required, for example on ancient monuments.

Once again, exactly what should be used, how much of it and in which combination will depend on the needs of the target market(s) to the site.

Finally, commercial activities seem to sit well with **customer expectations** (retail 'therapy' continues to grow as a leisure activity – shopping is not about need, but about want). It is not inconceivable to find a range of retail shops, restaurants (perhaps discriminating in terms of convenience and prices charged) and additional activities such as horse and carriage rides and temporary exhibitions charging an entry price even though the main attraction may not.

Specifically in terms of retail, the heritage sector has traditionally taken a gentle approach and therefore not maximized this revenue-generating opportunity, especially at heritage sites or attractions.

Heritage retail should learn from the best practise in other sectors to develop and extend their offers in three key ways.

First, store environments should reflect the product. The British Museum Shop takes an elegant Gallery approach to showcase its replica antiques, whilst MoMa in New York's design and merchandising compliments the funky objects and furniture . . . stores need their own personality.

Second, great retailers are great communicators. Point of sale should tell stories rather than sell price. Product displays should have a lifestyle focus that inspires and entertains.

Thirdly, all retail needs a critical mass to make it convincing. For example, instead of selling a few pots of home-made jam, teaming up with local farm suppliers could build a credible food offer that becomes a destination in its own right.

(Brown, 2004)

CASE STUDY 3.1: The Royal Pavilion, Art Gallery and Museums, Brighton, UK

The Royal Pavilion has played a key role in the development of Brighton and its international reputation.

(Brighton Borough Council, 2004)

The Royal Pavilion is a unique and extraordinary building that since its creation has both inspired and irritated, engendering enthusiasm or disdain in the visitor, but never indifference. J.W. Croker's claim in 1818 that it was '... an absurd waste of money and will be a ruin in half a century or sooner' fortunately proved to be ill-founded.

(Jessica Rutherford, Head of Museums and Director of the Royal Pavilion, 2004)

In the mid-eighteenth century, Brighton was transformed from a small fishing town into a fashionable resort, largely because of the discovery of the therapeutic qualities of sea water consumed both internally and externally. The success of this cure for many ailments drew many people to Brighton, especially from London, including the Duke of Cumberland, the Prince of Wales' disreputable and 'raffish' uncle.

Prince George (George IV, Prince Regent) first visited Brighton in 1783, to escape the court of his Father, for medical reasons and to enjoy the lively company of his uncle, which included gambling, the theatre and the races. This led him to instruct Louis Weltje, his Clerk to the Kitchens and Cellars, to find a suitable residence in Brighton. In 1786 he moved there, after installing Mrs Fitzherbert, a Roman Catholic whom he had secretly and illegally married, in a villa nearby.

In 1784, as his financial position had improved, he instructed Henry Holland to design the first impression of Brighton Pavilion, which was then to be a neoclassical structure with a central domed rotunda surrounded by Ionic columns. This was remodelled by John Nash in the early 1820s to the grand oriental design that is evident today, reflecting the changing status of George, Prince of Wales from Prince Regent (1811–1820) to King George IV (1820–1830).

However, there was earlier evidence of this oriental emphasis because the stable building, which was located in the grounds, had been designed in the 'Indian style' by William Porden (1775–1822). Built between 1803 and 1808, it soon dwarfed the Pavilion itself. 'A stupendous and magnificent building, it could house in elegant style some sixty horses and remains a monument to the Prince's passion for riding and racing' (*Guidebook:The Royal Pavilion*, 2004).

John Nash (1752–1835) was chosen as the architect because he had worked for the Prince Regent at Carlton House (demolished in 1827) in London. This house, too, had an exterior in the 'Indian style' and had been inspired by the architect Humphrey Repton (1752–1810) who had published, but not executed, several designs for the Prince. These, in turn, were taken from William and Thomas Daniell's four volumes of drawings entitled *Oriental Scenery*.

The interior of the Pavilion is largely credited to two designers, Frederick Crace (1779–1859) and Robert Jones. The Prince met with these two artists in 1817 in order to determine who would be responsible for the decoration of various rooms in the Pavilion. Most of the major rooms were decorated by Jones (the Banqueting Room, Saloon, Red Drawing Room and the King's private apartments) and Crace undertook the Music Room and Banqueting Room galleries. 'The final schemes, with their rich and sophisticated decoration combined with the superb quality of the furniture and furnishings, created a magnificent and appropriate setting for the new monarch' (*Guidebook:The Royal Pavilion*, 2004).

The presence of the Prince in Brighton encouraged a considerable entourage to follow, which increased the prosperity of many trades people in the town. By 1800 it had become very 'fashionable', and one of the most frequently visited towns in Britain. 'Over the next decades elegant town houses, squares and crescents were constructed reflecting the affluence and popularity of the town' (*Guidebook:The Royal Pavilion*, 2004), a phenomenon that was aided by the coming of the railway in the late 1840s.

George IV died in 1830 but the Pavilion was in continuous use by Royal families, first by William IV and then by Queen Victoria until 1845, after which she preferred to live at Osborne House in the Isle of Wight. However, prior to moving, Queen Victoria had stripped the interior of the Pavilion of virtually all its furniture and fixtures, including wallpapers, chimney pieces and other decorative features, although many have since been returned.

In 1850 the Royal Pavilion was purchased from Queen Victoria and this key act served to raise the profile of both the building and the town.

The restoration of the Pavilion, exterior and interior, to the schemes approved by George IV in the 1820s, started in the mid-nineteenth century and continue today. The most notable rooms are:

- the Octagon Hall, 'this octagonal room with its plaster ceiling resembling the interior of a tent and delicate "peach-blossom"-coloured walls was filled with light' and leads to
- the Entrance Hall, 'a cool coloured square room, decorated with panels and banners of serpents and dragons on a pale green background'. The Entrance Hall gave access on the south side of the building to The Red Drawing Room and on the north to the private apartments of the King. Adjacent is

- the Long Gallery, 'its name reflects its origins in sixteenth-century country house galleries, which were used for gentle exercise and for the display of pictures. The Gallery was dramatically lit by a large, central, painted-glass ceiling or laylight . . . in the evening the Gallery was lit with brightly painted lanterns . . . the interior was furnished with bamboo-pattern cabinets and pedestals, oriental jars and bottles, pagodas and Chinese figures'
- the Banqueting Room, 'remains one of the most magnificent interiors in the Pavilion. The interior . . . was designed with a shallow dome and canopies to the north and south, providing numerous arches, coves and elliptical shapes . . . the walls were hung with large canvases painted with Chinese domestic scenes . . . from the centre of the shallow dome hung a chandelier, 30ft long, a ton in weight, held in the claws of a silvered dragon . . . below through a fountain of glass six smaller dragons exhaled light through lotus glass shades. In 1816 the Prince Regent secured the services of the renowned French Chef Marie-Antoine Careme, who devised elaborate menus with as many as sixty dishes'.

Other exquisitely decorated and notable rooms available for visitors to see include:

- the Table Decker's Room/Page's Room
- the Great Kitchen
- the Banqueting Room Gallery
- the Saloon
- the Music Room Gallery
- the Music Room (severely damaged by fire in 1975, followed by extensive damage following a hurricane in 1987)
- the King's Apartments
- the Yellow Bow Rooms (the bedrooms of the King's brothers, the Duke of York and the Duke of Clarence)
- Queen Victoria's Apartments and
- the South Galleries.

Outside, there are landscaped gardens with many rare trees, flowers and shrubs, together with an ice house and the India Gate, which was given to the Pavilion by the people of India to commemorate Indian soldiers who had died in the First World War.

The Royal Pavilion, partly as a result of its unique structure and the materials used to create it, has suffered problems from the outset, including water leakage, dry rot and structural problems, not to mention issues facing the interior over the timescale. Restoration is on-going, time-consuming and expensive. The Pavilion's various restoration projects are supported by numerous voluntary and non-voluntary groups, including Brighton Borough Council and The Friends of the Royal Pavilion, Art Gallery & Museums, Brighton.

Acknowledgment: The Royal Pavilion, Brighton, 2004.

Questions

1 Who is in the market to visit a site such as The Royal Pavilion, Brighton? Briefly explain what the purpose of the visit for each group would be.
2 Which national funding organizations could help the Pavilion in
   a) its restoration work?
   b) its developmental and marketing work?
3 What would the Pavilion need to do in order to create a relationship marketing strategy?

CASE STUDY 3.2: Warwick Castle – The Finest Mediaeval Castle in England

Warwick Castle is a visitor attraction that comes under the umbrella brand of venues owned by 'The Tussauds Group'; others in the portfolio include:

- *Madame Tussauds*, one of the most-visited heritage sites in London, known for its wax models of famous people;
- *Alton Towers*, a 'roller-coaster' theme park in Staffordshire;
- *Chessington World of Adventures* in Surrey, an attraction combining 'rides', a Circus and a Zoo;
- *Scenerama Amsterdam*, which is based on the Madam Tussauds concept and highlights the history of The Netherlands from the seventeenth century; and
- *The London Planetarium*, which is a three-dimensional show of the solar system.

The very first castle was built at Warwick in 1068, overlooking the River Avon. It was reflective of a new era in British history, the mediaeval period, which followed the Dark Ages. By the late thirteenth century, Warwick Castle had become significant as a major seat of power in England.

From 1338 to 1453, on and off, Kings of England engaged with the Hundred Years War. At the outbreak of hostilities, Warwick Castle was owned by the de Beauchamp family and Thomas de Beauchamp, who became owner in 1329, became the Black Prince's military adviser – his grandson, Richard de Beauchamp, was appointed to oversee the trial and execution of Joan of Arc.

Following these battles were others, just as fierce; in particular the Wars of the Roses. From 1450 to 1471 Warwick Castle was home to Richard Neville, the 'Kingmaker', after whom an attraction at the castle is named.

In 1478, ownership of the castle transferred to Richard of Gloucester (he became King Richard III) who was defeated at the Battle of Bosworth.

In contrast to dynastic life, the society which revolved around a major castle like Warwick was strictly ordered. An important earl would have a household of servants, soldiers, clerks and estate managers. He would have a retinue of knights, drawn from around the country, who served him in return for a payment. Beyond the castle walls, peasant farmers leased land from the earl. As well as the regular members of the household, the castle would see a number of passing visitors, monks, merchants, travellers, craftsmen and labourers. Mediaeval life could be harsh, brutal and brief, which explains why it could also be boisterous, noisy, earthy and exuberant.

(Guidebook: Warwick Castle, 2000)

The Tussauds Group have tried to capture this atmosphere at Warwick Castle, as well as the various periods of history through which the castle has survived (relatively intact). In addition to the castle building itself, there are various specific 'attractions', which include:

- *KingMaker* – wax models in recreated 'scenes' from history together with sounds reminiscent of the times and lighting to create visual effects are used throughout;
- *The Dungeon* – this occupies the lowest chamber of 'Caesar's Tower' and was built in the fourteenth century, accessed via 24 narrow steps. 'Set into the wall is a tiny, sunken chamber, a dungeon within a dungeon called an "oubliette". Lowered into this hole the prisoner would scarcely have room to breathe let alone move. And there he would be left' *(Guidebook: Warwick Castle, 2000)*;
- *The Towers and Ramparts* – the towers and curtain walls that protect the courtyard are the result of a large re-structuring plan carried out in the fourteenth and fifteenth centuries;
- *Bear and Clarence Towers* – these are all that is left of the very large Tower House, which Richard of Gloucester started to build in 1478. Clarence Tower is named after Richard's elder brother, the Duke of Clarence, and it is thought that the other tower housed bears that were used for bear-baiting;
- *The Armoury* – this has displays of many different 'blackened breasts' and 'backplates' worn by soldiers in the English Civil War. Sitting on a caparisoned horse and dominating the whole room is a knight in Italian jousting armour from the 1570s;
- *The Ghost Tower* – a fourteenth-century aspect of the castle decorated in Jacobean style with a gateway from its base leading down to the river. In 1604, James I granted the castle to Sir Fulke Greville (1554–1628) who died at the hands of his manservant, Ralph Haywood. Using sound and vision (wax models in period costume) a scene of the fatal stabbing is recreated – it is said that the ghost of Greville still haunts this tower;
- *The State Dining Room* – commissioned by Francis Greville in 1763, the dining room was designed and built by eighteenth-century craftsmen from England and, later, both George IV and Edward VII dined here, as well as Queen Victoria and Prince Albert in 1858;
- *The Blue Boudoir* – the last of the State Rooms and presented exactly the same as it was in the 1870s; finally there are scenes and rooms (all with 'positioned' and appropriately dressed wax figures) from the Victorian era.

Questions

1   Who is in the market to visit a site such as Warwick Castle? Briefly explain what the purpose of the visit for each group would be.

2   Which national funding organizations could help Warwick Castle in its restoration and preservation work?

3a   What are the benefits to the Tussauds Group from having a heritage site such as Warwick Castle in its portfolio?

3b   What are the benefits to Warwick Castle from being associated with the Tussauds Group?

4   Identify at least one other heritage site/attraction in the UK or Europe that would strategically fit with the portfolio of the Tussauds Group.

CASE STUDY 3.3: The Admirable Crichton, Events and Parties Organizers, London, UK

The Admirable Crichton (the name comes from the book by J.M. Barrie, which was about a butler who used his creative skills to look after the family he worked for after they were shipwrecked on a desert island) was founded in 1981 by the charismatic Johnny Roxburgh, a Chartered Accountant, together with his business partner Rolline Frewen, a chef and sculptress. Their combined talents of creative party design and cooking led to the formation of one of the first high-calibre party design and catering companies in London.

The Admirable Crichton company have undertaken many high-profile events and parties both in the UK and abroad, which is a general reflection of the growth in private and corporate entertaining. This has led to an increase in the size of the company to over 50 people, with a turnover in excess of £10 million per year. It has been the recipient of a Royal Warrant by The Prince of Wales and has other high-profile clients, including Sting and Trudie Styler.

'Corporate clients are always looking for something new and different (in particular, a venue which their guests will not have been taken to by their competitors)' (Sara Binns, Head of Business Development, The Admirable Crichton, London, 2004). To this effect, heritage venues have become increasingly popular because of their awe-inspiring characteristics; the business to business corporate events/hospitality market has responded accordingly. For example, 'Historic Royal Palaces', which comes under the Department of Culture, Media and Sport (see previous chapter), has a dedicated 'events team' aimed at the corporate hospitality market and which offers HM Tower of London, Hampton Court Palace, Kensington Palace and The Banqueting House, Whitehall – they advertise in a range of trade publications.

Heritage venues used by The Admirable Crichton are mainly 'historic' and usually in London but increasingly, more from overseas are being added. The following are a few from their website:

* *Amanjena, Marrackech, Morroco* – 'Amanjena is a walled resort with Moorish arches, 34 rose-toned pavilions and six two-storey mansions which radiate out from an ancient basin or irrigation pool inspired by Marah's 12th century

Menara gardens ... Amanjena's swimming pool is finished on glittering tiles of ecaille de poisson – cut zellij and its patio filled with chaises longues ... [and] bordered with hibiscus flowers. Flowing water is a gift in this desert country but a symbol of grace and abundance [to be found here]'.

- *The Natural History Museum, London, UK* – '[several parts of the museum can be used but the] Central Hall features beautiful terracotta archways intricately carved with animals and birds and a 60ft high ceiling decorated with delicately painted panels ... a sweeping stone staircase ... [all in the shadow] of the 150 million year old reconstructed Diplodocus dinosaur skeleton, one of the largest land animals that ever lived'.
- *The Palazzo Pisani Moretta, Venice, Italy* – 'owned by the Pisani family and was erected in the second half of the XVth century along the "Canal Grande", half way between the Bridge of Rialto and Ca'Foscani's vault. The architectural importance of the façade is due to the splendid Gothic mullioned windows on the two main floors. The elaborate Baroque decoration of the interior is the work of the most outstanding Venetian artists of the XVIIIth century; the magnificent staircase rising to the top floor of the Palace also belongs to the Baroque period and was built to replace the old Gothic steps. Thanks to the restoration work of the last decade, the re-establishment of its collections and the recovery of its original antique furnishings, the Pisani Palace has recovered its ancient splendour'.

By kind permission: Sara Binns, Head of Business Development, The Admirable Crichton, London, UK, 2004.

Questions

1 Do you think The Admirable Crichton and Historic Royal Palaces target any type of business with their services?
2 What is the 'added-value' to businesses in the use of 'historic'/heritage venues for corporate events?
3 How has The Admirable Crichton managed to keep its portfolio of venues 'fresh'?

CASE STUDY 3.4: The Lake Country House: Pure Tranquillity in the Heart of Mid-Wales

The Lake Country House is one of three 'Period House Hotels' in the UK (another example of an umbrella brand which also has in its portfolio Northcote Manor in Devon and Dinham Hall in Ludlow, Shropshire).

The house was constructed in 1840 and remodelled around 1900 and although architecturally it is mock-Tudor, the overall design and in particular the verandas and French windows '... Give it a colonial air'. It is most famous for the visit from

Wilhelm II, who made the long journey from Germany to this remote corner of mid-Wales in order to take the legendary barium spa waters, enjoy the hospitality and to relax.

Built as a hunting and fishing lodge, the hotel has a rich history. From the turn of the twentieth century until the Second World War, when hotels at the time were requisitioned for convalescent use, this hotel was the only barium spa resort outside of Germany. Post-war austerity and the exclusion of spa treatments from the National Health Service, meant that the hotel would no longer be able to rely on its health-giving virtues, instead having to focus on the traditional country house hospitality and the country pursuits that had made it such a success over the first 50 years of its life.

The Lake Country House stands in 50 acres of private parkland, adjacent to the river and with beautiful, flower-filled gardens.

The website has links to other heritage attractions nearby including:

- The Brecon Beacons National Park
- The Elan Valley (a man-made complex of lakes and reservoirs; an area of outstanding beauty)
- National Trust properties: Powis Castle and Garden, Dinefwr (an eighteenth-century landscaped park which includes Newton House, built in 1660 but now with a Victorian façade, and an exhibition which explains the importance of Dinefwr in Welsh History), Dolaucothi Gold Mines (Roman site, over 2000 years old), and Aberdulais Falls
- The Red Kite Feeding Centre – Gigrin Farm (rare birds)
- Carreg Cennen (castle)
- National Botanic Gardens of Wales
- The Brecon International Jazz Festival
- Dan yr-Ogof – The Welsh National Show caves
- Rhiannon Welsh Gold Centre
- Black Mountain Activity Centre
- Brecon Mountain Railway
- Abergavenney (heritage town)

Acknowledgment: The Lake Country House, Wales, UK.

Questions

1 What type of heritage consumer(s) is Lake Country House keen to attract?
2 What are the distinguishing heritage aspects of this Hotel?
3 If Lake Country House wanted to expand its market of heritage consumers, what sorts of additional activities could it offer?
4 What other sorts of partners could this Hotel align itself with in order to develop its market?

Summary

There are many ways in which the market can be segmented in order to attract consumers with an interest in heritage.

In this chapter we have seen that for most aspects of heritage, in particular heritage tourism (which is the biggest sector, at present, that leverages heritage for commercial purposes), the majority of consumers have an ABC1 socio-economic profile and are likely to be 'grey', i.e., over the age of 50 years, although there are many other growth markets, notably the 'Yummy Mummy' market who are largely seeking luxury goods and services with a heritage emphasis or within a heritage context. DINKS and Young Urban Professionals are keen on the cultural heritage of European heritage cities.

Demand is also growing for period homes, cars with a heritage and many other aspects, such as an increasing interest in the heritage of companies and sport; the corporate or business to business market, especially for heritage venues, is another growth sector.

Heritage marketing, appropriately targeted, is capable of adding value, either to the qualitative experience of the individual or group (more on this in the next chapter) or in quantitative/financial terms. For example, as we have established, period properties are usually more highly priced, either for purchase or rental, than their contemporary counterparts.

There also seem to be increasing and important strides being made by both the public and private sector in marketing many different aspects of heritage for education: for school pupils, university students, individuals, communities, teachers, both in terms of physical resources and virtual ones.

Discussion questions and activities

1 List all the target markets, following the generic principles of market segmentation in terms of demographic profiles, socio-economic groups, socio-cultural groups, occasional buyer behaviour, psychographics and business to business who are in the market for heritage. Briefly explain what you consider to be the expectations of each individual or group.
2 Look up a museum or other suitable heritage site and identify how a relationship-marketing programme is being delivered.
3 Find two 'heritage hotels' and identify the target market(s) at whom they are aimed.

Recommended reading

Atkinson, C. (2004) A beginners guide to the planning, design and operation of visitor centres. *Association of Heritage Interpretation Journal*, 5, 4.

Blythe, J. (2001) *Essentials of Marketing*. Prentice-Hall, London.

Brown, M. (2004) *Heritage Retail Journal*, March.

Dee, R. (2004) *Event Magazine*.

Dibb, S. and Simkin, L. (1996) *The Market Segmentation Workbook: Target Marketing for Marketing Managers*. Thomson, London.

Engel, J.F., Fiorillo, H.F. and Cayley, M.A. (1972) *Market Segmentation: Concepts and Applications*. Holt, Rineholt and Winston, New York.

Engel, J.F., Blackwell, R.D. and Miniard, P.W. (2001) *Consumer Behaviour*. West, Fort Worth.

English Heritage (2002) *Heritage Dividend: Measuring the Results of Heritage Regeneration from 1999–2002*. Department of Culture, Media and Sport, London.

Hoare, E. (2003) *EventSolutions Magazine*, October.

Hole, R. (2004) The next generation of attractions. *Heritage365 Magazine*, February.

Hooley, G. and Saunders, J. (1998) *Marketing Strategy and Competitive Positioning*. Prentice Hall, London.

Howard, P. (2003) *Heritage: Management, Interpretation, Identity*. Continuum Books, London.

Jenkins, S. (2003) *England's Thousand Best Houses*. Allen Lane, London.

McCall Smith, A. (1998) *The No. 1 Ladies' Detective Agency*. Abacus, London.

Myrvoll, S. (2003) *EventSolutions Magazine*.

Packman, C. (2003) *EventSolutions*, October.

Richards, G. (1996) *Cultural Tourism in Europe*. CAB International, Wallingford.

Robertson, D. (1974) *The King's School, Gloucester*. Phillimore.

Simkin, L. (2004) From sectorisation to segmentation in six simple steps. Paper submitted as part of a conference at Warwick Business School.

Urry, J. (1995) *Consuming Places*. Routledge, London.

Wedel, M. and Kamakura, W. (2000) *Market Segmentation: Conceptual and Methodological Foundations*. Kluwer Academic Publishers, Boston.

Wilson, I. (2003) *The Economics of Leisure*. Heinemann, Oxford.

Wind, Y. (1978) Issues and advances in segmentation research. *Journal of Marketing Research*, 15, 10.

Zikmund, W.G. (2003) *Customer Relationship Management*. Wiley International.

Chapter 4

The marketing mix and heritage tourism

Baloo looked at Bagheera in horror. The Cold Lairs! None of the jungle creatures dared go there — except the monkeys.

The Cold Lairs had once been a great city, built around a splendid palace. Now the place was no more than ruined houses and dark streets. Some said there were ghosts. The monkeys loved to play up and down the streets, pretending to be the kings and queens who had once lived there.

(Kipling, 1889)

Introduction

We have already examined in some detail the different target audiences that are in the market for all the alternative types of heritage tourism (the latter will be discussed fully, below). In short (and generally speaking), in terms of demographic profiles there is usually a slight female bias; in terms of age groups, almost all groups are in the market for different types of heritage tourism (e.g. children on school day-trips to a local castle or museum); and in relation to age group and position in family life-cycle, the 'grey' market, who also tend to be 'empty nesters', are predominant. In socio-economic terms, we have established that heritage tourism tends to attract the ABC1s

PRODUCT ←→ PLACE ←→ PROMOTION ←→ PRICE ←→ (plus

Process ←→ Physical Evidence ←→ People)

Figure 4.1 The main elements of the marketing mix.

for a variety of reasons: level of education, wealth and, in particular, disposable income, and their expectations (psychographics) of heritage tourism, i.e. they want to experience and learn about the heritage of their own and other countries' cultures. The profiling of consumers up to this point is relatively straightforward.

Socio-cultural characteristics create more cause for concern (i.e. higher risk factors for the heritage marketer) as we do not know enough about the relationship between race, religion, ethnicity, sub-cultures and heritage tourism, although there is evidence to suggest that identity and genealogy has spawned heritage tourism amongst minority groups, together with the fact that some will visit religious heritage sites abroad, at least once in their lifetime.

However, from the discussion in the previous chapter we also know that customers themselves (whatever their profile) *are* involved in the production process, their individual use of the product will reflect their own attitudes, expectations and experiences, and if this is understood, for example through **ethnographic (observational) research**, it can be used in targeted marketing campaigns (the description of developing a marketing campaign for Madame Tussauds in the section 'Tourism research' below illustrates this point well).

In this chapter the elements of the marketing mix will not be treated discretely, as has been the case in the book previously. This is because, in the context of both heritage tourism and food and drink (the two heritage sectors that form the basis for this chapter and the next), the marketing mix elements are so inextricably linked that to separate them would make the text more difficult to follow.

In short, the key to success in the development of heritage products (whether these are in the heritage tourism sector or indeed any other) depends on the ability to *match* the product or service being offered (which is, of course, based on an understanding of consumer wants or aspirations) with the **benefits** sought by the customer (these can be both tangible and intangible, i.e. a tangible benefit is the *actual* consumption of the product or service itself and an intangible benefit might be the status or other 'feel-good' factor that arises either during the research process, during consumption or following consumption, such as being 'environmentally friendly' in supporting organic foodstuffs). If possible, the heritage marketer should be 'one step ahead' of the customer in terms of their needs, in particular to circumvent any potential problems that could arise in the heritage provision. All of this requires meticulous research, which is expensive, both in terms of time and money, and therefore needs to be planned and executed in advance of any marketing initiatives undertaken.

Product – definitions

A product is:

1 **Physical**, i.e., tangible (you can see it); for example, a museum building or an authentic food such as Parmesan cheese, as opposed to intangible, which is largely the case with services.
2 **Functional**, i.e., capable of doing something. That is, offering an experience or experiential insight into an aspect of the past; for example, in the case of spiritual heritage or nostalgia through the prompting of memories, or in the unique taste of a food or wine.
3 **Symbolic**, i.e., representative of something, such as the shrine to Mumtaz Muhal in the shape of the Taj Mahal in Agra, India or 'Tokaji', which is a liqueur made in Hungary and symbolic of that country in the same way that Pernod (perhaps a brand with which consumers are more familiar) is connected with France. All three examples stand as symbols of national identity in relation to each country and are frequently used as images in promotional material, not least for heritage tourism.

The vast majority of products also operate at three levels (a concept we have touched on earlier in the book). In other words:

1 **the core**, i.e., what is at the heart of the product, such as the monument or other aspect of heritage that has attracted the visitor;
2 **the actual**, which are the features or capabilities offered; for example, the facilities on-site for shopping and eating; and
3 **the augmented**, which can include any number of different 'added-value' variables such as brand name; an example therefore would be the visit to a National Trust-branded property or landscape.

We also know that products go through 'life-cycles' and we will therefore examine the application of this concept in the context of heritage tourism.

Service aspects of marketing heritage products will also be considered and, as a quick reminder, have three main characteristics:

1 they are **intangible** (i.e., cannot be 'seen', but are experienced during consumption);
2 they are therefore at once **perishable**; and
3 they are **heterogeneous** (never the same).

Further to this, over the last few decades several measures of *service quality* have been developed in order to fill the gap between customers' expectations and their perception based on what they receive. The notable example of a model that has addressed this gap is SERVQUAL, which has five main aspects, as follows.

1 *Tangibles*, i.e., the physical facilities and other resources, including the appearance of staff, that make up what the visitor or customer actually sees.
2 *Reliability*, i.e., a measure of how well an organization can deliver the promises made in the name of service quality, both reliably and accurately.
3 *Responsiveness*, i.e., how far an organization is prepared to go in order to help a customer.
4 *Assurance*, i.e., the level of knowledge (through appropriate training) acquired by the staff which benefits the consumer. The staff involved in producing and delivering the product are part of the product itself – their attitudes, behaviour and appearance are crucial to visitor perception and confidence; they are in the 'front line' in terms of **customer relationship building and marketing**, whether this is for a tangible or intangible product. 'Volunteers'/stewards at built heritage sites are one example of key service providers as they are readily available to answer visitor questions and address problems. Specifically, the 'Blue Badge Guides' who give their services free of charge to local community environments/towns and cities in the UK are one type of volunteer group who provide tours and information on the heritage aspects of a locality. However, in the context of heritage products (including sites and attractions), we could be referring to other types of 'sales' staff, for example those who operate in retail environments such as shops, restaurants and cafés.
5 *Empathy*, i.e., the level of care and individual attention that the organization at large and specifically its personnel are willing to offer the consumer.

Following on from SERVQUAL, another model has been developed to specifically address the service quality provision of historic houses. The HISTOQUAL model contains all the service quality aspects of SERVQUAL, together with examining communication, for example how potential consumers are made aware of the product offering and, when on site, how they should be guided around (use of signs, literature, etc.) and consumables, i.e., addressing their expectations (and subsequent perceptions) of catering facilities, shopping opportunities, etc.

Consumer's appreciation of service brands depends on a variety of factors such as the role played by the staff; the role consumers play and the interaction between consumers. All employees, as they embody the organisation in consumers' eyes, can influence perceptions of the service brand. Marketers therefore need to carefully consider their recruitment processes; the role staff is expected to play and their technical support to ensure they are able and motivated to deliver high-quality services.

(De Chernatony, 1998)

De Chernatony has advocated a complex concept that needs to be considered carefully in the context of marketing heritage tourism, i.e., we need to go deeper from the previous chapter on segmentation to consider the notion of experiential tourism when addressing heritage. In short, we must fully understand the expectations and perceptions of consumers in terms of their demand for heritage tourism if we are to offer them a satisfactory (or excellent) experience. This must be the case from the point of product launch, through the experience itself (including the interface with staff) and beyond; there should be no room for cognitive dissonance at any point, as far as practically possible.

Finally we shall consider the concept of branding, which is a name, term, design, symbol or any other feature that **identifies** a product or service.

Tourism research

All tourism providers, whether an individual heritage site or a 'grand tour' of heritage attractions spanning the world, will carry out research to determine all aspects of marketing before launching the brand.

The research process is generic, as can be seen in Figure 4.2.

The [specific] purposes of tourism research can be summarised as follows:
1 constructing and testing theory
2 profiling, inventory making and collecting baseline data
3 assessing social, cultural, environmental and economic impacts
4 identifying educational needs
5 assisting in planning and management activities
6 contributing to monitoring and evaluation
7 providing a temporal perspective – past, present and future trends.

(Jennings, 2001)

We have previously either touched on or covered in some detail many of the points mentioned in Jennings' view of the specific tourism research process.

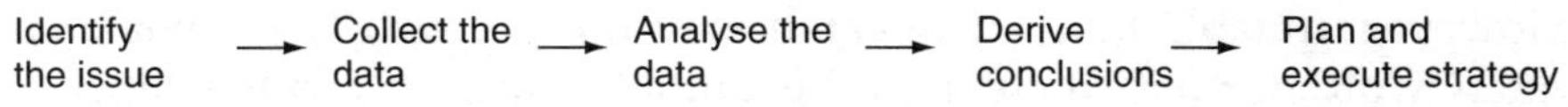

Identify the issue → Collect the data → Analyse the data → Derive conclusions → Plan and execute strategy

Figure 4.2 The research process.

In short, it is imperative to have data and be able to profile the target market so that they can be communicated with using an appropriate media campaign in order to stimulate either existing or latent demand, which may be for the past, present or future.

One critical aspect of tourism research that must be considered is the fact that there are different perspectives on what tourism is (depending on who you talk to) and, further, there are on-going paradigm shifts in terms of the social sciences that may affect the availability and validity of data. Therefore, the researcher must ask themselves three basic questions before any tourism research can begin:

1   How is the world perceived? (i.e., what is its ontological basis?)
2   What is the relationship between the researcher and the subject(s) of the research? (i.e., what is the epistemological basis?)
3   How will the researcher gather the data or information? (i.e., what will be the methodology?)

Once these questions have been addressed, the next two concern the collection of primary and secondary data, i.e., whether one or both are to be used, bearing in mind the costs in terms of time and money that may preclude engaging in certain activities.

- *Primary data* are original and collected specifically for the task in hand and are therefore usually 'recent' and highly relevant. However, the collection of primary data tends to be both time-consuming and expensive and therefore must be planned for well in advance of the information being needed.
- *Secondary data* are already published and, although relatively easy to obtain (both in terms of time and finance), may not be specific or completely relevant for the tourism research task. These data may also be obsolete and, further, a comparative analysis between different countries for example may be problematic, either because of the ways in which the data have been collected or because some data may not be available.

Secondary data for the purposes of tourism research are available from a wide variety of sources, including public documents such as the World Tourism Organisation's *Inbound and Outbound Tourism Statistical Reports*; archival documents such as public records and historical data; administrative documents, for example the annual reports and statements of accounts of companies; and formal studies and reports as well as travel guides and books.

However, suitable tourism research may not necessarily be available in written word format, there may be audio recordings, video tapes and images that are just as valuable in determining facts.

In 1992, the Tussauds Group (as it is now known) advertised for the first-ever Marketing Director. The incumbent came from a traditional fast-moving consumer goods (fmcg) background at CadburysSchweppes, a far cry from the museum/exhibition environment of Madame Tussauds.

The new Director of Marketing found many statistical analyses of visitor numbers and used these as a starting point to determine the 'peaks and troughs' for the attraction; this later led to promotion and price discrimination activities in order to manage better the demand. However, it was unclear (and indeed no such research had ever been conducted) as to *why* visitors came in their thousands, from home and abroad, to this albeit unique attraction, especially when very little advertising had ever taken place.

Some ethnographic/observational research based on video recordings was set in motion to 'see' what visitors actually did with the exhibits; the results were very revealing and showed a range of emotions and 'participation' (for example, 'kissing', shaking hands, etc.) with the wax models. This information was then 'played back' to potential audiences through a poster, and later a television advertising, campaign featuring some of the exhibits themselves. It was highly successful and became the launch pad for a more sophisticated strategy that subsequently saw the representation of Madame Tussauds in other venues, such as Warwick Castle as described in Chapter 3.

How did heritage tourism begin?

There is no doubt that the number of heritage attractions worldwide and the number of people visiting them have grown dramatically in recent years. In part, this is a reflection of the large-scale and rapid growth in international tourism, in particular since the early 1950s, which in itself is partly a function of the increase in marketing of destinations and attractions, including the raising of awareness and stimulation of demand.

In a biography of Audrey Hepburn, the distinguished film critic and biographer Alexander Walker argues that tourism from the USA to Europe was almost non-existent until the release of the film *Roman Holiday* in 1953, when visits to the 'eternal city' began to soar. Audiences in the USA were captivated by the baroque architecture that was evident in almost every shot, as this was the first film ever to be made completely on location.

However, in terms of trips taken by Europeans, the literature is able to relate back to Roman times when this community took their love of water-based attractions to all areas of colonization, creating for themselves the type of 'theme park' they adored. One fine example of this is the Roman Baths at Bath, UK (see Case study 4.1 on the new Thermae Bath Spa project).

During the mediaeval period in Europe, there was a rise in tourism based on religion (which some towns and cities around the world still use as a point of differentiation for tourism). Moving swiftly on to nineteenth-century England, industrialization generally, and the development of the railways specifically, stimulated the growth of attraction visiting. Museums and galleries sprang up, often funded by wealthy, paternalistic industrialists and which displayed items including those of the eighteenth-century tourists, especially those that had undertaken the fashionable (for the wealthy elite) 'Grand Tour'.

The modern public museum was invented from the mid-eighteenth to the late nineteenth centuries in Europe, Australia and North America. The main ideology behind the development of these specific places (which has become a heritage tourism sector in its own right), was the purpose of celebrating and dramatizing the unity of the nation-state and to make visible to its public the prevailing notion of 'national culture' – an ideal which we have critiqued in Chapter 1.

In the twentieth and twenty-first centuries there is an important link between the growth in heritage attractions and government investment in many countries, as governments have sought to use heritage attraction visiting as a way of regenerating urban areas (this has already been discussed in Chapter 2).

Table 4.1 illustrates that heritage attractions feature heavily in visitor 'days out'.

Table 4.1 allows us to make a correlation between the most popular visitor venues in the UK and those that charge admission; in other words, the top six are all free entry whilst all those that follow charge, except for two further museums, the National Maritime Museum in Liverpool and Tate Britain. A number of the attractions listed used to be free, notably Stonehenge, Canterbury Cathedral and Westminster Abbey; it is useful to think about the ethics of these places of worship charging admission because the trend is likely to continue, particularly in the UK as English Heritage continues to withdraw financial support from Cathedrals in particular.

A few other points worthy of note are that the Eden Project is a relatively new visitor attraction and situated in a remote part of the UK (Cornwall) but features at number eight in the table – is this because it is new, because of the unique architectural structure, because it featured in a *Bond* film which gave it exposure that would have been expensive to achieve and a glamorous link, or because it has content that consumers are keen to visit (although Kew Gardens has as much, if not more, of the same and is also a World Heritage site)?

The majority of these visitor attractions are based in London, which reinforces the position of the capital as a place of culture. Most of the London attractions are museums and all are free to enter because of the present UK government's change of policy on charging admission to these venues.

Table 4.1 The top 20 visitor attractions, 2004

Rank	Attraction	Visitor numbers	Admission charge
1	Blackpool Pleasure Beach	5 737 000	free
2	British Museum	4 584 000	free
3	Tate Museum	3 895 746	free
4	Natural History Museum	2 976 738	free
5	Science Museum	2 886 859	free
6	V&A Museum	2 257 325	free
7	Tower of London	1 972 263	pay
8	Eden Project	1 404 737	pay
9	Legoland Windsor	1 321 128	pay
10	National Maritime Museum	1 305 150	free
11	Edinburgh Castle	1 172 534	pay
12	Tate Britain	1 106 911	free
13	Kew Gardens	1 079 424	pay
14	Chester Zoo	1 076 000	pay
15	Canterbury Cathedral	1 060 166	pay
16	Westminster Abbey	1 022 718	pay
17	Roman Baths	983 392	pay
18	London Zoo	839 865	pay
19	Stonehenge	776 279	pay
20	St Paul's Cathedral	10 975	pay

Source: Association of Leading Visitor Attractions.

Why has heritage tourism grown in popularity?

We have touched on some of this in the introduction above and in previous chapters but there are many more theories on this point.

The majority of writers agree that tourists have become bored with conventional forms of tourism – they want something more 'authentic'. Others argue that tourists are now more mature, demanding and discriminating in their choice of travel. Cultural tourism (a term that includes heritage tourism and is sometimes used interchangeably with it, as we have discussed before) enables this type of tourist (as profiled above) to engage in more intellectualized and specialized activities.

People now have wider horizons because of an increased and changing emphasis on the way in which they wish to spend their leisure time. Undoubtedly, advances in technology have contributed to these rising and changing expectations; better and cheaper forms of transport (such as the 'low-cost' airlines and Eurostar), computer literacy (especially an ability to 'surf' the Internet – vast amounts of information on any aspect of the world, past or present, can be bought into the home at the touch of a button and with a little patience) and increasing wealth (not just in the developed West but also in the newly industrializing countries and those that have more recently opened their doors to the 'free market' – countries such as India and China. The former, in particular, has a 'burgeoning middle-class' with considerable disposable income to spend) has led to an increased demand for shorter, more frequent and more intensive tourism experiences. There is also an increasingly evident link between holidays and the pursuit of personal interests and identity (see Case study 4.2), for example, genealogy (tracing family history and roots).

In 1996, the Department of National Heritage stated that heritage and an interest in the past had become one of the most significant growth industries in the UK (this is mirrored in many other countries around the world, especially throughout Europe, the USA, Australia, South America, South Africa and, increasingly, the middle-eastern countries such as Syria) during the last ten years, managing to attract 250 million visitors per year to a complete range of heritage attractions.

Figure 4.3 encapsulates much of what tourists and locals wish to visit (and preserve for time to come).

WORLD HERITAGE SITES
(e.g. The Pyramids at Giza, Cairo, Egypt or Kew Gardens, London).

EUROPEAN CITIES/CAPITALS OF CULTURE
(e.g. Cork, Lisbon, Madrid, Krakow, Edinburgh, Glasgow, Paris, Frankfurt, Budapest).

REGIONAL HERITAGE TRAILS
(e.g. The Cradle of Humankind in Africa).

NATIONAL HERITAGE
(e.g. The Anglo-Sikh Heritage trail which is both physical and virtual. The Queensland Heritage trail in Australia and National Museums such as MOMA in New York, The National Museum of Singapore and The Natural History Museum in London. Coastlines such as the Red Sea area which spans both Jordan and Egypt. Conservation areas and trusts such as the giant 'Redwood' trees in California and rivers such as the Nile and Ganges).

LOCAL HERITAGE

(e.g. 'Local' places of worship, monuments, landscapes, vernacular buildings or others of architectural interest, townscapes, city-wide heritage marketing).

Figure 4.3 A taxonomy of heritage tourism attractions.

The relationship between tourism and heritage

Tourism (and its rise and rise) is the sector in which the concept of heritage has been leveraged to maximum benefit for the providers and, one might argue, for customers, although it is catching on fast in the marketing and branding of all manner of goods and services, as we shall see in subsequent chapters.

Tourism is one of the largest industries (if not the largest) for many countries around the globe. It is growing at a faster rate than many other industries and this trend is likely to continue – but with a significant challenge ahead for all concerned in the provision of access, i.e., for the growth to be managed in a **sustainable** way (see Insight 4.2).

Figures 4.4 and 4.5 show the visits (in volume, millions of people) to and from the UK from 1983 to 2003 and 2004. The conclusions that can be drawn from these are that the number of visits to the UK made by overseas residents doubled between 1983 and 2003. The number of visits abroad made by UK residents has tripled during the same period.

A further illustration of the extent to which international travel is taking place is evident in the number of UK residents travelling to the USA in 2003, which was unchanged at 3.6 million, and *vice versa*; there were 3.3 million visits by USA residents to the UK and their total spend was £2.3 billion.

In 2002, Spain became the favoured country for a visit by UK residents, overtaking France for the first time. In 2003, similar numbers visited Spain, i.e., 13.8 million UK residents, compared with 12 million to France. The third

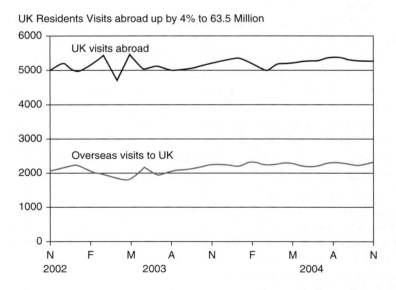

Figure 4.4 Overseas residents' visits to the UK and UK residents' visits abroad (seasonally adjusted). Source: National Statistics.

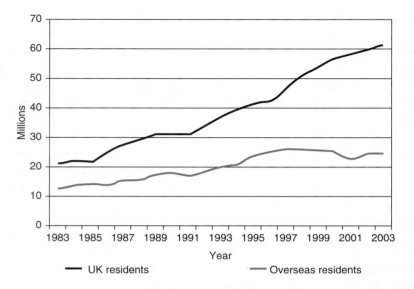

Figure 4.5 **Visits to and from the UK. Source: National Statistics.**

most popular destination for UK residents was the Irish Republic and then the USA.

Table 4.2 identifies the top 12 holiday destinations for the British, 1992–2001.

Tables 4.3 and 4.4 illustrate the top ten long-haul destinations overall and those made by US citizens.

The data in Tables 4.3 and 4.4 present no more than a 'snapshot', as the trends are changing in terms of favoured long-haul destinations. There is no doubt that an increasing global interest (particularly from certain regional areas, which we can collectively call the developed West) in heritage will see relatively new destinations for mass-market travel, for example places such as China will feature more highly in years to come, together with other newly industrializing countries such as those in Eastern Europe where increasing wealth is enabling the development of infrastructure for heritage tourism (among other types). I anticipate much more 'religious heritage tourism' to places such as Mecca, Rome, the original home of the late Pope, John Paul II (i.e. Krakow in Poland), and Israel and Palestine, notwithstanding the continuous conflict. India and Pakistan have recognized the enormous tourism potential of the jointly controlled Kashmir province and have begun moves to provide the catalyst for change in that war-torn area where both indigenous tourism and that from outside the two countries was once very popular, all year round.

Heritage, like culture, is increasingly being drawn into a globalized tourism industry that uses local, regional and national markers of **uniqueness and identity**. Heritage is intimately linked to identity (personal,

Table 4.2 Top 12 holiday destinations for the British, 1992–2001

	1992		1997		1999		2001	
	(thousands)	*(%)*	*(thousands)*	*(%)*	*(thousands)*	*(%)*	*(thousands)*	*(%)*
Spain	5120	22	7658	26	9526	27	10797	28
France	5740	25	6724	23	6903	20	7083	18
Greece	1820	8	1366	5	2275	7	3025	8
US	1670	7	1946	7	2611	7	2448	6
Italy	1820	8	1213	4	1447	4	1667	4
Ireland	630	3	1050	4	1929	6	1591	4
Portugal	1110	5	1170	4	1282	4	1384	4
Cyprus	n/a	–	645	2	854	2	1356	4
Netherlands	720	3	805	3	840	2	1022	3
Belgium	420	2	628	2	682	2	796	2
Turkey	280	1	910	3	749	2	772	2
Germany	570	2	495	2	547	2	561	1
Other	3340	14	4528	16	5378	15	6168	16
Total	**23240**	**100**	**29138**	**100**	**35023**	**100**	**38670**	**100**

Source: Mintel.

Table 4.3 Top 10 long-haul destinations

Rank	Destination
1	Barbados
2	Mauritius
3	Thailand
4	St Lucia
5	Mexico
6	Singapore
7	Hong Kong
8	Bali
9	Antigua
10	China

Source: Travel Trade Gazette (2001).

Table 4.4 Long-haul destinations, top 10 from the USA

Rank	Destination
1	Florida
2	Australia
3	Thailand
4	Barbados
5	New York
6	California
7	Dubai
8	South Africa
9	Mauritius
10	New Zealand

Source: Travel Trade Gazette (2002).

community and national, see Chapter 1) and to core value systems, therefore the commodification of heritage (see below) as a tourist product is inevitably fraught with tensions, not to mention the fact that tangible aspects of heritage such as buildings are a non-renewable resource and always in a state of decline and deterioration.

Tourism is a diffuse industry and coordination of this sector in an economy is required both *vertically*, i.e., between local, regional and national institutions, and *horizontally*, i.e., between agencies at the same level of activity. Some examples of this, mainly in the UK context, are discussed in Chapter 1, in particular with respect to funding heritage provision, especially heritage attractions.

We mentioned above that governments are increasingly interested in using heritage tourism (and other types of tourist activity) as a catalyst for positive change, in particular for the regeneration and/or growth of localities. Governments can act as a stimulator of tourism in at least three ways:

1 through offering grants and tax incentives, low-interest loans and other benefits such as networking opportunities;
2 through marketing initiatives such support of national and regional tourist boards or specific projects, such as Puerto de Culturas, Cartagena, Spain (see Insight 4.10);
3 through advertising.

These are 'large' generic government principles which vary in the type and level of support. Sometimes, both governments and other organizations (private and public sector) will engage with specific marketing communications activities, one of which (that has not been covered in the previous chapter, in detail) is **advertising**.

There are two types of advertising, 'above' and 'below' the line. 'The line' is an accounting term and, broadly speaking, defines the level of expenditure on advertising. Any spend above the line is deemed to be 'very expensive', for example advertising on television, and below the line is relatively cheap, for example initiatives such as spending on sales promotions, money-off coupons, etc. However, the concept of drawing an accounting line is now largely disregarded, as some sales promotions can cost as much (and indeed may be more appropriate in terms of the marketing communications objectives) as using broadcast media, if not more.

In the previous chapter I identified several different types of marketing communications that can be used for target marketing, such as newsletters, websites, press releases and so on; these are, of course, types of advertising so we now need to define the terms more specifically.

Advertising is a *paid for and non-personal* type of marketing communication and usually includes the use of newspapers, magazines, television, radio, outdoor advertising on billboards, websites and other media such as direct mail, both mail shots and mail drops through the post, in order to transmit a message.

An advertisement is rarely used as a stand-alone method of communication (partly because it is well known as a somewhat 'hit and miss' affair) but in combination with other types of communications. All these initiatives need to be carefully planned and phased-in during the lifetime of the marketing plan in order to maximize the opportunity for meeting the goals or objectives, both *quantitative and qualitative*.

In Chapter 2 we saw the different types of advertising used by English Heritage as part of their relationship marketing strategy, which is demonstrated by their 'ladder of loyalty'. Depending on whom they are targeting, i.e., existing, new or lapsed customers, whether it is to raise awareness, educate or interest (perhaps with a specific/new issue), encourage a decision (such as to take out a subscription, which may require an additional sales promotion incentive) or to take action, for example, there may be a specific cause requiring urgent donations, and the timeliness of the communication will all determine exactly which types of advertising will be used.

Norwegians have a heritage distinct from other cultures in many ways but the creation and recognition of 'LEGO' is one aspect with which almost everyone throughout the world is familiar. In 1996, 'Legoland', a theme park based on the familiar plastic bricks that can be made into almost anything, opened in Windsor, UK (it is now the third most visited theme park in the UK). Before the park opened to the public, and certainly during each year, a promotional mix consisting of television advertising, commercial radio, local, national and regional newspapers, trade publications, educational literature and direct marketing initiatives both through the Internet and mail drops, are used.

In recent years it has become increasingly popular for two organizations to 'piggy-back' off each other for the purposes of advertising strategically in terms of specific target markets. For example, at the time of writing, Disneyland Paris is offering deals in conjunction with National Express Coaches in the UK in order to encourage families with very young children to travel to the theme park by coach. The best available prices are 'out of season', i.e., not in school holidays – parents who are not tied to the school calendar because of their job(s) or the ages of their children can take advantage of these offers and this helps both Disneyland Paris and National Express Coaches to remain (fully) operative at what would otherwise be quieter times in terms of volume of business.

Advertising specifically, and marketing communications activities generally, are very important in service industries such as heritage tourism because there is no opportunity to 'try' the product, unlike a car which can be taken for a test-drive or a new food or beverage which can be sampled at a grocery retail outlet or at an event. Both the slogan or strapline and image(s) that are to be used must be carefully tested on the target before being launched in public and the organization must be ready to respond, for example to enquiries, bookings and so on. In short:

in addition to effective research, an advertising brief needs clearly expressed goals that answer:
- What should the advertising achieve?
- How does an advertiser want to influence consumers?
- Does the advertiser want to raise their awareness?
- Does the advertiser want to change their perceptions?
- Who is the brand competing against?
- How does the brand stack up against them?
- How can it truly be differentiated from the rest?

(Morgan and Pritchard, 2001)

Heritage tourism – marketing the UK

Travel and tourism in the UK form one of the largest economic sectors, worth approximately £74 billion per year (4.5 per cent of GDP). The sector employs approximately 2.1 million people and contributes much-needed income, in particular to local economies. The official website promoting tourism to Britain is known as VisitBritain and can be accessed at http://www.visitbritain.com; this site categorizes tourism in Britain as follows:

- Hidden Britain
- Britain's Garden
- Outdoor Britain

- Sporting Britain
- UK City Experience
- Youth.

One important feature is the promotion of a travel pass called **The Great Britain Heritage Pass**, which enables visitors to access 600 heritage sites all for a one-off payment (**a pricing consideration**), currently £22/US$35 (4 days), £35/$54 (7 days), £46/$75 (15 days) or £60/$102 (one month).

The two largest markets targeted by VisitBritain are European visitors and travellers from the USA. In 2002, it spent £10 million (out of a £20 million budget) on a marketing communications campaign to attract US visitors back to Britain following terrorist attacks and the 'foot and mouth' epidemic in the UK. The marketing communications strapline/slogan used for this campaign was 'Only in Britain: Only in 2002'.

Following the War in Iraq in 2003, a similar campaign was undertaken but the approach on this occasion was on 'timely' rather than 'timeless' marketing, with specific communications aimed at promoting limited offers such as a Globe Theatre tour of Shakespeare's Britain.

Interestingly the travel trade to Britain seems to have recovered remarkably well following major international events, relative to that experienced by other European countries. In 2002 alone, American visitors to Britain spent £2.3 billion, as much as the combined spend of tourists from Germany, France, Ireland and Austria. Currently, overseas visitors to the UK number approximately 25 million annually and they spend about £14 billion.

VisitBritain has been criticized for not trying to win business from **emerging markets** such as China and India, in particular because only 15 per cent of Americans actually possess a passport. The problem, however, is the lack of hard data on the viability of these markets, even if a significant amount of marketing investment takes place. Although the American market may be volatile and possibly 'small', their spend in Britain offers a positive return, at least for the time being.

The current emphasis in terms of strategic marketing of tourism by VisitBritain relies on **brand architecture** and there are two main brands in the portfolio: England specifically (as most visitors want to come to London and never make it beyond) and the UK generally; they are keen to develop separate **brand identities** for England, Scotland and Wales.

Communications' resources are moving increasingly into online and digital channels, within the context of a comprehensive **customer relationship management strategy** aimed at personalizing information for particular categories of overseas visitors. This includes targeting independent travellers, short 'breakers' and business-related visitors (see Chapter 3). By 2006 VisitBritain's goal is to have more than 6 million active records on an overseas customer database. For the overseas market, they are dividing the UK's 'product' into four 'pillars': culture; history and heritage; country and coast; and sport and activities.

Heritage tourism products

Heritage products in this sector are usually referred to in the literature as attractions and have three main types of impact on an economy: economic/financial, environmental and socio-cultural.

Economic:
1 Inward tourism brings in valuable foreign currency and domestic spend keeps money in the economy;
2 a significant indigenous economic benefit from the growth of tourism and associated spend is the creation of jobs, which
3 creates a multiplier effect (see Chapter 2) for the local and regional economy, i.e., it stimulates the demand for many additional goods and services such as housing, transport, etc.;
4 revenue subsidizes the heritage attraction itself.

On balance, the effect is positive.

Environmental:
On the whole, the balance in terms of environmental effects seems to be negative. In the case of natural attractions and human-made attractions that were not originally designed as tourism products, theft, vandalism and erosion caused by visitors has become increasingly of concern to curators and managers and these detriments have to be balanced against the economic benefits of revenue and the fact that the heritage attractions should be more accessible to the public.

Socio-cultural:
We saw in the previous chapter that some of the main 'presenters' of heritage in the UK such as English Heritage are keen that not only should a nation's heritage reflect the interests of all sections of society but that there should be greater public access, in particular to generate greater domestic tourism but also for the purposes of education, especially for the young. If these aims are 'successful' they should then create a greater degree of responsibility and responsiveness to aspects of heritage, which might go a long way to alleviating some of the long-term problems mentioned above.

Definition of attractions, the product life-cycle and three levels of product

An attraction must be a permanently established excursion destination, a primary purpose of which is to allow **public access for entertainment,**

interest and/or education. It must be open to the public without prior booking (this is not always possible or practical for heritage attractions) and should be capable of attracting day visitors or tourists.

(British Tourist Authority, quoted in *Travel and Tourism Analyst*, 2000)

Although the majority of this definition applies well to heritage attractions, it does not allow for the inclusion of temporary attractions such as exhibitions and other events, for example festivals, which may not exist permanently. Another unique feature of heritage attractions is that there may not be an entry charge, either regularly for some groups or individuals such as 'local' residents, or at certain times of the day or year, for example 'Heritage Open Days' during September each year enable free access to participating sites, as discussed in the previous chapter.

September was chosen deliberately to 'extend' the main season for visiting heritage sites, which is usually from May to late August/early September. This is one example of the notion of the **product life-cycle** applied to heritage sites, i.e., the 'growth' stage in the season is usually May to early July when the number of visitors is increasing greatly, week on week; the 'maturity' stage is mid-July to early September when the greatest amount of spend takes place, not least because this is when the majority of people, at least in the developed world, take annual holidays; and the 'decline' stage is from mid-September when some sites may even close for the winter period. This has implications for all the other principles of the marketing mix and we shall explore this in subsequent chapters.

Insight 4.1: *VUTA KUXA (New Dawn)* – The monthly web-based newsletter of the International Marketing Council of South Africa

Another country that celebrates heritage in the month of September is South Africa. Indeed, September is Heritage month (defined in the newsletter as 'who we are and what we have . . .') but the focus is not on buildings and landscapes but on national **symbols**, notably the national flag and national anthem. 'The central theme for our campaign is "Show your true colours – fly your flag". The key objective of this theme is to instil national pride in all South Africans, by encouraging and motivating them to fly the flag in word, thought and deed and to properly sing our national anthem. As we celebrate our heritage we need to take stock of where we come from to find root and pillars of who we are as a nation, united in diversity. September is also Tourism Month [remember that this is the Southern Hemisphere]. With it comes Spring . . . [and we will] . . . work together with South African Tourism to encourage South Africans to visit and explore South Africa.'

South Africa has much to be proud of in terms of all aspects of heritage, not least its diverse people and the fact that the country has five World

Heritage sites (at the time of writing), namely: Robben Island (where Nelson Mandela was kept prisoner for many years), Drakensburg/Ukhahlamba Park, greater St Lucia Wetlands, The Cradle of Humankind (this is an ancient site where it is reputed that South Africans originally lived and which has evidence of fossilized remains) and Maphugubwe.

Acknowledgment: International Marketing Council of South Africa, 2004.

Victor Middleton, in *Sustainable Tourism* (1998), establishes the principle that travel and tourism products have to be understood on two levels. Firstly, the overall tourism product that comprises a combination of all the service elements which a tourist will consume from the time of departure to their return; 'this "product" is an idea, an expectation, or a mental construct in the customer's mind'. For example, museums have physical artefacts (often housed in a 'period' building) but many also offer visitors the opportunity to indulge different types of feelings and emotions (this is again the psychographic element of market segmentation, in particular the personality aspect, rather than lifestyle) such as nostalgia, pride, belonging and perhaps awe. Another example is that in visiting cathedrals, pleasure is derived both from the physical features of the building and also the intangible elements, such as the general atmosphere and specifically the spiritual 'value' to the individual.

Secondly, the commercial activities that are part of the overall product offering and might include sales promotions (special offers, for example, as mentioned above), accommodation and transport; these might be as much of the 'pull' as the heritage attraction itself.

We can apply this to the **three levels of product** mentioned at the beginning of the chapter, i.e., in this context, the **core** is what the customer expects in terms of the tangible or intangible, the **actual** is the 'added-value' facilities on offer at the place of visit and the **augmented** would include benefits such as other ('added-on', i.e., not directly related, such as accommodation, food and transport) facilities and services, brand characteristics or 'feelings' engendered through the process of 'being there'.

Middleton argues that attractions are the elements within a destination's environment that, individually and combined, serve as the primary motivation for holiday tourism visits. They comprise natural attractions, built attractions, cultural attractions and social attractions.

Natural attractions

Natural attractions include:

1 *Landscape* – for example areas in the UK that have come to be labelled 'Areas of Outstanding Natural Beauty' (AONBs), such as the Malvern

Hills in Herefordshire or Snowdonia in Wales; examples abroad include The Grand Canyon in the USA or the Himalayas, which span a number of different countries, India, China and Tibet included.

2   *Seascape* – for example the 'Jurassic Coast of Dorset', declared a World Heritage Site; Chesapeake Bay in the USA and the Gold Coast in Australia.
3   *Beaches* – for example many of those in Thailand and the Indian Ocean islands and countries such as The Maldives and Seychelles.
4   *Wildlife* – most of which is found in rural areas, one example is The Wildfowl and Wetlands Trust at Slimbridge, Gloucestershire, UK, set up by the Antarctic explorer Sir Peter Scott.
5   *Climate* – a big 'pull' to countries such as those in southeast Asia, particularly for north European tourists during the coldest months of the year.

Built attractions

Built attractions include:

1   *Historic townscapes* – for example, Amsterdam or Bangkok.
2   *New townscapes* – as evident in newly built resorts, for example Disneyland Paris.
3   Urban areas tend to be rich in the heritage of *places of worship* such as cathedrals (in the UK, I can think of Durham, Salisbury, Gloucester (see Insight 4.2) and Liverpool); heritage *centres* and *health spas* (such as Cheltenham, Leamington and Bath (see Case study 4.1) in the UK) and *museums* such as the Dali Museum at Figueres in Spain.

In the UK there is no doubt that 'spa' towns, existing or previously known for their natural properties are using this as a source of competitive advantage in the heritage tourism marketplace, particularly at a time when there is a general interest in all things heritage and specifically amongst certain target markets in the spa concept, for historical interest and also to use physically the extension of this in 'luxury' environments, as discussed in the previous chapter.

My own home city of Gloucester, UK, was previously a spa town but very few people are aware of this fact; indeed, the place where one used to be able to 'take the (healing) waters' is now a dentist's surgery. This is in sharp contrast to the neighbouring town of Cheltenham, which in its tourism marketing literature has always used the fact that the waters can be 'taken' and has emphasized the heritage of the buildings in which they can be sampled, although perhaps this is not as 'widely' associated with Cheltenham as it is with Bath.

Destinations with genuine spa connections are also cashing in on the spa trend, none more so than Monaco. During 2004, the principality will be highlighting 'spas and all aspects of well-being', launching a 'Simply Spa' concept at

its famous Thermes Marins de Monte-Carlo and promoting related products
such as new spa property Le Port Palace.

(Wild, 2004)

In the previous chapter we touched on the fact that many heritage buildings,
especially grand houses or 'stately homes', are considering the use of their
premises for the business market and have identified that this segment,
whilst lucrative, is increasingly looking for a combination of old and new,
for example, 'new' facilities such as an up-to-date spa, accommodated in a
heritage building.

> Spas are a selling tool nowadays and they are one of the criteria clients are includ-
> ing in their briefs. Organisers looking for spa properties are already spoilt for
> choice and options are increasing, with spas opening daily around the world.

(Berry, 2004)

Organizers have found that the benefits of spas are that the busy conference
delegate or businessman can work out before or between sessions, enjoy a
lunchtime swim or book spa treatments after business. The overall concept
of the spa is now based on the seven pillars of well-being: beauty, life-bal-
ance, harmony, aqua, vitality, nature and nutrition – a significant development from the purely medicinal reasons for which taking spa waters were
advocated in the past.

Joanna Karmowska, in her excellent study *Cultural Heritage as an Element of
Marketing Strategy in European Historic Cities* (2004), argues 'city marketing . . .
involves, above all, the fashioning of the product and its image in such a way
that . . . the potential represented by the city, and the use of this potential for
the local society . . . [will be positively perceived]. European historic cities . . .
form cultural centres with a strong local identity . . . [generate income and] . . .
are alive in the minds of many people living far away . . . and of people who
will probably never visit them'.

Karmowska cites four main reasons for marketing a city's heritage:

1 Attraction of tourists (see below).
2 Attraction of investment and development of industry and entrepreneur-
   ship (European historic cities usually have a disproportionate number of
   well-educated residents and the entire place is often associated with high-
   quality living because of the facilities, for example domestic and business
   accommodation, and opportunities for leisure, sport and other recreation).
3 Attraction of new residents (this usually increases a city's income).
4 (Positive) influence on the local community, which Karmowska calls
   'internal marketing'. In terms of attracting tourists, she also recognizes
   that attracting unlimited tourists will generate detrimental environmental
   effects, in particular for a city, increased traffic, greater people congestion
   and, importantly, that as most tourists stay outside a city's boundaries,
   most of their valuable spend will be in that locality and not the city itself.

The city therefore has to balance how long it wishes the tourist to stay in order to generate spend, versus the negative effects of having them. Karamowska suggests a solution, 'if the city is able to present its heritage in a specialised, focused way in order to attract people truly interested in the uniqueness of the city and somehow discourage others to come, there will probably be fewer tourists, but they will stay longer . . . spending their funds in the city itself'.

The point above brings into play a wider debate in terms of tourism and sustainability.

As millions more people travel and seek personal rewards from their experiences, massive development of resources is the consequence. This pervasive tourism growth is a significant part of the global expression of the new services economy. With the weakening of many other aspects of the economy, nations and communities see tourism as a quick and easy solution.

The truth is that tourism development is being done by those who focus primarily on individual parts rather than tourism as a whole. Tourism can enrich people's lives, can expand an economy, can be sensitive and protective of environments and can be integrated into a community with minimum impact. But a new mind set is called for, that demands more and better planning and design of all tourism development, especially how the parts fit together.

(Gunn, with Turgut Var, 2002)

Insight 4.2: A heritage townscape: Gloucester, UK

Gloucester is a 'Cathedral City' in the southwest of England and, like most cathedral cities in the UK, has a rich heritage (mainly built heritage, i.e., buildings) including many sites of national importance. The majority, if not all, of these are usually owned by the local council and this is the case in Gloucester, where the City Council takes care of nearly all these sites. However, one unique feature of Gloucester in terms of its heritage is the religious aspect. Gloucester's **religious heritage** is the key to its identity and this is 'demonstrated' by the Cathedral and numerous churches in and around the city.

In the city there are 13 ancient monuments and the equivalent number of others that come under the jurisdiction of the local council for their care. Most are 'accessible' by virtue of being visible in the city but some require special entry, whilst others are totally hidden underground.

The council considers the key sites in Gloucester to be the following:

* St Oswald's Priory, founded by the daughter of Alfred the Great in order to provide a suitable resting place for the remains of her father (a saint), herself and her husband.

- The East Gate, which lies in a chamber under the Eastgate shopping centre and was until the eighteenth century, throughout the history of
  Gloucester, one of the four main gateways through the defences; it is
  open to the public on Saturdays throughout the summer and by special
  request for booked parties.

The City of Gloucester has two 'coats of arms', the first, known as the 'Tudor
Coat', was granted in 1538 by Henry VIII and the second, the
'Commonwealth Coat', was presented to the city in 1652. These can be seen
at various heritage sites throughout the city. Gloucester also has ten ancient
'Seals of the City', the first of which dates from about the year 1200 and
which are also accessible to the public.

Gloucester's religious heritage is further emphasized in the following saying: 'As sure as God's in Gloucestershire' because of its variety of English
Shrines to religion, these include the following.

- The *Cathedral* – one of the most impressive mediaeval buildings in
  Europe. The site was originally founded in the seventh century but has
  largely Roman origins in evidence. It has always been a significant place
  for pilgrims but in recent times has become more widely known as
  'Hogwarts School' as depicted in the *Harry Potter* films and books.
- *St Mary de Lode*, a church dominated by its memorial to the martyred
  Bishop Hooper and in which, in 1982, a beautiful Roman pavement was
  uncovered whilst treating the building for damp; this has left many new
  questions about the site and building unanswered.
- *St Oswald's Priory* is Gloucester's oldest standing building and was orig-
  inally dedicated to the martyred King of Northumbria.
- *Blackfriars* is a perfectly preserved example of a Dominican Friary but
  because of restoration work being undertaken by the local council, it is
  only open during the summer months for guided tours and during the
  National Heritage Weekends in September of each year.
- *Greyfriars* is a fine example of an early sixteenth-century Franciscan
  Friary, which was largely destroyed during the dissolution of the monasteries.
- *Llanthony Secunda Priory* was a neglected heritage site for many years but
  is undergoing restoration through the combined efforts of the local council and English Heritage. During the summer it hosts outdoor plays for a
  diverse audience.

Other buildings which bear testament to Gloucester's religious heritage
include the churches St Mary de Crypt; St John's, the tiny Mariner's Church
which is located at Gloucester Docks adjacent to the city, which was
founded for the spiritual well-being of sailors; St Nicholas's Church and a
Ukrainian Church and Mosque.

Figure 4.6 A city-wide heritage timed provision, linked to a national heritage initiative. Courtesy of Gloucester City Council and The Civic Trust.

Acknowledgment: Gloucester City Council, 2002.

On the peripheries of many towns and cities (usually close to villages), especially in the UK, it is common to find 'large' houses that were once the domain of rich, 'noble' or aristocratic people. Today, they may be used (if at all) in any number of different ways, as:

1　hotels (as discussed in the previous chapter), heritage tourist attractions, either for the architectural significance of the building itself and/or the contents contained within (see the Case studies 3.1 and 3.2 of Brighton Pavilion and Warwick Castle in the previous chapter and Insight 4.3 on Blenheim Palace which follows);
2　local museums;
3　schools or other educational centres.

As mentioned previously, sometimes the owners of these heritage buildings still reside in them. For some target markets this adds value to the visitor experience, even if they do not see the residents – this is the case with Knebworth House in Hertfordshire mentioned in the previous chapter and also Blenheim Palace, which is the main home of the Duke and Duchess of Marlborough. The revenue generated from 'visitor activities' can be substantial and at the very least help with the maintenance and repair of these heritage properties and landscapes.

Insight 4.3: Blenheim Palace, Woodstock, Oxfordshire, UK

As custodians of a priceless national heritage we are endeavouring to ensure that this magnificent house and its treasures will be preserved for future generations of visitors in these beautiful surroundings.

(Duke of Marlborough, 2000)

As we passed through the entrance archway and the lovely scenery burst upon me, Randolph said with pardonable pride 'this is the finest view in England', looking at the lake, the bridge, the miles of magnificent park studded with old oaks ... and the huge stately palace, I confess I felt awed ... but my American pride forbade the admission.

(Lady Randolph Churchill)

We have nothing to equal this!

(King George III)

Queen Anne came to the throne of England in 1702 and in return for his services, granted to John Churchill the Royal Manor of Woodstock, where she stated that there would be, at her own expense, a house to be called

Blenheim. John Churchill became the 1st Duke of Marlborough when Blenheim Palace was finally completed in 1722.

John Vanbrugh was chosen as architect; he already had a sound track-record, having designed both Greenwich Hospital in London and Castle Howard in Yorkshire.

Most parts of the Palace, inside and out, are accessible to the visitor and several 'scenes' from the history and life at Blenheim have been recreated. One significant reason cited by many visitors for their trip to the Palace is its association with Winston Churchill, son of Sir Randolph and Lady Churchill, who was born at Blenheim, proposed marriage there and is buried in the nearby village of Bladon, which itself has become a site of pilgrimage.

A bronze statue of Sir Winston Churchill (which he later became) and Lady Clementine Churchill, together with Sir Winston's painting of the Great Hall at Blenheim, are the two most notable features of the Churchill Exhibition at the Palace. 'The exhibits vary from Churchill's lively letters to a piece of shrapnel which, in the 1914–18 war, fell between himself and his cousin' (*Blenheim Palace*, 1999).

In the building there are numerous rooms with many displays of paintings, china, antique furniture and furnishings, artefacts and curios that belong to generations of the family. The total 'grandeur' inside and the scale of the building, not to mention its architecture with many unique facets, is indeed an extraordinary sight and, I believe, leaves a lasting impression on the visitor; one could argue that it is overwhelming.

One key distinguishing feature at Blenheim Palace is 'The Grand Cascade', a waterfall designed by the famous landscape artist 'Capability' Brown in the 1760s. 'When the full stream devolves from the rocky barrier and bounds from one point to another in foamy pride with deafening roar, nothing can be more grateful to a contemplative mind than such a scene and such a situation' wrote one visitor in 1790.

From the falls the path continues beside the lake and back towards the Palace. The boathouse was built for the 8th Duke in 1888 and here there are motor-launches or rowing boats for visitors to hire.

The other two key features at Blenheim are the 'Grand Bridge' (built by Bartholomew Peisley under Vanbrugh's direction in 1710. It is 31 m wide and was the source of much dispute with Sarah, Duchess of Marlborough, as she contested its 'extravagance') and the Column of Victory, which is 40 m high. Both are extraordinary feats of design, engineering and construction, bearing in mind the period of history and the techniques and tools available to designers and artisans.

The facilities on offer include all the usual 'hygiene' factors, together with a tea shop/restaurant in the 'Arcade Rooms' from which the formal gardens, mostly in the 'Italian style', can be seen. These comprise water terraces, statues, fountains and many rare trees, shrubs and flowers that have been added to the collection over the centuries. In addition to all that has been described above, there is a 'Butterfly House', the 'Marlborough Maze', Adventure Play Area, other areas specifically for children's play, giant chess and draughts sets and a garden shop.

The Palace is open daily from mid-March until October of each year for which an entrance charge is made; 'The Park' is open daily and no charge is made for its use. Visitors are encouraged to participate in a guided tour (one hour duration), which runs at five- to ten-minute intervals throughout the day, but they are also free to view the rooms independently.

Visits from educational establishments are catered for and reflect the National Curriculum. In addition, there is a nature trail, education rooms and picnic huts for school visitors. Blenheim has been the recipient of the Sandford Award for **Outstanding Contribution to Heritage Education** and is a **UNESCO World Heritage Site**.

Cultural attractions

Cultural attractions also fuel heritage tourism, such as theatres, museums and presentations of history and folklore, many of which are organized as festivals and pageants with heritage themes.

One example is the Cheltenham Festival held every March for three days and which attracts hundreds of visitors from the UK and overseas (particularly Ireland). The Cheltenham Festival is an example of **sporting heritage** (horse-racing) culminating in the race to win the much coveted (by the racing fraternity) Cheltenham Gold Cup, an event which has been depicted in many films and television programmes over the years.

Yet another international event held in the same town is the Cheltenham Festival of Literature, which makes use of many local heritage buildings including the Everyman Theatre, Cheltenham College and Cheltenham Ladies' College (English 'public schools', see previous chapter) and the Pitville Pump Rooms, built in the eighteenth century for the purposes of the arts and festivals but which were originally the site of a natural spring that attracted many people to 'take the waters' as a cure for all sorts of ailments ('spas' at heritage sites, in particular hotels, are beginning to enjoy a revival in many European countries, as discussed above).

'Living history' and 'open air museums' have the potential to bring an awareness of the past to many individuals and groups, in particular those that do not visit conventional museums or read historical books. There are many examples of these around the world and one from the UK, 'Blists Hill' in the World Heritage site of Ironbridge is mentioned below. However, let us pause for a moment to consider the art of interpretation.

Interpretation is defined by the Association of Heritage Interpretation as 'the art of helping people explore and appreciate our world' (Association of Heritage Interpretation website: http://www.heritageinterpretation.org.uk,

2004). In other literature, interpretation has been defined as the art of explaining the past by bringing it to life, usually in thematic or story form. At natural sites, interpretation is the art of revealing the relationships between people and environments and in the explanation of the character of an area.

There is a considerable amount of research being undertaken in this area with many new initiatives, ever more-sophisticated and innovative, with the aim of enhancing the visitor or consumer experience, particularly at heritage sites and attractions.

There is no doubt that interpretation should remain uncompromising in its **authenticity** and not lapse into pure entertainment. Good interpretation therefore should raise the 'value of an aspect of heritage' (such as a heritage site) amongst those people who come to enjoy or acquire – greater value creation should lead to an increased conviction to preserve and protect.

However, not everyone is a fan of interpretation, even though it might be used as a subtle and sophisticated art and is often criticized for removing the 'spirit' of a place. '[A]s soon as I see notice-boards, display cases, floor druggets, velvet ropes and teaching aids, a gulf opens between me and the spirit of a place. A home has become a museum' (Jenkins, 2003).

In summary, the strategic marketing objective (quantitative) of most cultural attractions, in particular special events and festivals is to have as many visitors as possible and to maximize this revenue-generation opportunity, as well as to make sure that visitors have a good or excellent qualitative experience, as measured by their (customers') expectations, as discussed at the beginning of this chapter.

Insight 4.4: The Terms of Reference of the Heritage and Museum Coordinating Committee, London

The following is a clearly constructed **strategic marketing plan** to address a range of target markets for the heritage and museum provision in London. It is detailed and covers many well-known principles of marketing, including market segmentation, customer relationship management, the AIDA principle and strategic marketing considerations together with their implementation. Specifically in terms of the heritage sector, it draws our attention to the need for funding, lobbying governments and councils, and volunteer management.

Mission

To establish the City of London as a well-known and highly valued culture and heritage tourist destination while strengthening the community's heritage resources and promoting a better understanding of London's heritage and culture.

Goals

1 To increase heritage and culture tourism in London.
2 To improve awareness of London's heritage and culture by those that live within and outside of the community.
3 To collaboratively market museums, heritage sites and heritage organizations.
4 To provide visitors of all ages with a choice of many heritage and culture experiences.
5 To improve the quality of the visitor experience offered by museums, heritage sites and organizations.
6 To increase attendance and membership at museums, heritage sites and heritage organizations.
7 To enhance and promote heritage neighbourhoods and buildings to provide a rich context for heritage and culture tourists.
8 To develop business partnerships with other tourist-related groups in London and within the surrounding region.
9 To establish a peer funding review and allocation process to be administered by the heritage and museum community.
10 To improve the financial viability of museums, heritage sites and organizations.
11 To minimize duplication and maximize coordination through communication, collaboration, partnerships and resource sharing.

Strategic planning

1 Develop, and periodically amend, a strategic plan and sector-wide vision for coordinating, marketing and improving the heritage and museum sector in London.
2 Develop benchmarks for success and continually measure and monitor the sector's performance against these benchmarks over time.

Marketing

1 Prepare marketing research to identify target markets, understand opportunities, determine strengths and weaknesses and develop strategies for increasing tourism.
2 Prepare marketing strategies, collaborative marketing packages and cross-marketing programmes to maximize the impact of the sector's marketing resources.
3 Develop strategic partnerships with other tourist attractions within the City and the surrounding region.
4 Develop a web presence.
5 Explore opportunities for product development to promote the heritage and museum sector in London.

Internal communication

1 Coordinate communications within the sector.
2 Develop 'best practices' for tourist/customer service and communicate these to the sector through workshops and other education initiatives.

Volunteer management

Coordinate and manage volunteer resources through recruitment programmes, database development, cross-site volunteer opportunity programmes and volunteer opportunity and rewards.

Funding allocation

1 Develop strategic performance criteria for allocating operating funds to the sector.
2 Create a funding allocations sub-committee to accept and adjudicate funding applications and allocate funding accordingly within the sector.

Grant applications and fund-raising

1 Collaboratively apply for secure grants from other levels of government and other funding organizations.
2 Develop collaborative fund-raising campaigns for the benefit of the sector.

Acknowledgment: Heritage and Museum Coordinating Committee, London, 2004.

Social attractions

Social attractions are defined as opportunities to meet with, or 'encounter' the residents of destinations and to some extent experience their way of life.

Attractions that are 'local' mainly draw visitors from within a few miles and, as such, strictly speaking, are leisure pursuits rather than tourist products. Examples of these local attractions include country parks and museums. Others may have mainly regional catchment areas, such as theme parks, which tend to be situated in relatively rural areas but close to at least one large metropolis, for example, Thorpe Park (a 'roller coaster' theme park) in the UK is close to London.

National catchment areas include most capital cities such as Budapest, Madrid and Cairo and usually one or more provincial towns or cities, for example Pecs (Hungary), Barcelona (Spain) or Port Said (Egypt). Visitors to these places are willing to travel and take (usually) short breaks. In fact, short breaks made by Europeans are a fast-growing segment of the tourism market, comprising 25 per cent of the 9 million visits made to Britain last year. City-break spending is worth £808 million a year to the UK economy, but this comes at a 'price' to the city, as we saw in Joanna Karamowska's study.

Festivals and events

There are many tangible and intangible reasons why communities host festivals and events, including social, political, cultural, economic or environmental factors and, often, it is a combination of these motivations. Specifically, the reasons may include the following:

1 celebration and identity – the festival or event reinforces bonds;
2 external revenue generation;
3 internal revenue generation;
4 recreation or socialization;
5 agriculture;
6 natural resources;
7 tourism;
8 culture and education.

The features of festivals and events that may make them appeal to individual and groups include:

1 the *satisfaction of multiple roles* – e.g., such as tourism, heritage, community development, urban renewal or raising/reinforcing cultural awareness;
2 the *satisfaction of basic needs* – physical, interpersonal and psychological;
3 *festival spirit* – sharing values and developing a sense of belonging;
4 *uniqueness* – the creation of unique sights and experiences;
5 *authenticity* – an opportunity to reflect indigenous or historical cultural values and processes;
6 *tradition* – a 'celebration' of history or past ways of life;
7 *symbolism* – honouring cultural rituals and their special significance;
8 *nostalgia* – 'celebrating' or reliving a feature of the past that can reinforce community bonds.

In an article entitled 'Festivals bring the world together with musical diversity' (2002), Ray Waddell offers the following insight into 'world' cultural tourism with an emphasis on music. 'While artists who fall under the broad "world music" umbrella may find mainstream venues like arenas, amphitheatres or even theatres out of reach, numerous **niche-oriented** music festivals provide ample performance opportunities', these include the New Orleans Jazz & Heritage Festival and the Montreal Jazz Festival; the latter had an audience of over 100 000 in 2002.

One group for whom this type of cultural celebration has proven to be exceptional is King Chango. Their mix of reggae, rasta, dub, kumba and island became known all over Canada on the strength of playing just the Montreal Jazz Festival; '. . . smaller festivals are also useful for exposure, in particular for small bands – the Reggae Festival Guide lists several hundred festivals . . . people who may not be familiar with all the particular artists enjoy the shows, support the festivals and enjoy the atmosphere . . . [and] over the last 30 years, people seem to have become more interested in world goods, food, clothing and now music' (Waddell, 2002).

Towns with a rich industrial heritage might present this to market (perhaps in a commodified way, which may be for practical reasons), in particular to educate or remind the local populus of their heritage and to encourage visits or to attract inward tourism or other forms of investment, such as conferences from the **corporate market** (see Chapter 3). One example of a town with a rich industrial heritage that is used for tourism and other marketing purposes in the UK is Ironbridge. The Ironbridge Gorge Heritage Centre has recently been declared a UNESCO World Heritage site. Apart from the iron bridge itself, there are many additional tourist products, including an open-air museum (Blists Hill), several other museums (some of which are in period buildings and others in purpose-built buildings), a picturesque landscape and many 'seasonal', educational and temporary activities that make up the overall provision. There are different pricing structures to reflect the needs of the various target markets and varying promotional activities, depending on priorities and whether the aim is to raise awareness, educate, remind or persuade.

World Heritage sites

Myra Shackley argues, as we did above, in terms of built heritage: 'World Heritage is a fragile non-renewable resource which has to be safeguarded both to maintain its authenticity and to preserve it for future generations' (Shackley, 1998). Shackley recognizes that although an interest in most things heritage, and in particular heritage tourism, has grown dramatically in recent years, the majority of visitors may not actually have any prior knowledge of the site before their visit; therefore, the provision of adequate information and interpretation is critical.

'The significance of a World Heritage Site is such that it will act as a magnet for visitors, meaning that issues of accessibility, transport, accommodation and other service provision have to be tactfully dealt with in order to avoid swamping the site itself' (Shackley, 1998), a situation with which other cities have to contend, whether they are a World Heritage site or not, as we shall see below.

To date, although the majority of World Heritage sites tend to be built environments, this is not exclusively the case and, recently, two wine-growing

Figure 4.7 A heritage festival that is held in conjunction with two neighbouring cathedral cities, Worcester and Hereford. Courtesy of Gloucester City Council.

regions have been added to the list, the Alto Douro wine region in Portugal and the Tokaji wine region in Hungary. Both are busy exploiting this recognition, primarily for tourism and also to promote the wines themselves through a range of promotional initiatives in specialist media, at exhibitions and on their respective websites.

In terms of pricing, Shackley states that most sites have **no pricing strategies** because to charge an entry fee would be culturally unacceptable or because it would be impossible to administer or collect.

Insight 4.5: Hadrian's Wall Tourism Partnership, UK

Hadrian's Wall is located in Northumbria and Cumbria in the northeast of England. It covers an 80-mile coast-to-coast stretch across the narrowest part of England and is one of the most well-known and popular (as evident in visitor numbers, local, national and overseas) cultural assets of that part of England. It has also been designated a World Heritage site (in 1987), a site of particular and significant importance internationally, especially in terms of understanding aspects of the culture and history of Roman Britain.

The Northumbria Tourist Board recognizes and promotes Hadrian's Wall as a tourist attraction but has increasingly become concerned that 'the needs of today should not be met at the expense of future generations'. This attraction therefore needs to balance public access and the fact that jobs have been created because of the monument, with conservation and protection of this unique Wall and its surrounding landscape and ecology. Indeed, Hadrian's Wall is considered to be the most important monument to have been built by the Romans in Britain, not least because it served as the best-known frontier in the entire Roman Empire.

Several issues, including changes in visitor patterns, the fragmented nature of ownership and variability in marketing as well as the on-going need to protect and conserve this monument, led to the formation of the Hadrian's Wall Tourism Partnership. The objectives of the Partnership are to:

- develop a tourism product which meets the needs of the independent, environmentally aware tourist;
- generate and spread benefits for businesses in the area by improving communication and access to markets, attracting more high-spending visitors and extending the tourism season into the quieter months;
- encourage more people to leave their cars at home and to travel in and around the area by public transport, cycling and walking;
- stimulate visitor interest in the management and conservation issues surrounding the site and encourage them to play a part in caring for the area's special features.

The Partnership works with other agencies concerned with the care and conservation of the overall site and continuously seeks to demonstrate that tourism can play a positive role in the locality but that this should be in the context of sustainability.

Acknowledgment: Hadrian's Wall Tourism Partnership, 2004.

European Cities/Capitals of Culture

The concept of European Cities/Capitals of Culture was born in 1985 with the aim of 'contributing to bringing the peoples of Europe together' (Melina Mercouri, Council of Ministers of the European Union, 1985) and has been perceived by most interested parties as a way of boosting tourism, urban regeneration (partly through the new inward investment) and, in general, strengthening the city brand in an internationally competitive marketplace. It has therefore become a much coveted title for many cities in Europe.

European Cities of Culture include Lisbon, Madrid, Liverpool, Edinburgh, Dublin, Helsinki and Stockholm, to name a few. Until 2004 they were chosen on an intergovernmental basis, i.e. the Member States of the European Union unanimously selected cities worthy of the title, which was followed by a grant from the European Commission. However, from 2005, cities will be chosen by the Council of the European Union on a recommendation from the Commission and will include a 'jury' of seven independent members of the public, each of whom is an 'expert' in the field of culture.

In 1990, the Ministers of Culture created the European Cultural Month, a similar principle to creating cities of culture but which was designed to last for one month rather than a year and was targeted mainly at central and eastern European economies.

Insight 4.6: The King Harry Maritime Trail, Cornwall, UK

The King Harry Maritime Trail (KHMT) was a UK-based (southwest Cornwall) initiative, created in 2002, with the specific aim of reducing the fluctuations in yearly trade. It therefore has a significant impact on the financial stability of many small businesses in that region and has the general aim of attracting new and increased numbers of visitors to southwest Cornwall. The project was supported by many organizations including national ones (the National Trust and English Heritage) and local ones such as South West Tourism. The Trail concept fits with the priorities set out within the Tourism Task Force Strategy, which is allied to the Cornish Tourist Board.

The name 'King Harry Maritime Trail' (KHMT) was taken from the name of the King Harry Ferry that crosses the upper reaches of the Fal Estuary and was one of the main routes for Pilgrims to the holy sites. The 'Maritime' reflects the influence of the sea and the coast on Cornish people, through the climate, gardens, beaches and walks, through history.

The overall marketing aim was to promote southwest Cornwall, both nationally and internationally, using a variety of techniques, including **PR, direct marketing** (CD-Roms), **sales promotions, a wide variety of national print media and a fully interactive website**. Businesses that want to be included in the Trail pay a membership fee and must prove that their business meets 'previously agreed standards for quality of service'.

The project also designed and produced a **KHMT brand** in order to make all information relating to KHMT clearly identifiable.

KHMT targeted primarily the over-45 age group from ABC1 socio-economic backgrounds as they are a market willing to travel 'off season'. KHMT recognized that, as this was a new venture, the AIDA principle would have to be followed and implemented through the marketing communications initiatives. That is, the awareness of KHMT would have to be generated amongst the target market through use of a combination of media to stimulate interest, mainly by clarifying that visitors would be assured of a 'fully functioning destination', to reinforce desire by using images of Cornwall and to facilitate action in a number of different ways, including use of the website and a much more 'traditional' method, the telephone.

'The KHMT also aims to incorporate sustainable principles and adhere to environmental best practice. The Trail is a promotion of Cornwall's unique and beautiful landscape, beaches, estuaries and harbours, gardens, hotels and pubs, all of which depend on caring for Cornwall's environment.'

The total cost of the project for the first three years was £322 904, gained from a mix of public- and private-sector contributions, but it is expected to be self-funding, based on revenue, after that period.

Acknowledgment: Carrick Community Alliance IAP, Truro, Cornwall, UK, 2003.

Insight 4.7: The Queensland Heritage Trail, Australia

The Queensland Heritage Trails Network is a partnership between the State and Federal governments and local communities in Queensland. It is an extensive programme funding 32 major cultural tourism attractions in rural and regional Queensland with the overall aim to grow regional tourism and a specific goal to encourage visitors to venture beyond the usual tourist places and into rural and regional Queensland. AUS$110 million and three years have been invested in developing the infrastructure of the Queensland Heritage Trails Network.

The various projects from the network, which links the Outback to the coast, will be marketed using '. . . established, successful channels . . . . [the marketers] will be working within the existing Tourism Queensland desti-nation framework and leveraging off the activities of Tourism Queensland and the regional tourist associations'.

The key target market is motoring holiday makers and the promotional aim is to communicate the network as authentic heritage experiences in a contemporary, educational, fun and interactive manner that adds another dimension to Queensland's destinations. Strategic marketing is being devel-oped in conjunction with industry partners, individual attractions, regional tourist organizations, Arts Queensland and Tourism Queensland.

'The Queensland Heritage Trails Network provides a great opportunity for visitors to learn about the heritage that helped develop Queensland's character and spirit.'

Acknowledgment: Queensland Heritage Trails Network Partnership, 2004.

Insight 4.8: Heritage trail tips – from the Utah Heritage Tourism Toolkit, USA

The Utah Heritage Tourism association recently issued a set of guidelines based on 'HandMade in America's' experience in promoting folkcraft in rural North Carolina through the establishment of a 'craft heritage corridor' and guidebook.

In order to establish a heritage trail, they offer the following advice.

1 Use National Trust for Historic Preservation (USA) guidelines to estab-lish criteria for eligibility to be on the trail system.
2 Ask citizens of each county or town to define their assets or sites to be placed on the trail.
3 Ask citizens of each county or town to identify 'sacred sites' where visi-tors are not welcome but which are important to local citizens.
4 Hire a 'quality control' person to ride the trails and visit each site through the eyes of a visitor – i.e., authenticity of retail items to the trail (made in Taiwan or locally)(!).
5 Select volunteer focus groups (similar to the characteristics of a heritage visitor) to review the guidebook – i.e., size of book, clarity of language, visual appeal, size of print and cost of guidebook.
6 Have volunteers call every phone number listed in the guide from the 'blue line' to ascertain correctness of phone numbers.
7 Conduct a training session for volunteers and staff of all sites on how to 'hand-off' visitors from one site to the next and prepare all site partici-pants for questions from visitors.
8 Have fun! This is your community, your history and your heritage; it is a wonderful way to overcome stereotypes and provide a visitor with insight and knowledge about your community.

Business tourism

Business Tourism is a tourist trip that takes place as part of an individual's (or group's) professional commitment to that location and therefore takes place in work time, rather than leisure time.

Tourism and leisure pursuits 'bolted-on' to business trips are becoming increasingly popular, not least because the individual or group is paid to attend for a professional reason and may therefore extend this with some vacation time, taking advantage of the fact that the cost of getting to and from the destination has been covered by their firm.

One aspect of business tourism (defining this broadly) is that detailed in Chapter 2, namely the use of a heritage site or landscape (or possibly heritage music or sport) in order to create a unique setting or atmosphere during a business meeting; this is another growth area for the marketing of heritage.

Insight 4.9: Business tourism in Barcelona and France – facts and figures

Business tourism in Barcelona, Spain (based on 2002 figures):

- 1104 conferences were held in the city;
- more than half of all conferences (51 per cent) involved up to 100 delegates;
- Barcelona has 11 five-star hotels and 80 four-star hotels with a total of 39 632 hotel rooms;
- the congress, convention and incentive travel market has grown by 500 per cent in the past two decades and the city hosted 281 078 delegates in 2003 against 50 000 in 1984;
- The Barcelona Convention Bureau celebrated its 20th anniversary in February 2004; and
- during this time the meetings tourism industry has succeeded in bringing more than 3 million visitors to the city;
- the Catalan capital has the largest portfolio of international congresses of any city worldwide.

Business tourism in France:

- France bought 77 million visitors to its historic country in 2003 and has the aim of increasing this to 100 million by 2010;
- business tourism earns the country €4.57 billion per year (£3.1 billion);
- each year since 1992, France has attracted more international organizations than any other country, except the USA;
- Paris is France's premier business tourism destination, followed by Strasbourg, with Lyon and Nice in joint third place;

- Strasbourg Convention Centre holds more than 400 events a year and is the first major French convention centre to obtain ISO 9002 certification;
- Lyon Palais des Congres holds more than 300 events a year, attracting in excess of 76 000 visitors;
- conventions and trade fairs generate around 300 000 room nights a year;
- the expanded Lyon convention centre is due to open in 2006 with a new 3000-seat auditorium;
- in 2003, low-cost airlines carried 2.5 million passengers to Nice, France's second national airport, an increase of 37 per cent on 2002.

Heritage tourism brands

The word 'brand' was originally used by 'Norsemen' (men of Scandinavian origin) and meant the process by which they identified their cattle; this was by 'branding' a name or symbol with a hot instrument, such as an iron poker, on to the animal itself.

In marketing, much has been written on branding as a concept applied to consumer goods and services and briefly states that it is a process by which messages are conveyed to the consumer, or potential consumer. These messages need to be simple and consistent and reinforced by experience; the **messages can be either rational or emotional** – slogans/straplines, names, advertising and PR are some of the communication tools used to reinforce the brand.

One of the great advantages of branded products is that they are an infinitely renewable resource, as long as their value is maintained through careful marketing – their **value resides primarily in the mind of the consumer** and this must be created and nurtured.

New brands are increasingly expensive to launch and maintain, therefore the use of big 'umbrella' brands with a smaller number of sub-brands is becoming more common. For example 'Shakespeare Country' includes Shakespeare's birthplace (a period building), other architecture, theatres and museums from the same period/connected with the author, and the surrounding landscape of Stratford-upon-Avon and Warwickshire, UK.

Country branding can include many aspects of heritage, including the following:

- the nation's famous people, for example Dylan Thomas (see Case study 4.3); former US Presidents or other notables such as Mahatma Gandhi (India, and South Africa where he was a law student and lived for many years);
- the role it has played in world events, this may be sporting events, literature, music, art, dance, food;

- major historical moments can be 'celebrated' or re-enacted to remind people (for example of tragic events such as the holocaust, the American Civil War or the partition of India and Pakistan, which is in part an ongoing conflict);
- particular pieces of architecture (including whole buildings such as the Guggenheim in Bilbao, Spain) and natural beauty (discussed previously);
- national, regional and/or local food and/or drink;
- language, people and folklore.

Uniqueness is marketed by combining the heritage offerings of a destination and other benefits which consumers may want, as mentioned above, but it must create an impact. There is also an increasing trend, in particular in the UK, to 'marry' aspects of heritage with a modern-day emphasis; this may mean use of the latest technology to explain the past, present or future, the latest cosmetic products used with time-honoured beauty techniques/applications or the up-to-date cuisine offered in a period dining room, in a traditional/period house or hotel – all these concepts are fast gaining ground in the competitive marketplace, whether for tourism, leisure or recreation or even medical reasons (see Case study 4.1).

Steve Anholt, in his article 'Nation brands: the value of "provenance" in branding' (Morgan *et al.*, 2003) states that a country's brand image can profoundly shape its economic, cultural and political destiny. 'Japan, Ireland, Germany and Scotland are often-quoted cases of countries whose public perception has dramatically altered over a relatively short period.' This means that, as a result, they have prospered, in spite of some of their (recent) records in terms of violence and human rights, or just apathy. Marketing communications have played a key role in changing these perceptions, or perhaps in enabling the public to 'see another side' of each country and to reflect on its possibility as a tourist destination.

For example, Ireland used a strapline in its campaign in summer 2004 entitled 'the island of memories' and maintained a consistent campaign, irrespective of type of communication channel used. Images of its World Heritage site at Giant's Causeway have featured prominently, together with other 'well-known' heritage brands such as Guinness and Jameson's Irish Whisky and the intangible aspects of Irish culture with which many people are familiar (or at least they are now): hospitality (lots of food and drink), smiling and 'friendly' faces.

Brand advantage therefore is secured through communication, which highlights the specific benefits of a product and creates a specific image or set of images in the mind of the consumer. It must have a created value, which has the potential to reduce substitutability, i.e., the demand for other tourist or leisure pursuits. This value in terms of heritage products includes (as has been briefly mentioned above in the general discussion under 'product', 'atmosphere' and 'friendliness' of a place) locality, people and, indeed, the overall impression.

Consumers are looking increasingly less for escape and more for discovery (experience or experiential tourism) and that creates the basis of an emotional connection that marketers can exploit through branding – the challenge beyond that is to make the destination brand 'live', so that visitors experience the promoted brand values and feel the authenticity of a unique place. This latter point is very much debated and disputed in the literature, briefly, mainly in terms of the fact that political ideologies and the power of the majority influence what is presented as 'authentic' or historical to the present-day market.

> The positioning of Scotland as a land of fire and stone is translated into the rational benefit of encountering rugged unspoilt wilderness, romantic history, heritage and folklore and warm and feisty people . . . at a deeper emotional or salient level these benefits offer the overseas visitor the emotional benefits of feeling in awe of the elements, embraced by the warmth of the people and rejuvenated by the experience of Scotland. Finally, the culmination of these brand attributes is a destination personified by independence, mystery and warmth; this becomes the essence of Scotland the brand, with values rooted in the experience of past visitors, credible and relevant to potential visitors and which the product can deliver.
>
> (Morgan *et al.*, 2003: 47)

Suprabrands: main and second-level brands

Morgan *et al.* (2003) also establish the principle that one of the most successful European suprabrands is Spain and whilst Spain is the main brand, its cities and regions are the second-level brands. '[A]t the country level Spain has remained remarkably constant in its advertising, with each campaign promoting the diversity and variety of the country, focusing on its heritage (especially culture) as well as the staple sun and sand product . . . [and] at the heart of the brand for almost 20 years is Miro's logo' (Morgan *et al.*, 2003: 47).

India has also recently engaged in an extensive marketing campaign, essentially as one brand and, in doing so, has prevented any dilution of the message that the promotion of individual regions of the country would have created. The core brand values mainly emphasized aspects of Indian heritage such as religion, landscape, diversity of people and spirituality, while a variety of different channels of communication have been used to promote India.

> The development of electronic commerce now offers new opportunities for collaboratively marketing tourism destinations. There is the potential to cre-

ate 'virtual co-operation', whereby potential tourists can browse through web sites of individual facilities at a destination and develop a coherent picture of the destination experience on offer. Electronic commerce offers great flexibility . . . the promotional message can be changed much more quickly than is the case where the requirement to print brochures leads to long lead times.

(Palmer, A., 'Destination branding and the web' in Morgan *et al.*, 2003: 47)

Insight 4.10: Puerto de Culturas, Cartagena, Spain

Cartagena is a naval port and city that lies in the southeast corner of Spain, in the region of Murcia. Cartagena has a very long history and interesting heritage, having come through Punic, Roman and Byzantine periods, all of which have helped to shape its unique physical and cultural landscape and identity. It is now aiming to use this in a marketing campaign.

The Cartagena Puerto de Culturas project has the main overall goal of locating Cartagena city as a significant tourist destination in the mind of the Spanish holiday maker (indigenous or overseas) because of its cultural heritage. A further objective is to create a thematic space that offers visitors and local residents a wide range of leisure possibilities using the historical resources of the city generally and the port specifically. The providers are well aware that this project will raise awareness of Cartagena, create interest and a positive tourist image of the city and strengthen its unique identity, but will also greatly benefit local businesses.

The partners in the project include the Consortium Cartagena Puerto de Culturas, the City Council of Cartagena, the Port Authority, the Confederation of Cartagena Businessmen, the Chamber of Commerce Cartagena and the Polytechnic University and as many private investors as possible.

The facilities on offer for visitors include the following:

- An Interpretation Centre, which is located inside the local castle (Conception Castle) and has the further advantage of offering panoramic views of the city; state-of-the-art telescopes are provided to view the landscape and an exhibition is displayed in the 'Tower of the Homage'.
- An Interpretation Centre has also been created at the 'Punic Wall', with the specific aim of explaining the culture and history of the period using interactive screens, games and exhibitions which include the use of film and projected images.
- The Three Kings Square in the city has been designated an area best reflective of the Roman Period and a street, the Decumano, has been used to 'demonstrate' the customs and how trade was exchanged at that time.

- A special tourist tram will take visitors to all the major heritage aspects of the city.
- Specific tourist signs will direct visitors, whether or not they are following one of the special heritage themes.
- A tourist boat will sail around the Cartagena inner harbour and allow visitors to see coastal fortifications, which defended strategic parts of the city, from the sea, offering an alternative way of seeing the city.
- The Fortune House is a recreated Roman House with all main ornamental features that it would have had at that time, including paintings and mosaics.
- The Autopsy amphitheatre, which was originally a place for the study of anatomy, will house temporary or travelling exhibitions and offer concert facilities as well as meeting/conference rooms for businesses.

Acknowledgment: Puerto de Culturas Consortium and Murcia Turistica, Cartagena, Spain, 2004.

Insight 4.11: The work of the English Heritage Custodian and a job description of a 'Heritage Manager'

There are many aspects of 'service' in tourism both generally and specifically in terms of managing a heritage site at the level of the customer. English Heritage has published some details on the work of a custodian and these are summarized below:

The main purpose of an English Heritage Custodian is to maximize visitors' enjoyment of English Heritage properties and to keep the site well presented and secure.

The key to doing the job of a custodian well is effective customer service achieved through communication and product knowledge. A custodian must ensure a high standard of customer care is provided when:
- welcoming and managing visitors;
- answering queries about the site, educational facilities and the local area;
- giving information about the site, its history, contents and merchandise.

Website: http://www.english-heritage.org.uk, 2004

They also specify health, safety and security responsibilities, which include controlling access to the site, up-holding any by-laws that might apply and safeguarding against potential damage and theft.

The job description of a 'Heritage Manager' issued by the Association of Graduate Careers Advisory Service (AGCAS) states the following:

Heritage managers are responsible for conservation and all aspects of heritage sites: these encompass landscapes, ancient monuments, historic buildings from

A Port. Thirty centuries. A city

"Cartagena Puerto de Culturas" invites you along on a journey that will take you from the Punic times until the present.

1 Interpretation Centre of Cartagena History
The Interpretation Centre of Cartagena History is inside Conception castle. From the hill where it is located, you will discover a beautiful view of the city. State of the art telescopes will help you to know Cartagena better and inside the Tower of the Homage you will learn about its history.

2 Interpretation Centre of the Punic Wall
The Punic Wall will open a door to the past, where an interpretation centre of the punic culture has been devised for everone. Games, exhibitions, projections, everything is devised in order to experience the life of the Punic Cartagena.

3 Decumano – Three Kings Square
The Three Kings Square will take you into the Roman period. We invite you to see one of the main streets of the Roman cities, the Decumano that will introduce you to the trade and in the customs of the Roman times.

4 Touristic tramway
If you want to admire in confort the history of Cartagena, take the tourist tram. During the journey it will stop at the most representative places of the city so no detail is lost.

5 Tourist signs
Tourist signs will help you to stay un track while you walk in the city. Follow a thematic itinerary and discover the remains and monuments conserved from the III century B. C until present.

6 Tourist Boat
Take the tourist boat and sail around Cartagena inner harbour. You will see an alternative image of the city and you will discover a landscape of coastal fortifications which defended strategic places.

7 Fortune house
View the structure of the Roman houses and their main ornamental features, including paintings and mosaics. Feel at home and perceive the daily life of the Roman world.

8 Autopsy amphitheatre:
A building belonging to Marina's Real Hospital. A place where anatomical studies were taught and autopsies were carried out in the XVIII century. Inside, you will be able to listen to concerts, chats, readings, as we are preparing it to be an open multidisciplinary exhibition room.

9 Panoramic lift:
Dicover a bird eye view city. We shall be working in a panoramic lift from which you will ascend to Concepción Castle. See the fantastic views of the old Cartagena and some of its main architectural elements.

10 Refuges of Civil War
We are conditioning the antiaircraft refuges that were used during the Civil War. Daily life of that time would not have been the same without these excavations.

Figure 4.8 Cartagena Puerto de Culturas.

all periods, including industrial archaeology, as well as museums. Managers . . . are required to be multi-skilled and to operate within commercial constraints . . . [and] the need to balance preserving the character of sites with the need to promote them appropriately.

Work activities vary depending on the specific function and seniority of the post . . . [managers] will undertake combinations of the following:

1   Supervising and motivating staff and/or volunteers.
2   Managing budgets, securing funding from external sources, generating income from entry charges, trading and membership.
3   Planning projects.
4   Managing strategic development.
5   Marketing your heritage attraction(s) through literature, advertising and the media, exploring, evaluating and implementing new ways of presenting the heritage attraction, to facilitate interpretation, interaction, enjoyment and interest.
6   Analysing and interpreting results of customer surveys and other statistical data.
7   Ensuring high standards of visitor care at sites which are open to the public.
8   Writing reports, promotional leaflets, etc.
9   Liaising with outside funding agencies, regional tourist boards, etc.
10 Keeping up to date with developments in the field, for example new technology, and with historical research into topics related to the attraction.

The salary for this type of job, quoted at May 2002, started at approximately £13 000.

Acknowledgment: AGCAS/University of Bristol, 2004.

CASE STUDY 4.1: A new era for spas in the UK

Britain's most ambitious spa in nearly 200 years is due to open in the historic city of Bath in April 2006. A combination of a new state-of-the art spa and two restored eighteenth-century buildings will contain thermal pools, steam and treatment rooms and offer bathing in natural spring water. There is also a free Spa Visitor Centre that describes the colourful social and cultural history that grew round Bath's natural thermal waters, using interactive displays and exhibits that unfold the story and an on-site drinking fountain enables visitors to sample the unique waters.

The rebirth of Bath's spa – first established by the Romans – is just one element of a countrywide renaissance as hotels invest millions of pounds in modern facilities. Spa towns, such as Cheltenham and Buxton, are changing and re-emerging as centres for medical and stress treatments. The 'sociable' aspect still continues, with many spa towns offering such pleasures as afternoon tea to music or arts and literature festivals.

The location of the country's only hot springs is appropriate in the twenty-first century for the first of a new generation of centres: the Thermae Bath Spa. Housed in a glass-enclosed building, it will utilize Bath's unique naturally heated waters that, at up to 47°C, are among the warmest in Europe. There are actually four baths in three buildings and the facilities will be open year-round.

There is archaeological evidence that there was human activity around the hot springs on which the City of Bath is built at least 8000 years BC, and it was Prince Bladud, cured of leprosy after bathing in the hot waters, that founded the City of Bath in 863 BC.

In AD 43, the Romans developed 'Aquae Sulis' as a sanctuary of rest, relaxation and healing, and in AD 70 they built a reservoir around the hot springs, followed by baths and temples, dedicated to the goddess Sulis Minerva. These facilities, and the fact that the complex was also a religious shrine, attracted visitors from across Britain and Europe and set Bath on its path to becoming a major tourist destination.

In 1088 John of Villula was appointed Bishop of Somerset and bought this royal property from the king. The baths were almost certainly rebuilt over the Temple Precinct and in 1138 were described as: '. . . through hidden pipes, spring supply waters, heated not by human skill or art, from deep in the bowels of the earth to a reservoir in the midst of arched chambers, splendidly arranged, providing in the centre of the town baths which are pleasantly warm, healthy and a pleasure to see . . . from all over England sick people come to wash away their infirmities in the healing waters and the healthy gaze at the remarkable bubbling up of the hot springs' (Gesta Stephani, 1138).

Visits from Royalty in 1574, 1613, 1615, 1634 and 1663 increased the awareness, fame and attraction of Bath; these visits set off a period of development in which Bath became 'the premier resort of frivolity and fashion' and led to the rebuilding of the city to produce the eighteenth-century layout and architecture of today's UNESCO World Heritage site.

In 1948, following the establishment of the National Health Service, the health authorities of Bath made arrangements to provide water-cure treatments on pre-scription, but the Hot Bath finally closed in 1976. Bath was the third from last of the eight great hydropathic centres in England to close; the last, Buxton, closed in 2000. However, as museums the Roman Baths and Pump Rooms became one of the UK's leading tourist attractions and this helped to re-establish a demand for the opening of the new spa facilities.

The opening of Thermae Bath Spa is behind schedule, caused in large part by the complex nature of the project and the difficulties of working with Grade 1 listed buildings in a very restricted site. Other factors include the period of time dedicated to archaeology and the necessity of going through the planning process three times, mainly in order to increase the capacity of the spa.

The Bath Spa Project is a combination of new building and restoration. The centrepiece is the state-of-the-art New Royal Bath; the new building had to be 'of its time' to celebrate the new millennium, however as much of the old buildings as possible had also to be restored. All the buildings on the site are linked in a very transparent way by enclosing the 'cube' in a translucent envelope and by using glass walls and bridges between the buildings.

The cost of the project is approximately £26 million, with the Millennium Commission contributing almost £7.8 million, Thermae Development Company (UK) £6 million, Bath and North East Somerset Council (B&NES) £12 million, and £0.5 mil-lion coming from the Bath Spa trust, local fund-raising and some smaller grants.

To qualify for Millennium Commission Lottery funding, the Bath Spa Project had to:

- enjoy public support;
- make a substantial contribution to the life of the community it is designed to serve;
- look back over this millennium and/or forward to the new one;
- be seen by the future generations as marking a significant moment in national or local history;
- include partnership contributions to demonstrate the real support of the local community;
- not be possible without Millennium Commission funding and not normally be supportable from public funds nor fall within the scope of another Lottery distributor;
- be of high architectural design and environmental quality.

The main partners in the scheme are B&NES, the Millennium Commission and the operating company, Thermae Development Company (UK). Three themes were emphasized in the application: the thermal waters are a natural phenomenon that should be used and enjoyed; five listed buildings should be restored with genuine economic purpose and good provision of jobs; and, with tourism trends changing, Bath's position as a leading tourism destination should be consolidated and developed by adding health tourism (a growth area) to the heritage and cultural attractions.

Acknowledgment: by kind permission, Fiona Humphreys, Thermae Bath Spa, Bath, UK, 2004 and Bob Barton, VisitBritain, 2003.

Questions

1 Which target market(s) do you think the Thermae Bath Spa concept is keen to attract?
2 What types of heritage activities do 'spa towns' in the UK also offer to visitors?
3 How do you think that Thermae Bath Spa will promote its heritage to the target market(s) and which aspects of the AIDA principle are particularly important at this point in time?
4 Apart from heritage, what are the characteristics of this facility that might be useful in the overall promotion of a city such as Bath and in adding value to a 'Visit Britain' campaign?
5 Thermae Bath Spa is a year-round facility but when are the 'peaks and troughs' likely to be and how could promotional activity help to smooth these out?

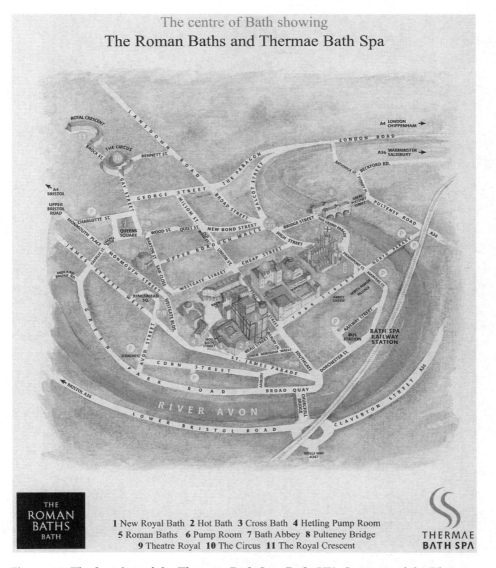

Figure 4.9 The location of the Thermae Bath Spa, Bath, UK. Courtesy of the Thermae Bath Spa Project.

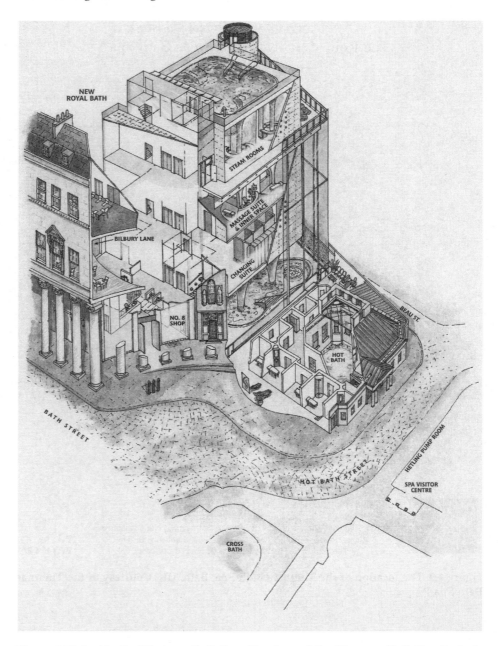

Figure 4.10 Inside the Thermae Bath Spa. Courtesy of the Thermae Bath Spa Project.

CASE STUDY 4.2: In the market for a traditional Christmas

The scenes could be straight out of a box of old-fashioned Christmas cards. Dickens characters in top hats, ladies in bonnets and full-length dresses; chimney sweeps and urchins stroll past shops and inns decorated for the festive season. Flakes of snow cling to a mediaeval castle and cathedral, and fall onto groups of carol singers and warmly wrapped ice-skaters. Christmas trees and colourful lights are everywhere; roast chestnuts and mulled wine being enjoyed.

These are not images from long ago but memories of last year's Dickensian Christmas held in Rochester, Kent, UK. This compact city, just an hour southeast of London, has many links with Victorian writer Charles Dickens – not least that he lived here and wrote three of his best-known novels here.

Rochester's fun-filled extravaganza is just one of a growing number of Christmas-themed events held in towns and cities all over Britain. Each year there seems to be another historic location added to the annual roll-call of places celebrating in style: Lincoln, Edinburgh, Durham, Bath, Portsmouth and Swansea, to name a few. They all offer opportunities for Christmas shopping in historic settings; these are not only good opportunities to buy gifts, but also a chance to enjoy British festivities and traditions. Cathedrals, abbeys, castles – even renowned battleships – can be backdrops, and many people dress in period costume.

The British expression 'having a Dickens of a good time' is never more appropriate than at one of these atmospheric events. Just like Oliver Twist, you will be asking for 'more' if you go.

Acknowledgment: by kind permission, Bob Barton, VisitBritain, 2004.

Questions

1 What do you think is the primary aim of a Dickens-themed event?
2 What do you think is the secondary aim of this type of event?
3 Why do 'historic cities' make good venues for this type of event?
4 What is the potential/real environmental problems caused by these types of events?
5 What other ways could 'historic cities' exploit their heritage?

CASE STUDY 4.3: On the Dylan Thomas Trail

Guided walks, an arts festival and a sea cruise were among the events planned in 2003 in Wales to mark the 50th anniversary of the death of Welsh poet Dylan Thomas. It was an opportunity to visit other literary locations in this beautiful land where music, poetry and Celtic heritage are given due importance in everyday life.

When Thomas collapsed at New York's Chelsea Hotel a few days before his death in 1953, he was on his fourth tour of America, holding audiences spellbound with readings in his mellifluous voice. He was at the height of his literary power and had just completed *Under Milk Wood*, his 'play for voices', lyrical poetry so rooted in his home country and which was known around the world.

Even he might have been surprised at the longevity of his fame and by the extensive preparations for the 50th anniversary of his death. The highlight was the Dylan Thomas Festival, held annually in his home city of Swansea; with exhibitions, film shows, guided tours and readings from his short stories and poems – and more.

The focal point for many anniversary events is the Dylan Thomas Centre in the city's maritime quarter; guided walks start here, taking in the scenes of his childhood.

Wales is a land of festivals, including the national Eisteddfod, the largest and oldest celebration of Welsh culture and language, which is held each year in different parts of the country.

Behind these celebrations of Wales' rich literary heritage is the magical, mystical Wales, well described by another poet who captured the spirit of the country, R.S. Thomas, who hinted at a past history 'Brittle with relics, Wind bitten towers . . .' . There is a rich seam of bardic Welsh literature, myths – the legend of King Arthur is said to have originated here – and stories going back to before the Romans; some of these writings are preserved in the National Library of Wales, Aberystwyth, with its outstanding collection of ancient Welsh books and illuminated manuscripts. In nearby Machynlleth, Celtica employs the most modern of technology to explore 2000 years of Celt history, legend and culture.

There is another, more recent aspect of Welsh history that is commemorated at Rhondda Heritage Park in Mid-Glamorgan, a recently declared World Heritage site and which celebrates the world of *How Green was my Valley* (the most popular novel in English by a Welshman, Richard Llewellyn).

Acknowledgment: by kind permission, Hilary MacSkill, VisitBritain, 2003.

Questions

1   What aspects of Welsh heritage are identified in this article and how are these:
  a)   celebrated and
  b)   presented to the marketplace?
2   Why do you think Dylan Thomas 'took' his poetry to America?
3   What do you think the heritage of Welsh literature means to Welsh people?

Summary

In summary, in most of the world today, interest in heritage tourism is at an all-time high; from visits (actual or virtual) to World Heritage sites (which may be of specific archaeological importance, such as the city of Krakow in Poland, horticultural importance, such as the Royal Botanic Gardens at Kew,

London or for many other reasons), some of which are 'themed' by marketers, such as the 'Cradle of Human Kind' in South Africa which includes many aspects of heritage including the natural environment, the 'past' and people.

With respect to man-made phenomena that were not originally designed to attract visitors, such as castles and cathedrals or other World Heritage sites, the strategic marketing objective should be to manage demand so that the attraction is not damaged by overuse but also to seize the potential of the place in order to generate income (sometimes much needed), raise awareness, educate, remind or persuade.

Heritage and or cultural tourism is very often associated with the past, evoking ideas about ways of life and other people that has been criticized by many academics, who believe that this aspect of heritage is often 'sanitized' and 'commodified' and therefore not a true reflection of the situation or issue being presented. Some writers have gone further and argue that the approach of some organizations to the marketing of aspects of heritage/cultural tourism have stripped 'locals' of their dignity and, sometimes, even their rights.

In terms of marketing strategy, the recommendation is for precise customer segmentation (a niche market, rather than a mass market, which we established in the previous chapter); to consider not just a tourist market but to recognize that the business to business conference market is another lucrative opportunity for historic European cities, as cultural heritage is often a consideration for organizers when comparing competitive environments; and finally, targeting these segments through specialist media.

Discussion questions and activities

1 Give some examples of 'heritage products'.
2 What are the main reasons for the growth of heritage tourism in your country (or another country)?
3 What are the possible environmental consequences of the growth in heritage tourism?
4 Look up and research a 'historic city' and compare your findings with those of Joanna Karamowska – are the reasons for promoting the city's heritage the same as those she has identified? Briefly explain your findings.
5 Are there any 'heritage theme' events that take place in your country (or another country)? If so, briefly provide some details and explanation as to why they take place.

Recommended reading

Berry, D. (2004) *Conference and Incentive Travel Magazine*, April.
Blenheim Palace (1999) Jarrold Publishing, Oxford.

De Chernatony, L. (1998) *Creating Powerful Brands in Consumer, Service and Industrial Markets*. Second edition. Butterworth-Heinemann, Oxford.

Doswell, R. (1997) *Tourism*. Butterworth-Heinemann, Oxford.

Douglas, N. (ed.) (2002) *Special Interest Tourism*. Wiley, Australia.

Finn, M., Elliot-White, M. and Walton, M. (2000) *Research Methods for Leisure and Tourism*. Longman, London.

Gunn, C., with Turgut Var (2002) *Tourism Planning*. Routledge, London.

Hall, M. (2000) *Tourism Planning*. Prentice-Hall, London.

Henderson, J.C. (2002) Conserving colonial heritage: Raffles Hotel in Singapore. *International Journal of Heritage Studies*, 7(1), 7–24.

Jenkins, S. (2003) *England's Thousand Best Houses*. Allen Lane.

Jennings, G. (2001) *Tourism Research*. Wiley, Australia.

Karmowska, J. (2004) *Cultural Heritage as an Element of Marketing Strategy in European Historic Cities*. Centre for European Studies, Jagiellonian University, Krakow, Poland.

Kipling, R. (1889) *The Jungle Book*. Penguin, London.

Middleton, V. (1998) *Sustainable Tourism*. Butterworth-Heinemann, Oxford.

Morgan, N. and Pritchard, A. (2001) *Advertising in Tourism and Leisure*. Butterworth-Heinemann, Oxford.

Morgan, N., Pritchard, A. and Pride, R. (2003) *Destination Branding*. Wiley, London.

Shackley, M. (ed.) (1998) *Visitor Management*. Butterworth-Heinemann, Oxford.

Swarbrooke, J. (2002) *The Development and Management of Visitor Attractions*. Butterworth-Heinemann, Oxford.

Waddell, R. (2002) *Festivals Bring the World Together With Musical Diversity*.

Wahab, S. and Pigram, J.J. (eds) (1998) *Tourism, Development and Growth*. Routledge, London.

Wild, S. (2004) *Conference and Incentive Travel Magazine*, April.

Chapter 5

The marketing mix and food and drink heritage

One evening, Oliver thought he would go mad with hunger. He had finished his allotted bowl of gruel and still felt a raging emptiness inside him. Desperately, with his bowl and spoon in hand, he approached the master of the workhouse. 'Please, sir' said Oliver, 'I want some more'.

The master was stupefied. No one had ever dared to ask for more. '*What?*' he roared. 'Please, sir', Oliver repeated quietly, 'I want some more'. Enraged, the master struck Oliver on the head, and locked him up in a dank and dismal cell. He remained there for weeks.

(Dickens, 1837)

Introduction

The relationship between many aspects of heritage and food and drink is so extensive that one could write a whole book on this matter alone. I have therefore had to select a limited range of issues for discussion here but have tried to apply marketing concepts that have not been covered elsewhere in the book. However, as in previous chapters, you will find that there are links with concepts and issues that have been discussed elsewhere.

In Chapters 2 and 3 we explored the fact that there has been an increasing interest and demand in many countries for food and beverages that have

been grown and are being offered in 'traditional ways'. This does not necessarily mean that they have to be organic, rather there is a growing market of
consumers who want to be able to trace the source of the product they are
buying and also perhaps want to acquire it outside of the usual supermarket experience. However, there is no doubt that the demand for organically
grown produce has grown and continues to do so in many countries; this is
illustrated in Tables 5.1–5.6.

The majority of the products listed in Tables 5.1–5.6 are premium-priced
and are therefore largely for the relatively price-insensitive consumer.
However, with the **elasticity** of premium goods, there is a finite amount that
can be charged before demand reverses dramatically – something that needs
to be calculated carefully before the price is established.

One example of this relatively new phenomenon in the UK (and in other
European countries, especially in northern Europe) is the firm establishment
of increasing numbers of 'Farmers Markets' in many towns and cities.
A 'Farmers Market' is where local producers and suppliers bring their fresh

**Table 5.1 UK retail sales of organic fruit and vegetables,
by value, 1998–2003**

Year	£million
1998	223
1999	303
2000	341
2001	402
2002	451
2003	481

Source: Mintel.

**Table 5.2 UK retail sales of organic dairy products, by
value, 1998–2003**

Year	£million
1998	35
1999	55
2000	95
2001	124
2002	137
2003	145

Source: Mintel.

Table 5.3 UK retail sales of organic meat and poultry, by value, 1998–2003

Year	£million
1998	42
1999	53
2000	65
2001	80
2002	92
2003	99

Source: Mintel.

Table 5.4 UK retail sales of organic breads and cereals, by value, 1998–2003

Year	£million
1998	29
1999	40
2000	58
2001	64
2002	68
2003	75

Source: Mintel.

Table 5.5 UK retail sales of organic eggs, by value, 1998–2003

Year	£million
1998	3
1999	6
2000	17
2001	18
2002	20
2003	21

Source: Mintel.

Table 5.6 UK retail sales of organic non-alcoholic drinks, by value, 1998–2003

Year	£million
1998	8
1999	12
2000	15
2001	19
2002	22
2003	24

Source: Mintel.

produce directly to the consumer in a central location (usually close to a main shopping centre), throughout the year.

Surveys have found that many people (especially the grey market) are nostalgic about this concept, as it is the way in which shopping took place in the past. (Of course, shopping continues in this way in many countries throughout the world, even if people have refrigeration facilities, because it is part of the culture to shop on a daily basis – this particularly tends to be the case where women largely do not work outside the home and therefore do not have the same pressures of time that affect many women in the developed West and increasingly elsewhere.) The grey market is a primary target for most aspects of heritage, as we have established previously.

Before we embark on a discussion of target markets with a particular focus on the emerging grey market in Europe as a significant opportunity for many organizations, we need to devote a little more time to the segmentation principle known as **psychographics** (which has been mentioned in previous chapters), as I believe that this is the critical success factor in terms of understanding consumers and their behaviour(s) for all types of business organizations.

The level of coverage of psychographics in most marketing textbooks extends only as far as the generic concepts. Therefore we shall begin with the perspective on **personality** advocated by Hippocrates.

Hippocrates was a philosopher, born in 460 BC. The love of wisdom led him to study both medicine and philosophy and he was the first known man to keep careful documentation on the progression of diseases.

Hippocrates firmly believed that good health was a function of both physical and mental well-being and that there are four basic temperaments (humours), which are the products of four liquids in the body:

1   *Blood* (sanguis), which makes for the sanguine in a person, i.e., their relative 'liveliness'. This type of individual has a friendly, 'outgoing' character

that is the envy of timid people. The relatively negative aspects of this temperament are that these individuals are easily impressed by others and have a tendency to bursts of anger, although these are quickly forgotten.

2   *Yellow Bile* (chole), which makes one choleric, i.e., active. The temperament of this group is that they are quick-witted, practical, strong willed, independent, decisive and ambitious. The negative aspects include being unsympathetic, hot tempered, 'thick skinned' and a strong dislike of sentimentality.

3   *Black Bile*, which can make a person melancholy, i.e., 'dark' or sad. The characteristics of this group of individuals are that they can be analytical, self-sacrificing, perfectionist and tend to have a sensitive nature. The negative aspects are that they can be self-centred because they are inclined to self-analysis, are prone to depression and constantly worry about their own mental and physical well-being.

4   *Phlegm* (phlegmatic), which makes an individual slow and steady. The characteristics of this group are that they can be 'cool', calm and collected, are relatively 'easy going', have a 'dry' sense of humour and a good retentive memory. However, they can also be 'slow' and lazy, resent being pushed into action and can be stubborn.

These four classifications of temperament are still widely used by medical practitioners today, but they could equally be applied in a marketing context to understand the differences between individuals. Therefore, four homogeneous groups can be proposed, each of whom could be targeted separately and differently to reflect these humours: for example in the use of images on promotional material and in advertising; the approach of 'front of house' or sales staff; the use of music, light and sound generally in enhancing the media message.

Definitions of terms used

Temperament is the combination of inborn traits that subconsciously affects our behaviour and which have been inherited genetically.

Character is the 'real' you (see Insight 5.6 on Coca-Cola, where the same principle has been applied to a heritage brand), the natural temperament of an individual that is modified through the passage of time by the process of socialization and creation of attitudes and beliefs, norms and values.

Personality is the outward expression of ourselves that may or may not be the same as our character.

Target markets

In Chapter 2 we discussed the grey market in some detail, as consumers in this increasingly mainstream market for suppliers everywhere are growing in number, have the highest levels of disposable income and, more often than not, the leisure time in which to spend it. They are therefore a prime target for almost all things heritage and, in terms of psychographics, they are the group most likely to respond emotionally (specifically, nostalgically) and in other psychological ways to anything that has a connection with the past.

Mintel has recently advocated that in as little as two years time the grey market will account for over one-half of all UK expenditure on food, drink and household products. *The Older Consumer*, a report from Reuters Business Insight and TNS (2003) revealed that, by 2006, the over 55-year-olds will account for £53 billion of what is predicted to be a £104.4 billion market for food, drink and household goods.

The changing nature of the European consumer market is highlighted by another recent report (King, 2004). 'Europe's population is aging. Consumers aged 55 and over will grow by 60 per cent in the next 15 years, whereas the under-50 group will remain stable. Unless they are in the business of selling retirement homes or hearing aids, companies have turned a blind eye to this greying market . . . [and specifically in terms of advertising] 86 per cent feel that advertising isn't aimed at them.'

The vast majority of worldwide organizations such as Coca-Cola are still overly concerned to target the 'younger consumer' in Europe (under 50-year-olds and most notably the 15–35 age group). One of the reasons for this is because they feel that this younger group can be made 'loyal' to a brand and therefore investment in them will produce longer-term benefits. However, there is a lack of appreciation that older consumers are living longer and the same degree of loyalty penetration can be created, however this does require a different targeting approach, particularly in terms of advertising and especially the images that are used.

> The key elements are to keep the message direct. The over-50s are experienced consumers so they don't want to read flowery language. You also need to give them a lot of information. Seniors have a lot of time on their hands and so you must be prepared for answering many more detailed questions than you would for 20-year-olds.
>
> (King, 2004)

The Mintel report further identifies that in terms of their shopping behaviour, older consumers shop five times a week compared with 3.5 times a week for other consumers, which therefore creates more selling opportunity than is the case for younger consumers.

Another point from the report (which can be applied to most countries) is that these consumers are significantly concerned about the 'Britishness' (or 'Belgian-ness', 'Frenchness', etc.) of the products and brands that they buy (50 per cent of this group claim to buy 'British' whenever they can, compared with 28 per cent of younger consumers) and prefer to 'shop around more and plan their purchases' (http://www.foodanddrinkeurope.com, 2003).

One further interesting fact from the report is that older consumers spend more on take-home drink products than younger consumers (£44 per head more), yet it is largely the younger drinkers who are targeted with promotions by alcohol manufacturers and suppliers.

'The over 55s tend to trust more in established brands and are more likely than under 55s to stick with a brand that they like' (http://foodand drinkeurope.com, 2003). UK brands popular with this group include PG Tips, Kit Kat, Glenmorangie Scotch Whisky (see Insight 5.1) Silver Spoon and Tetley Tea. The over 55-year-olds are also more likely to try new brands than are their younger counterparts in the marketplace.

With respect to this and other target markets (see Chapter 3 and the section below), travel abroad in particular has exposed consumers to many new food and drink experiences, including the way in which the raw ingredients are sourced, prepared, presented and consumed – for many food and drink products that have a heritage, these processes will have remained virtually unchanged for hundreds of years.

One set of unique drink products that have a very long history both in their indigenous place of manufacture and in their consumption throughout the world are Scotch Whisky, Gin and Vodka. Collectively known as spirits, they are mainly produced in the UK, especially Scotland, and contribute significantly to the community, directly and indirectly.

Although the target market for these heritage drinks has always traditionally been the grey market, there has been a sustained campaign both by the industry and individual companies to bring in new consumers with a 'younger' profile, particularly for Gin and Vodka, especially the 25–35 years age group with a DINKY profile. 'Marketers want to expand this sector to attract drinkers below the age of retirement, but they can't afford to alienate their core market . . . tradition is everything in this market' (Bainbridge, 2003).

Scotch Whisky and white spirits have conferred much wider benefits than their sales alone – as we stated in Chapter 2, the economic benefits through the multiplier-effect have been far-reaching in the local community (and beyond) as a result of the success of these heritage drinks. This is further explored in Insight 5.1.

Insight 5.1: Scotch Whisky – a unique heritage product and a unique heritage industry, and the white spirits industry: Gin and Vodka, Scotland

Scotch Whisky is a unique heritage product, not only because it has been made for hundreds of years but also because it can *only* be called Scotch if it has been distilled and matured in Scotland. Scotch Whisky is the world's leading alcoholic drink with a distinct national heritage.

Whisky is a natural drink, made from the natural products of Scotland such as barley and wheat, clear waters that have passed through glens of granite and moors of peat, all of which have benefited from the pure air of Scotland. Each bottle of whisky takes a minimum of 12 years to mature and therefore cannot be bought to market before that time.

The exact origins of the distilling process which makes Scotch Whisky so unique are unknown but it is certain that the Ancient Celts practised this art and they gave their fiery spirit a distinctive name – *uisge beatha* (the water of life); this art has been perfected by the Scots over the years. 'Scotch Whisky is, by definition, an industry unique to Scotland and is one of the country's longest established manufacturing sectors' (DTZ Pieda Consulting for the Scotch Whisky Association, 2004).

In previous chapters we have explored the relationships between various aspects of heritage and how these can have a significant (regeneration) impact on an economy. This is very much the case with the production of spirits (which includes Gin and Vodka) in Scotland.

In Scotland, the production of spirits employs more than 10 000 people and also creates a multiplier effect for other parts of the economy. The total amount in excise duty and VAT contributions paid annually is more than £1.6 billion. Scotch Whisky contributes in excess of £2 billion a year to the balance of trade and is one of the UK's top five export-earning manufacturing industries.

In the year 2000, 41 000 Scottish jobs depended on Scotch Whisky production, which accounts for almost 2 per cent of all jobs in Scotland. The industry generated over £800 million in income for Scottish employees and, at the level of the UK, approximately 65 000 jobs are supported by this industry, generating £1.3 billion in income for the economy. In terms of the multiplier effect, in the year 2000, capital expenditure by the industry was £689.72 million in Scotland and £1018.87 million in the UK as a whole; this includes the purchase of cereals, packaging, bottles, plant and machinery, energy, transport and distribution and other services. 68 per cent of the industry's expenditure is on goods and services from companies based in Scotland, the largest part of which is packaging and bottles (33 per cent); this expenditure generates almost 20 000 jobs in Scotland and approximately 34 000 in the UK.

Specifically, about 40 per cent of employment in this industry is for the distillation processes, which employ 3470 people directly, but which indirectly generate another 12 204 jobs in Scotland and 22 483 for the UK as a whole. The other activities associated with this industry support 25 000 jobs in Scotland and 38 800 in the UK.

In rural areas of Scotland, over 7000 jobs depend on the Scotch Whisky producing processes, which generate an income of £148.16 million annually; this industry also purchases over £90 million of cereals from Scottish suppliers.

The infrastructure of Scotch Whisky production has enabled producers of Gin and Vodka to take advantage of these economies of scale and now 'over

70 per cent of UK Gin and Vodka comes off bottling lines in Scotland' (DTZ Pieda Consulting for the Scotch Whiskey Association, 2004).

The production of Gin and Vodka in Scotland has created 750 jobs and, in the year 2000, purchases from Scottish companies to make these products amounted to £32 million and, at the UK level, £46 million. It is therefore a significant industry, both directly and indirectly, in its own right – if these figures are added to those of Scotch Whisky, we can calculate the total economic impact of producing these spirits specifically for Scotland and generally, the UK.

Gin and Vodka – some facts

1 'Vodka is now the world's most popular (white) spirit drink' (The Gin and Vodka Experience in a report by The Gin and Vodka Association, 2004).
2 Gin and Vodka are exported to over 200 countries around the world.
3 Over 70 per cent of the Gin and 20 per cent of the Vodka produced in the UK is exported.
4 Gin and Vodka producers employ 2000 people directly and 8000 indirectly in the UK.
5 Gin and Vodka production also stimulates the rural economy by using 135 000 tonnes of wheat grown in the UK.
6 Gin and Vodka now form the largest sector by volume in the UK spirits market.
7 The UK production of Gin and Vodka has now reached 274 million 70 cl bottles.
8 Growth is on average 6 per cent year on year.
9 Annual exports of UK-produced Gin and Vodka were worth nearly £205 million in 2002.
10 Vodka is now the biggest selling spirit in the USA.
11 Exports of UK-produced Vodka have expanded 439 per cent since 1990.
12 UK companies produce Gin and Vodka in many other countries, including the USA, Canada, Australia, Italy, India, South Africa and The Philippines.
13 The top two export markets for UK-produced Gin in 2002 were the USA (£74 million) and Spain (£31 million).
14 Exports to EU countries in 2002 were worth nearly £79 million.
15 Exports to the rest of the world in 2002 were worth nearly £126 million.
16 The two top export markets for UK-produced Vodka in 2002 were the USA (£6 million) and Greece (£2 million).
17 Exports of Vodka to EU countries accounted for £13 million of sales in 2002.
18 Exports to the rest of the world accounted for over £19 million of sales in 2002.
19 Over £700 million per year is paid to the UK Exchequer in excise and VAT from UK-produced Gin and Vodka.

20   The alcohol trade in total contributed over £7 billion in 2002 to the UK Chancellor through excise duties and over £2100 million was contributed by the spirits sector.

21   On average 70 per cent of the price of a bottle of gin and vodka is taken as tax revenue in the UK, compared with the following European counterparts: Italy, 43 per cent; Spain, 44 per cent; France, 56 per cent; and Germany, 65 per cent.

The Scotch Whisky Heritage Centre, Edinburgh, Scotland

Interest in the heritage of Scotch Whisky led to the creation of a dedicated heritage centre in Edinburgh, Scotland's capital, which is in itself a heritage townscape (see Chapter 4) and an increasingly popular short-break destination as well as a 'stop off' for longer stay holidays in Scotland. Edinburgh has also been a European City of Culture, together with its neighbouring heritage townscape, Glasgow.

The Scotch Whisky Heritage Centre is located at the top of Edinburgh's 'Royal Mile', which contains many of the city's heritage sites and attractions such as Edinburgh Castle, Holyrood House and Princes Street – all these sites have royal connections, both past and present.

The aim of the heritage centre is to provide visitors with an insight into the manufacturing process of Scotch Whisky and traces the history of this product over 300 years. The centre has a number of innovative ways of providing this information including a 'barrel ride', a chance to meet the resident ghost and, to encourage tasting, adults are given a free dram of whisky. The retail outlet at the site offers 250 different whiskies and there is also an eating area and gift shop.

The target markets are locals and visitors but the centre is also used by the corporate market and is available for private functions by the general public.

Scotland in particular and the UK generally also have a number of other *'Food' museums*; each of these has their own website for further information and are listed below:

- The Bass Museum, Burton-on-Trent
- Bell's Blair Athol Distillery, Pitlochry
- Bell's Cherrybank Centre, Perth
- Biddenden Vineyards & Cider Works, Biddenden
- Bramah Museum of Tea and Coffee, Tower Bridge, London
- Cadbury World, Birmingham
- Car Tayor Vineyards, Hastings
- Chilford Hall Vineyard, Cambridge
- Dalwhinnie Distillery Visitor Centre, Dalwhinnie
- Denbies Wine Estate, Dorking
- Edradour Distillery, Pitlochry
- Freightliners City Farm, Islington, London

- Glen Grant Distillery and Garden, Rothes
- Glen Ord Distillery Visitor Centre, Muir of Ord
- Glenfarclas Distillery, Ballindalloch
- Glenkinchie Distillery, Edinburgh
- Glenlivet Distillery, Ballindalloch
- Glenturret Distillery, Crieff
- Isle of Arran Distillery, Arran
- National Fruit Collection, Faversham
- Scottish Fisheries Museum, Anstruther
- Sedlescombe Vineyard, Sedlescombe
- Sheppy's Cider Centre, Taunton
- Stathisla Distillery, Keith
- The Teapottery, Leyburn
- Tenterden Vineyard Park, Tenterden
- Three Choirs Vineyard, Newent, Gloucestershire
- Westons Cider Visitor Centre, Ledbury, Gloucestershire
- Womersley Crafts & Herbs, near Doncaster.

Acknowledgment: DTZ Pieda Consulting for the Scotch Whisky Association, 2004. The Gin and Vodka Association of Great Britain, Salisbury. The Scotch Whisky Heritage Centre.

Food and drink is consumed in any number of different ways and in contrasting environments, depending on the prevailing culture of that country or specifically the culture of a food. For example, 'corn dogs' and 'hot dogs' are symbolic of being eaten 'on the go', i.e., in an outside setting, as they are a convenience food that can be hand-held and consumed whilst doing other things – they are also symbolic of 'New York' culture and confirm the 'fast pace' of this city and are often used in marketing communications when highlighting the benefits of New York.

In contrast, elegance and sophistication are symbolic of the eating experience at 'grand' hotels and restaurants around the world, such as The Ritz Hotel and, specifically, the 'art' of taking tea at The Ritz, as described in Insight 5.2.

Insight 5.2: The Ritz Hotel, London – taking tea at the Ritz

In Chapter 3, and very briefly in Chapter 4, we discussed the demand for heritage hotels, which particularly in recent years, partly as a result of better targeting, have enjoyed an increase in 'sales'/occupancy, not least by members of the grey market but by other target markets too, such as the business to business market who might use the facilities on offer for a range of different corporate events.

One of the most famous hotels in the world is The Ritz Hotel, Piccadilly, London and, whilst I shall give a brief history of its unique heritage, the main purpose of this insight is to explore the relationship between The Ritz Hotel and tea, especially 'Afternoon Tea at The Ritz', a ritual which has become known as a unique heritage phenomenon in its own right.

The Ritz London opened in 1906, following the success of the Paris Ritz, both of which were designed by Mewes and Davis who were appointed by the hotelier, Cesar Ritz. The Ritz was praised at the time by both press and public for its 'brilliant refinement of detail and articulation' (*The Ritz Hotel Publication*, 2004). The seven-storey building of steel frame (the first of its kind in London) was designed to resemble an elegant French Chateau and therefore has an imposing façade and frontage, complete with large copper lions at each corner of the roof.

The interior is designed with perspective effects to make it appear larger than it actually is. The focus of the eye is along the long main corridor through to the Restaurant at the far end and, beyond that, to the Italian Garden and London's Green Park.

The Ritz Hotel has 95 bedrooms and 38 suites, most of which retain the Louis XVI style and in which four principal colour schemes are used: salmon pink, rose pink, yellow and blue.

The Ritz is the only hotel in the world to hold a Royal Charter, in this case for the supply of banqueting and catering services to HRH The Prince of Wales. In addition to this, it holds many other awards and commendations including membership of The Tea Council, for which it won The Top London Afternoon Tea Award 2004.

The Ritz London is a Grade 2* listed building (see Chapter 1) that was returned to private British ownership in 1995, at which point it underwent a refurbishment that eventually cost £40 million and took eight years.

The 2004 rates for one night (exclusive of vat) were as follows:

- Superior Queen £300
- Superior King £365
- Deluxe King £430
- Junior Suite £500
- One Bedroom Suite £780
- Green Park or Piccadilly Suite £1500
- Two Bedroom Suite £1850
- Two Berkeley Suite £1950

Short breaks and weekend packages have been branded as follows:

- *Putting On The Ritz* – a one-night programme including accommodation and English Breakfast, with a bottle of Ritz Champagne, fruit and flowers. Prices start from £390.

- *The Ritz Finale* – a one-night programme with accommodation, English Breakfast, two theatre tickets and either a pre- or post-theatre supper in The Ritz Restaurant. Prices start at £535.
- *Ritz Romance* – a one-night programme including accommodation, English Breakfast, Table d'Hote dinner with wine in The Ritz Restaurant, and fruit, flowers and Ritz Champagne in the room. Prices start at £535.

The eating and drinking areas are also branded and called The Ritz Restaurant, The Palm Court and The Rivoli Bar.

The Palm Court was originally known as the Winter Garden and was designed as a 'dramatic stage set to delight those entering from the Piccadilly entrance . . . [it] makes imaginative use of a mirrored backdrop reflecting the impressive marble columns which flank the entrance to the restaurant; much of the appeal lies in the charming centrally focused fountain sculpture of a reclining female figure wrought in gilded lead' (*The Ritz Hotel Publication*, 2004). The Palm Court is where the famous 'Afternoon Tea at The Ritz' is served, but reservations are required (months in advance for members of the general public) and it begins with sittings at 12 p.m. in order to cater for the demand. The cost is £342 per person.

The Ritz Restaurant 'has one of the most magical interiors in London and is considered by many to be the most beautiful hotel restaurant in the world. The rich and varied use of soft pink, pale green and veined white marble and the dazzling garlands of chandeliers combine to create the feeling of a room permanently *en fete* and as charming by day as by night' (*The Ritz Hotel Publication*, 2004).

In June 2002, The Ritz London became the capital's first hotel to offer diners certified organic meals, following its successful move to be licensed by the Soil Association, the UK's largest organic certification body.

The Rivoli Bar was designed to reflect the opulent grandeur and luxurious style of the 1920s. 'On entering the bar, from the hotel's Long Gallery, attention is immediately caught by five gilded ceiling domes each with their own delicate Lalique style chandelier. The bar . . . has an onyx marble top which glows with lighting set both below and above. The glasses, bottles, silver cocktail shakers and bowls also sparkle with brilliant reflections from the rear wall set in glass' (*The Ritz Hotel Publication*, 2004). The Rivoli Bar offers a range of beverages including the signature drinks of the hotel, which are Martinis and Champagne Cocktails, but also offers its own afternoon tea.

In order to mark its forthcoming centenary, The Ritz London has recently announced a unique partnership with the 16 historic Champagne Houses that form 'Les Maisons Grandes Marques de Champagne'. Champagne is a product that has EU-protected designation origin and was briefly discussed above. The product might now be synonymous in consumers' perception with the highest qualities of lifestyle and enjoyment, but it did in fact have very humble beginnings, being made by Benedictine Monasteries in sixteenth-century France, primarily for their own consumption.

However, in 1882, in order to protect the growing status and reputation of Champagne, the predecessor of the Grandes Marques was established and the sixteen member houses now continue to maintain the stature of the wines they produce. In 1956, L'Academie du Champagne was founded to foster and promote the members' reputation in the UK. The Ritz Hotel's management are active members of this Champagne Academy and have therefore created this alliance, which acts as another point of differentiation with respect to the competition. The alliance hosts a different Champagne each month and a special dinner at the end of the month (see Table 5.7).

Afternoon Tea at The Ritz

Afternoon Tea at The Ritz has been popular since the hotel first opened and 'regulars' over the years have included King Edward VII, Charlie Chaplin, Sir Winston Churchill, General de Gaulle, Noel Coward, Judy Garland and Evelyn Waugh.

The concept of afternoon tea was started by Anna, 7th Duchess of Bedford, who grew tired of the 'sinking feeling', which she experienced

Table 5.7 Grande Marque Champagne calendar at The Ritz

Date	Champagne House	Foundation
March 2004	Ruinart	1729
April	Lanson	1760
May	Veuve-Clicquot	1806
June	Bollinger	1829
July/August	Mumm	1827
August/September	Krug	1843
October	Perrier-Jouet	1811
November	Tattinger	1743
December	Moet & Chandon and Dom Perignon	1743
January 2005	Laurent Perrier	1812
February	Heidseck Monopole	1834
March	Charles Heidseck	1851
April	Louis Roederer	1827
May	Piper Heidseck	1785
June	Pommery	1836
July	Pol Roger	1849

around 4 p.m. every day and which was the interlude between meals. 'In 1840 she plucked up courage and asked for a tray of tea, bread and butter and cake to be brought to her room. Once she had formed the habit she could not break it, so spread it among her friends instead. As the century progressed, afternoon tea became increasingly elaborate. By the 1880s ladies were changing into long tea gowns for the occasion, appetites sharpened by the customary afternoon drive in a carriage' (Simpson, 1986).

At The Ritz, tea is served on fine Limoges china, decorated in an exclusive design of gold, pale green and rose colours to complement the décor of The Palm Court restaurant. Tea is served in silver teapots with silver milk jugs and tea strainers. The Ritz's own Traditional English tea is offered, together with a range of variants including China Oolong, Lapsang Souchong, Earl Grey, Ceylon Orange Pekoe, Darjeeling and Jasmine tea. The tea is accompanied by sandwiches on a three-tier stand, together with scones, home-made jam, clotted Cornish cream and a selection of afternoon tea pastries and fresh cream cakes.

> Tea at the Ritz is the last delicious morsel of Edwardian London. Here is one of the few places outside church or royal garden parties where a woman may wear a hat and feel entirely at ease. In fact, those approaching the Palm Court clad in such garments as jeans, shorts or trainers will be reluctantly but firmly turned away.
>
> (Simpson, 1986: 12)

By kind permission of Gerrie Pitt, Director of Press and Public Relations, The Ritz London, 2004.

Emerging target markets for indigenous heritage food and drink products or brands

In the section above I have largely focused on the indigenous (UK) market for its own heritage food and drink products and brands, but there is an interesting and rapidly changing international scene for those heritage food and drink products that may have fallen out of favour with the UK market. This is a concept that translates around the globe.

For example, malt- and chocolate-based hot beverages (the former in particular) are no longer consumed in the quantities that they were in the past in the UK – the two 'well-known' brands, each of which has a long heritage associated with these products in the UK, are Horlicks and Cadbury's Drinking Chocolate, respectively. However, whilst the market for these two drinks has declined in the UK and other developed markets in the West, sales have increased, year on year, in other countries, particularly Latin America. '[The two products are] marketed mostly as an excellent source of nutrition in countries where food quality is often poor. Global retail volume sales of both malted and chocolate-based hot drinks reached 956 702 tonnes in 2003 . . . with Latin America alone accounting for over one-third of total sales' (http://www:foodanddrinkeurope.com, 2004). India is the largest market for malt-based drinks and accounts for 22 per cent of world sales. The Horlicks brand (which is now owned by the multi-national organization Glaxo) accounts for 70 per cent of all sales of this drink in India.

Whilst the market for processed cheese products continues to show marginal or steady growth in the UK (depending on the product or brand), in another emerging market, the Middle East, sales of the same products are rising on average 18 per cent per year. UK market analysts Proteus Insight claim that there are 370 million consumers in this market who presently consume 200 000 tonnes of processed cheese. Saudi Arabia, Egypt, Algeria and Morocco accounted for approximately 65 per cent of the total volume of sales, primarily made by multi-nationals such as Kraft (Australia), although local companies are beginning to challenge the strength of these players in the market.

We can turn this concept on its head and come back to the increasing demand in the UK (and other countries) for products, or just flavours incorporated into high demand goods, which are not indigenous to the native shores and the pull for which has not necessarily arisen out of travels to those countries but has perhaps been led by exposure to citizens who have migrated permanently to the nation. For example, in the UK, demand for hospitality generally and specific brands in particular has been fuelled by an increasing interest in ethnic foods (this was recognized by Theodore Levitt and is referenced in Chapter 1). The development and accessibility of ethnic restaurants and the popularity of ready-made meals (because of social changes) has seen a steady growth in demand for 'Asian', in particular 'Indian' flavours in anything from dedicated sauces from which meals or convenience food can be produced to crisps and other snacks. Table 5.8 shows UK retail sales of Indian foods, 1998–2003, and Table 5.9 shows a breakdown by food type.

> The popularity of food products formulated with ethnic ingredients is far from waning in the UK, and Thai cuisine continues to hold the number one slot in emerging cuisine, with food makers such as Jacob's rolling out finished foods positioned with a Thai appeal.
>
> (http://www.foodanddrinkeurope.com, July 2004)

Jacob's was originally a British company and most famous for its branded (by the same family name) cream cracker. It is now owned by the French group Danone (Danone is worth £186.4 million) who have launched rice- and potato-based crackers made by Jacob's under the brand name of Fusion's, although the Jacob's name still features heavily both in broadcast advertising and in the written media.

Table 5.8 UK retail sales of Indian foods, 1998–2003

Year	£million
1998	391
1999	432
2000	483
2001	535
2002	565
2003	613

Source: Mintel.

A recent report from Mintel has valued the ethnic food market in the UK at £115 million and states that Thai-flavoured food is the fastest growing element, worth approximately £65 million, of this overall ethnic market.

I could refer to literally thousands of examples where foods indigenous to one nation (or region) have succeeded equally well (or better) elsewhere, even before the concept of marketing, and in particular branding, was born. Two examples follow below.

The Conquest of Mexico in 1521 gave rise to one of the richest culinary revolutions in history. When the Spanish explorer Cortez and his followers came to the 'New World' in search of fortune, they found a wealth of culinary specialties such as chocolate, peanuts, vanilla, beans, squash, avocados, coconuts, corn and tomatoes. In turn the Spanish brought to the Americas products such as pork, beef, lamb, citrus fruits, garlic, cheese, milk, wheat, vinegar and wine.

Table 5.9 UK retail sales of Indian foods, 1998–2003, by food type

Food type	1998 (£million)	2000 (£million)	2002 (£million)	2003 (£million)
Ready meals	254	308	372	404
Accompaniments	75	96	120	135
Cooking sauces	52	68	64	65
Curry powder	10	11	9	9
Total	**391**	**483**	**565**	**613**

Source: Mintel.

Montezuma, the great Aztec emperor, had been warned that one day bearded men mounted on animals like giant deer would come to take over his territory, so when he heard that men had landed at Vera Cruz, he was not surprised. He made every effort to keep them in Vera Cruz by offering them great riches, but seeing these had the counterproductive effect of urging the men on to see where the riches had come from. On 8 November 1519, Cortez entered Montezuma's capital, along with 7000 native soldiers he had recruited along the way. He was received by Montezuma and given a great feast but the cordial relations between the Spanish captain and the Aztec emperor were short-lived and, after many fierce battles, on 13 August 1521, Cortez claimed the capital. The conquerors systematically destroyed the Aztec empire and replaced it with Spanish structures and institutions, but they never succeeded in extinguishing the native culture and traditions, which are still part of Mexico today.

Mexican cuisine has evolved (as is the case for most countries) and was constantly enriched from many different countries. In particular, recipes and ingredients from Africa, South America, the Caribbean, France and the Orient found their way through the Spanish – Mexico conduit. One of the best known Mexican worldwide culinary exports has been 'Tex-Mex' food, which is a cultural blend of Northern Mexico and Southwest US (southern Texas) foods, representing the areas where Native Americans, cowboys, Texans and Mexicans intermingled; it is available in almost every country of the world.

South Carolina in the USA is noted for many aspects of heritage (a driving force for tourism into the region) and, not least, its rich heritage of culinary preparations, which have been learned from the Native Americans and from settlers who came from Spain, England, France, Scotland, Ireland and Germany. African slaves, who were originally brought to the colony, have also contributed to the culinary heritage that has developed in the state of Carolina. The foods indigenous to this area are peaches, figs, muscadines, pumpkins, squash, game, fish, nuts and corn, which were discovered and enjoyed by the settlers when they arrived. In turn, they bought dairy cattle, swine and chickens. The Africans bought okra, field peas, eggplant, peanuts and yams from their native lands. The combination of these ingredients, different techniques of preparation and presentation have created a unique culinary heritage.

Adding value through heritage branding and 'piggy-back' marketing

The fact that a food or drink comes from a particular country creates a *natural heritage* and this concept can be used for marketing purposes (see Insight 5.1 on Scotch Whisky). The food or beverage may also be linked to 'wider'/international organizations who might assist in its promotion. For example, the Tokaji region in Hungary was designated a UNESCO World

Heritage site in June 2002 because of the area's tradition of producing wine, which dates back 1000 years. The product itself is similar to what we might acknowledge as a liqueur, such as more well-known brands like Pernod, but it is the unique taste of Tokaji (just like Pernod) and the historic landscape of hills and river valleys to which UNESCO responded positively and accordingly awarded the World Heritage status, which is used on many types of marketing communications.

The European Union has for many years involved itself in the protection of traditional ways of producing food and drink and has created legislation in order to forbid 'copycats' from using the same generic product name. The EU has created a list of over 500 European products that now have protected designation origin (PDO), which provides legal protection for the heritage of a brand. For example, Champagne is only allowed to be called such if it is produced in the region of the same name in France.

> Strong brands retain a close link to their origins by protecting and communicating their brand heritage. Big supermarkets have spent their time building their own brands at the expense of manufacturers' brands.
>
> (Ritson, 2003)

> Italy has one of the most diverse portfolios of protected food and drink products in Europe, a factor which marketers are increasingly using to promote their foods. But some of the best known names in Italian meat, cheese and wine are now being introduced to the ice-cream segment in a bid to further enhance their regional status.
>
> (http://www.foodanddrinkeurope.com, 2004)

Of the 649 food and drink products with protected origin status 137 are from Italy. Now, Italian products such as Vincotto balsamic vinegar, Gorgonzola, Parmesan and Squacquerone cheese, and wines such as Amarone, Barolo and Soave, are being incorporated into gelati (Italian ice-cream) as new flavours in order to combine the fact that they are PDO products with another significant culinary heritage of the country – that of ice-cream – to create a new **synergy** and an enhanced market for ice-cream. Although 60 per cent of ice-cream sales in Italy are dominated by another multi-national, Nestle, there are enough local artisan producers of this product to allow for product innovation and marketing to both locals and visitors.

Commercial organizations such as CadburysSchweppes, Nestle and others have recognized the added-value to branding that a focus on heritage can bring; at the very least it creates a temporary source of competitive advantage with a particular (limited edition) promotion. Although examples of this are evident throughout the year (for example to tie-in with an anniversary of the organization or specifically the time-lapse of a particular brand), they tend to occur more often at major mass-market celebrations such as Christmas. For many years the retailer Marks & Spencer, as part of its grocery arm, ran a branded range entitled 'Penny Bazaar', which depicted scenes from winter-time Victorian England on tins of biscuits, cakes, etc. However, just like any other sales promotion opportunity, this heritage branding opportunity in itself has a limited timescale and was removed after a few years.

Organizations, both large and small, will also use the fact that they have been in existence for some time (this need not necessarily be 'very long') in order to use heritage as a branding tool in sales promotions (see Case study 5.1). Clearly this is a notion to which consumers respond positively because it offers them reassurance and reflects an aspect of their personality, i.e., the perception that something which has been available or around for some time must be 'better' or 'good'. If we add to this the lifestyle aspects discussed above, we have a complete psychographic profile of an existing or potential consumer, and all that is needed to unlock the demand is the use of appropriate targeting promotional tools.

However, relying on 'reputation' or previous longevity alone can have dire consequences for market share in the long run. 'French wine exports are falling. Challenged by the success of New World wines, France's global market share fell four per cent in 2002 . . . it's time for French wine makers to uncork a better strategy than just relying solely on the strength of their origins' (King, 2003).

French wine makers have perilously ignored an important emerging market – that of consumers who want wines priced at between €5 and €10, which are both reliable in taste quality and are suitably branded. Marketers of wines from the New World, which includes countries such as Australia, the USA, Chile and South Africa (see Insight 5.4) have strategically pursued this niche market with a great deal of success. The cornerstones of their marketing strategies have been to create strong brands that are easily distinguishable in the marketplace, clear labelling with the right amount of product information and quality standardization.

A survey commissioned in 2003 by the British drinks company Threshers Group confirms that a growing number of wine drinkers are looking for just that. According to the study:

1   85 per cent of consumers are more likely to buy wine when they have been provided with clear information about it, either on the bottle or on the shelf;
2   almost one-quarter of consumers are seduced by imagery and make their purchase decision according to label design;
3   63 per cent of consumers do not care what country the wine they choose originates from;
4   over one-third of consumers polled feel confused about which type of wine is best to buy.

(Research conducted by Taylor Nelson Sofres in the UK, 2003)

French wine makers admit that they have a significant difference in approach to the market than their New World counterparts, the latter are demand-led whilst the former are supply-based. The New World wine producers have focused on what the customer wants and then used the appropriate marketing tools to reach them.

One other significant difference, and an explanation for the approaches taken, is that France has over 750 wine producers, many of which are small enterprises with limited funds for marketing and a tradition for doing business that has remained virtually unchanged over the generations – clearly this is going to make each and every one relatively uncompetitive against a large consortium which has pooled funds for collective marketing. In South Africa, for example, one company is responsible for distributing 80 per cent of the country's entire wine production, while in Australia four companies distribute all the country's wines.

France also has a complicated wine classification system, which was originally created to safeguard and ensure quality and consistency of the wines. The system of 'appellations' includes over 400 different categories, which has also resulted in hundreds of different names for the wines that can then cause confusion in the marketplace.

In the past, information pertaining to the wine was always on the bottle's front label. However, wine makers from the New World took the unprecedented step of putting this on the back, which has also helped them to generate extra sales.

> The label is the first contact people have with the product on the shelf. It must therefore be simple and easy to understand but also reflect the particular personality of the brand. For this reason, many wineries, especially in the New World have decided to put the required data on the back label of the bottle. The front can then be used to attract the consumer with colours, an identifiable logo or attractive graphics.
>
> (F. Crouzet, Castel Groupe (French drinks company), 2004)

Finally, there has been a cultural reluctance by French wine makers not only to embrace the power of marketing but also to question its immediate benefits, and therefore to plough any extra cash into machinery and operations rather than marketing. Further, there has also been a definite desire *not* to engage with others to create a joint brand, as this goes against the tradition of emphasizing the individual vineyard or family tradition that has gone into making the wine. However, this scenario is slowly changing and there is an increasing recognition by some wine producers of the threat posed by the New World; in 2003 the Castel Groupe created a specific new line for the export market. 'We created the "Castel" brand to counteract the rise of New World wines: we wanted to meet consumer demand with simple and accessible wines' (F. Crouzet, Castel Groupe, 2004). The range brings together under the Castel brand name different table wines, which are divided into three separate categories according to taste: light, fruity wines; stronger, aromatic wines; and richer, more complex wines; each bottle is priced from €3 to €8.

In the previous chapter we mentioned the concept of 'piggy-back' marketing, i.e., two (or possibly more) organizations getting together for mutual (promotional) advantage. For example, in Autumn 2004, the *Daily Telegraph* ran a promotional campaign in conjunction with the National Trust to give readers the chance of a free visit (subject to collecting tokens from the newspaper) to a National Trust site. The choice of the *Daily Telegraph* must have been deliberate, as its readership profile reflects closely the profile of National Trust members or advocates. However, as existing members can visit sites for free at any time, the campaign was targeted to stimulate demand from either lapsed members or potential new ones, or both.

The example of the National Trust and the *Daily Telegraph* joint campaign illustrates a type of marketing activity with which promoters of heritage brands also engage. Look for examples on supermarket shelves on packaging, at point of display and possibly also taste testings/samples, which will usually be backed up by an incentive to purchase the brand through a below-the-line sales promotion such as a money-off coupon.

Insight 5.3: Knights Cider Company Ltd. Malvern, Worcestershire, UK. 'From Blossom to Bottle'

One organization that uses not just the heritage of a product such as cider (which has been around for hundreds of years) in its marketing activities but also the fact that the product is made in a heritage area, indeed an AONB – the Malvern Hills – and that 'traditional' methods are used in its production, is Knights Cider Company.

During the past 25 years, Knights Cider has grown from a small family company (three generations) making a few thousand gallons of traditional cider using a labour-intensive wetbed press and having a cider apple orchard of 25 acres, to become one of the country's independent commercial and traditional cider makers. Now, a new belt press is used, with all the apple-moving and -cleaning operations controlled by computer, and the press processing takes just one hour as opposed to half a day.

In addition to making traditional ciders and perry (a pear-based product), the company makes a wide range of commercial ciders and perrys that are sold to the wholesale market for packaging into glass, cans and plastic containers of all sizes for distribution countrywide and for export.

The cider itself is a rich golden, natural colour with a clean, fresh taste. It is lightly carbonated and bottled in glass and, more recently, the firm has added a still, unpasteurised cider on draught, which is available exclusively from their retail outlet located at the production site.

The 'real' ciders produced by Knight's Cider Company Ltd have won many awards for quality, both locally and internationally and recently they have added two new brands to the existing range, Malvern Gold and Malvern Oak. Malvern Gold Medium Reserve is a full-bodied real cider, rich in tannins and flavenoids that create its natural flavour and golden colour. The product is made from the company's own apples, which are pressed, fermented and matured prior to the processes of filtration and bottling. It takes at least two and a half pounds of apples to produce every bottle of cider. Malvern Oak Dry Reserve is a refreshing, balanced cider made from a variety of traditional cider apples, including Yalington Mill, Harry Master's Jersey, Dabinett and Kingston Black. A natural process is used to ferment the cider to 6 per cent alcohol.

The cider orchards, which vary in age, have increased to occupy 200 acres and the later plantings of trees are all from their own nurseries. There are 60 000 established trees and a further 10 000 trees were to be planted in 2004. Specimens of old varieties are grown to prevent them from dying out and, in conjunction with the National Association of Cider Makers, experiments are being carried out to develop new varieties of tree for the future. The main varieties grown are Dabinett, Ashton Bitter, Michelin and Browns Apple, with smaller plantings of approximately 40 other traditional cider varieties.

The firm also buys in hundreds of tonnes of cider apples every season from local farms in the area, thereby helping to safeguard some of the traditional orchards of Herefordshire and Worcestershire.

The company is located in the foothills of the Malvern Hills, which has been declared as an Area of Outstanding Natural Beauty (AONB), and the owners take every opportunity to enhance this natural environment. The mature orchards are a haven for wildlife, receiving visits from an abundance of birds, rabbits and foxes living in the surrounding woodlands. 'The Worcestershire Way' passes through the main orchards and, in May particularly, walkers are encouraged to enjoy the sea of pink blossom that covers the area.

By kind permission of Knight's Cider Company Ltd, Crumpton Oaks Farm, Storridge, Malvern, Worcestershire, 2005.

Insight 5.4: South African wine: a 300-year-old heritage

We briefly mentioned above that South Africa is one of the countries that feature under the umbrella of the 'New World' in terms of wine production and marketing, but wine has been produced in this country for over 300 years.

The South Africans have been selling their wines outside the country of origin since the early 1900s but between 1986 and 1991 there was virtually no availability because of the sanctions that had been imposed on the country. Since these have been lifted, South Africa has pursued the world with its wines, with remarkable success, and now ranks 18th in the world in terms of acreage, 8th in the world in terms of output and accounts for 3.7 per cent of international wine production. South Africa exports approximately 8 per cent of its total production from a total vine crop of 270 million gallons, of which 50 per cent is made into wine.

Wine production is largely located in the Western Cape region and the industry is relatively small compared with that of other countries. The industry is made up of 78 estates and 97 independent wine cellars and there are also 70 winery cooperatives, which in total consist of 5000 grape farmers.

Vines were first introduced into South Africa in 1656 by Jan Van Riebeeck who was the first commander of the Cape Colony. On 2 February 1659, wine was pressed from the grapes he had grown. However, it was not until the seventeenth century when the French Huguenots arrived that more extensive wine-making took place, owing to their knowledge of vines and wine-making.

South Africa is in the Southern Hemisphere, which with its cool, wet winters and dry, hot summers makes it ideal for vine cultivation. The grapes are harvested from late December to late March when the cool maritime breezes offset the extremes in heat during this season.

The soil varieties vary from Table Mountain Sandstone in the west to granite compounds on the slopes of the mountains further east, and shale is the predominate type in the Karoo.

The vineyards are located in the three main regions: Coastal, Breede River Valley and Boberg. The Coastal Region includes the oldest wine-producing farms at Constantia, Durbanville, Paarl, Stellenbosch, Swartland and Tulbagh. The seven districts are Boberg, Overberg, Olifants River, Piketberg, Klein Karoo, Benede Oranje and Douglas. Fortified wines are produced in the towns of Robertson and Worcester, which are in the Breede River Valley.

The grape variety that is planted most densely in South Africa is the Chenin Blanc and accounts for almost one-third of total wine production. Other grape varieties planted include Chardonnay (about 5 per cent), Colombard and Palomino (8 per cent each), Muscat d'Alexandrie, Cape Riesling, Sauvignon Blanc, Semillon, Weisser or Rhine Reisling, Gewurztraminer and Ugni Blanc. The majority of wine produced is white, red grape production accounts for only about 15 per cent of total wine made and approximately half of this is made using the Cinsault (known locally as Hermitage) grape. Further grape varieties include Cabernet Sauvignon, Pinotage, Shiraz, Pinot Noir, Cabernet Franc, Merlot, Malbec, Gamay and Grenache. Pinotage is a unique variety having been created by Professor

Abraham Perlod in 1925 by cross-fertilizing Cinsault and Pinot Noir; the result is a fruity wine which is best drunk young.

Acknowledgment: http://www.thewineman.com, 2005.

Food and drink heritage and tourism

There is absolutely no doubt that tourism, regional, national and international, is linked by most consumers to the culinary uniqueness of an area – it is part of that area's heritage. In terms of a consumer's personality, this may reflect their curiosity, a willingness for adventure or their depth of knowledge, with the aim of both finding out and trying that which one understands.

Many consumers associate the concepts of food, drink, heritage and identity, i.e., they recognize that there is an inextricable link between the food and/or drink consumed (including how and when it is consumed) and the heritage and identity of both a geographical area and the people of that locality or region – even if they no longer live there, or never have. For example, for most first-, second- and third-generation Asians in the UK it would be inconceivable not to eat curries and associated foods regularly, whether made at home or not – though perhaps no longer with their bare hands because this is largely socially unacceptable in the UK. Many of these consumers will never have visited the Indian sub-continent but will have *inherited* the concept of eating indigenous foods from family and friends. The fact that 'curry' has overtaken 'Fish and Chips' as the UK's favourite food is testament to the fact that the UK is now a multi-cultural society. Increased exposure to these foods (over a period of time – they were not always popular) and a general increased awareness of other aspects of people and society are partly reflections of increased travel, education, tolerance and acceptance. There have been significant paradigm shifts in the understanding of different races and religions that reside in the UK over a period of time.

The type of heritage we have described above is just as important (some writers/students might argue that it is more so) as that associated with buildings, literature, music, museums, etc. (see previous chapters). This is increasingly being recognized by both governments and organizations as a marketing opportunity, not just for tourism into the country but for the sale of the indigenous brand elsewhere, perhaps made under licence if there should be sufficient demand.

Wine, food and tourism have long been closely related. For example, eating out is a major tourism activity. However, it is only recently that the roles which wine and food play in attracting tourists to a destination have come to be explicitly recognised by governments, researchers and by the wine, food and tourism industries. Food has become recognised as:

1   part of the local culture which tourists consume;
2   part of tourist promotion;
3   a potential component of local agricultural and economic development;
4   something at the local level that is affected by the consumption patterns and perceived preferences of tourists.

(Hall and Mitchell, 2001)

In the previous chapter we discussed the use of 'heritage trails' as a tourism differentiation opportunity. This concept has also been applied to the heritage marketing of food and drink and two examples follow, marketed under the 'umbrella' regional brand of 'The Heart of England', which is part of the wider remit of a regional development agency entitled 'Advantage West Midlands'.

Insight 5.5: The Heart of England Fine Foods Group: 'promoting regional excellence'

The Heart of England Fine Foods Group was established in 1998 in order to raise the awareness and promote the food and drink that is available in the 'Heart of England' region. The Heart of England region comprises the following counties: Herefordshire, Shropshire, Staffordshire, Warwickshire, Worcestershire and the urban conurbations of the West Midlands region; this group is the lead organization for promoting producers, growers and processors of speciality food and drink products and brands.

The aim is to assist member businesses develop and expand profitable, sustainable markets for their products, utilizing regional strengths whilst raising consumer awareness of all that is on offer in the region from these suppliers.

The Cheese Trail

The organizations selected to form the Cheese Trail occupy a large geographical area encompassing the counties mentioned above and specifically in terms of towns and cities, Leek in Staffordshire to the north, Coventry to the east, Hereford to the south and Shrewsbury and Ludlow to the west (see Figure 5.1). The latter has in itself become a 'gastronomic haven' in recent years, evident through the number of 'Michelin stars' awarded to chefs who ply their trade in hotels and restaurants in the town, although Ludlow has always had a rich heritage of street trade in all types of food and drink, including cheese.

The organizations are specifically chosen because of the traditional processes used (i.e., non-commercial), what one might call 'hand-crafted', in order to create the best possible taste and texture. One consequence of this selection criterion is that many are small family businesses that use cheese-making recipes and methods that have been handed down over generations. '[T]raditional processes capture the character and taste of individual counties, even resurrecting long-lost flavours of a bygone era, or with a modern twist to embrace our diverse culture' (K. Davies, Chief Executive, Heart of England Fine Foods Group, 2002).

The 12 companies on the Cheese Trail are:

1 *Ansteys of Worcester* – cheese-makers since 1985 on their Worcestershire farm. Cheeses are carefully handmade in small batches to ensure a rich creamy texture. They are then clothbound for a 6–12 month period to yield the distinct character and flavour of the brands which include: Old Worcester White – a full-flavoured cheddar-style cheese with unique creaminess; Double Worcester – a variation on the famous Double Gloucester; Worcestershire Sauce Cheese – a marriage of two famous flavours from the area, Ansteys' cheese and Worcester Sauce made by Lea & Perrins.

2 *Appleby's of Hawkstone* brand is known as Appleby's Hawkstone Cheshire, which is produced from their own herd of cows on the edge of the Cheshire Plain. They have been making cheese for 50 years in the same traditional way.

3 *Fowlers of Earlswood* are England's oldest cheese-making family. The milk for cheese-making is from a single herd, which is accommodated on their farm in the West Midlands and which gives the cheese a unique flavour and texture. The brands marketed by Fowlers include Warwickshire Truckle and Original Little Derby, both of which are traditional cloth-bound cheeses and matured in their cheese cellar. The company also makes another heritage cheese, Sage Derby, which is a sub-brand of the Little Derby. Sub-brands of the Warwickshire Truckle include Arden Oak Smoked Truckle, Garlic and Parsley, Black Cracked Pepper and Chilli. Warwickshire Forest Blue is a newly developed cheese that has been bought to market.

4 *Innes Cheese* is a small, family-run business. Cheese is made daily in their dairy, using the freshly drawn milk from their herd of 300 goats. The best-known brand from Innes' farm is Innes Button, which was supreme champion in the first-ever British Cheese Awards. They also produce the Gold Medal-winning Bosworth Leaf and the smaller Clifton Leaf, which is richly flavoured and mould-ripened with a sweet chestnut leaf. Another Gold Medal-winning variety is the Bosworth Ash, which is matured with a sprig of Rosemary.

5 *Lightwood Cheese* is another family-run cheese-makers that uses traditional and family recipes in order to create authentic tastes that have been enjoyed in the past – they are partly marketing nostalgia with their range of cheese. The milk used for their cheese comes only from the herd of Friesian cows which are kept at the farm. The brands have taken their names from famous local people and places, these include: Elgar Mature, which has a rich nutty taste; the Gold Medal-winning Olde Gloster, which has been created using a nineteenth-century recipe and

uses carrot juice to enhance the colouring – it is a moist cheese with depth of flavour; Severn Sisters uses semi-skimmed milk and is made following an eighteenth-century Worcestershire recipe and is distinguished by its racing green wax, softer texture and is acidic in flavour; Severn Vale uses an excess of cream and whole milk to form this white crumbling cheese, which has a slight hint of citrus; Lightwood Smoked is lightly cold-smoked over oak and becomes a moist cheese.

6   *Malvern Cheesewrights Ltd* is a company that produces a range of hand-crafted speciality cheeses from century-old recipes retrieved from the area; they are internationally renowned for cheese-making. The brands include: Hereford Hop (this was a triple Gold Medal winner at the British Cheese Awards); Worcestershire Gold; English Oak; Malvern Gold and Black; Gold and Herb; Red and Chives, and their latest additions are Gold and Sundried Tomato, and White Ladies Goat Cheese. The company supplies local and national retailers and also international airlines.

7   *Mar Goats* produce a variety of soft and hard goats cheeses on their farm using goats milk from goats that are naturally fed. The brands marketed by this firm include Capella, which includes herbs, pepper and oatmeal; Juglandis, which contains chopped walnuts in walnut oil; Haedi, which also has paprika, fine herbs and black pepper; and Albion, which is an aged cheese.

8   *Monkland Cheese Dairy* is a working traditional cheese dairy that is open to the public and is located close to an important built heritage area in Herefordshire known as 'The Black and White Village Trail'. The brands made by this firm include: Little Hereford, which has a creamy texture and is matured for 3–4 months; Monkland, which is brine-bathed and therefore has a 'fresh' flavour and crumbly texture; and two new brand variants are Monkland with Garlic and Chives, and Hereford Sage. The Dairy, which is located in Leominster, has visitor facilities that include a farm shop and café where produce can be bought and consumed.

9   *Neals Yard Creamery* is a small-scale producer of handmade high-quality dairy products and their range consists of two goat's cheeses, two cows' milk cheeses, yogurt, fromage frais and crème fraiche; the cows' milk products are totally organic. The firm supplies retail outlets around the country in refrigerated vehicles and by mail order using insulated containers packed with ice in order to maintain the quality of the cheese.

10   *Ram Hall Dairy Sheep* has one brand that is made using an old recipe. This is known as 'Berkswell' Ewes milk cheese, which is handmade at sixteenth-century Ram Hall, situated on the edge of Berkswell Village, from which the cheese takes its name. 'Berkswell' is a hard cheese, developed from a traditional Caerphilly recipe but which has been adapted and the cheese matured for 3–8 months to give it a unique flavour and texture – it is frequently compared with a mature Pecorino (Italian cheese). 'Berkswell' cheese has won many awards including six Gold Medals at the British Cheese Awards.

11   *Staffordshire Organic Cheese* are makers of specialist handmade cheese from both cows' and ewes' milk. The company was created in 1983 and has built up a national reputation for its cheeses, all of which are suitable for vegetarians.

12   *The Staffordshire Cheese Company*, based in Leek, Staffordshire, also make hand-crafted cheese and use both local cows and goats milk. The brands include: The Staffordshire, a cloth-bound cows' milk cheese, which is pressed in handmade moulds produced by local craftsmen; Archie's Choice, a hard-pressed crumbly cheese finished in a distinctive black wax; Captain Smith's Titanic, a cheese where the warm curds are washed in Captain Smith's Ale from the Titanic Brewery in nearby Stoke-on-Trent; the Abbey Beer and Garlic, another cloth-bound cheese that has a hops and garlic finish; the Moorlander, an oak-smoked cheese with a 'rust'-coloured skin – it is a moist, crumbly cheese with a distinctive smoked taste. Other brands are The Cheddleton Cheese, Abbey Delight, Dream of the Abbey, Loxley and Rudyard.

The Ice Cream Trail

Ice cream is a popular dessert the world over and of which there are many variants. The companies included in this trail use a range of different ingredients in order to create a variety of flavours, and have both seasonal and regional flavours such as Gooseberry and Elderflower, Damson and Sloe Gin, Blackberry and Apple Crumble and Christmas Pudding ice cream.

The literature on ice cream suggests that it was first made by the Chinese in the Tang Period (AD 616–907). In this period ice cream was made by heating buffalo, cows' and goats' milk, which was allowed to ferment and was then mixed with flour for thickening and 'frozen' by mixing salt with ice. The process was not evident in Europe until 1503 and even then it was considered a party trick by Italian chemists.

In Europe, ice cream was not used as a food until sorbets appeared in the 1660s in Naples, Italy. In the UK it gained recognition only after being served at a banquet for the Feast of St George at Windsor Castle in 1671, and even then it was only served to the guests on King Charles II's table as it was such a rare and exotic dish; 'one plate of white strawberries and one plate of iced cream' is a well-known quotation from that event – all the other guests had to watch and wonder at what the people at the King's table were eating and guess at the taste.

The subsequent growth in the phenomenon of ice cream led many wealthy people to build ice houses on their estates, some of which are still evident today and are normally pointed out on literature associated with a period building or its grounds/estate. Ice was 'farmed' from lakes, rivers and ponds in winter and stored under straw and bark until summer when it was used for many culinary purposes, including cooling drinks, making water ices and iced creams. The making of the latter was a closely guarded secret for many years in order to protect its exclusivity.

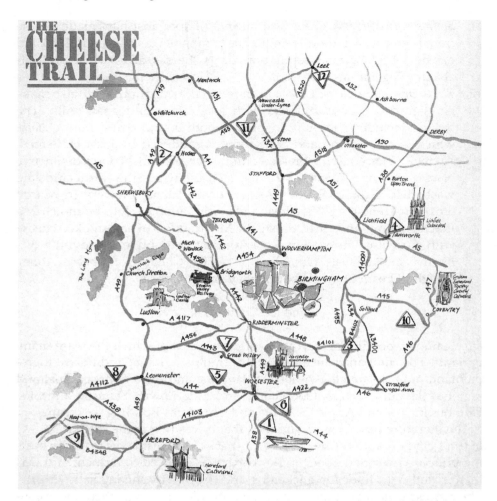

Figure 5.1 A map of the Cheese Trail. Courtesy of the Heart of England Fine Foods Group.

In 1843 an 'Ice Cream Machine' was launched. The machine was a simple structure consisting of a wooden bucket with a rotating handle and packed with salt and ice around a metal container – the slow churning process of the cream, sugar and any added ingredients in the metal container made ice cream. By the end of the 1800s the availability of mechanical refrigeration led to a growth in the ice cream industry, which is very buoyant in today's marketplace.

There are ten companies on the Ice Cream Trail (see Figure 5.2):

1   *Beaconhill Ice Cream* is made on a farm in Ledbury, Herefordshire, using their own Jersey milk and cream. The firm has 18 flavours of ice cream

and sorbets, which are available directly from the supplier under the brand name of Beaconhill Jerseys.

2 *Bennett's Foods Ltd* is an artisan producer of farmhouse ice creams, sorbets and frozen yogurts. The company uses fine ingredients including double cream, real fruit, natural flavours and milk from their own farm. Bennett's stocks over 30 flavours and can also make unique or unusual ones on request. They distribute directly in the south Midlands area and supply throughout central and southern England through wholesalers.

3 *Henley Ice Cream Parlour* is the home of the original Henley Ice Cream, which dates back to 1934. The ice cream was originally made using excess milk from a farm located at their Warwickshire site but it is now made on selected Midlands farms. The product is made from fresh whole milk and extra double cream and there are 31 flavours of ice cream, sorbets and frozen yogurts.

4 *Just Rachel Quality Desserts* was established in 1987 to produce top-quality pure ice creams (and other desserts) using real, whole ingredients that are additive free and locally sourced whenever possible. The firm has won many awards including the Small Producers Award and *The Times*/Waitrose Small Producers Award and their product has been listed as one of the top 50 ice creams in Britain by the *Independent* newspaper. The flavours range from traditional Vanilla, Strawberry and Chocolate to more unusual ones such as Gooseberry and Elderflower, Treacle Toffee and Damson and Sloe Gin. The firm also creates 'specials' using seasonal fruit such as Rhubarb, Orange and Orange Liqueur ice cream in April or Lavender ice cream in July.

5 *Red Lion Farm Ice Cream* is made to a traditional recipe with milk from their own Jersey herd. The firm offers over 25 different flavours, which include Honeycombe, Cappuccino and Ginger and Lime.

6 *Ringswood Ice Cream* produces a real dairy ice cream on a Warwickshire family farm from natural flavours and ingredients. There are ten flavours and each is offered in a range of sizes from 110 ml tubs, 0.5 litre, 1 litre and catering sizes.

7 *Shepherds Ice Cream*, located in the heritage town of Hay-on-Wye (famous for its literary associations and its built heritage as well as the heritage of the surrounding landscape), makes ice cream using whole ewes' milk, which means that it is lower in fats than conventional recipes. Shepherds Ice Cream was placed 15th in the *Independent*'s 'Best 50 Ice Creams'.

8 *Taj Products* make fine-quality Indian Kulfi Ice Cream using whole milk, cream and exotic fruits and nuts. Flavours include Mango, Pistachio, Almond, Coconut and Pineapple. The firm supplies shops, hotels, restaurants and wholesalers.

9 *The September Organic Dairy* makes dairy ice creams using milk, creams and eggs from their own organic dairy farm in Herefordshire. The

company was launched in 1987 and obtained full organic certification in 1999. The ice cream is available in many different outlets and also by mail order, as well as at the farm itself where visitors can also be shown the production process.

10   *Top House Dairy Ice Cream* is a small family business located in Shropshire that makes luxury Italian ice cream in artisan handmade fashion. Vanilla is the biggest-selling flavour and others available include Pannacotta, Malaga, Lemon, Raspberry and Mandarin.

Acknowledgment: Heart of England Fine Foods, 2004.

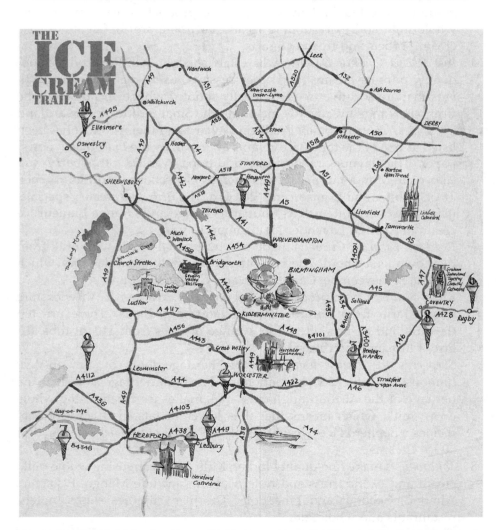

Figure 5.2 A map of the Ice Cream Trail. Courtesy of the Heart of England Fine Foods Group.

The relationship between food and drink and other types of heritage

In Insight 5.5 we identified firms that are included on two trails (Cheese and Ice cream), which form part of a regional branding initiative called 'The Heart of England Fine Food'. The majority of the firms identified are located on or close to the source of their ingredients, which in both cases is mainly milk, either cows', ewes' or goats', but are engaged in a range of different distribution opportunities such as their own retail outlets, use of wholesalers for national (and possibly international) distribution and mail order, the latter a function of the innovation in packaging but also the greater availability of 'postal' services from, for example, courier companies. The trails (or individual business(es)) can become tourist attractions, either for short breaks or part of a longer vacation in a regional area (see Chapter 3).

The fact that there are so many businesses in each of the trails, which only represent one region of the UK, serves to demonstrate the interest in and demand for heritage foods such as cheese and ice cream, both of which have a long heritage and exist, in some form or another, in every country of the world. There is also an attempt by some of the producers to reflect the heritage foods of other countries in their own, such as the use of sun-dried tomatoes (which will have been imported from Spain or Italy) in cheesemaking or the use of Pistachio nuts (definitely not indigenous to the UK but more than likely have been bought from wholesalers who will have acquired them from Pakistan or countries of the Middle East, such as Iran).

There are literally thousands of these types of links to which I could refer but one product that must be discussed, because it is the best-known beverage brand in the world and is also a unique product, is Coca-Cola. In Insight 5.6, I shall briefly discuss Coca-Cola and particularly the relationship between Coca-Cola and the 2004 Athens Olympic Games as, together, both directly and indirectly, they are marketing heritage.

Insight 5.6: Coca-Cola creating 'moments and memories' for local communities along the worldwide Olympic torch relay route

The Olympics

The first modern Olympic Games were held in Athens, Greece in 1896; however, the original homeland of the ancient Olympics, held approximately 3000 years ago was Olympia, in what were then known as the Peloponnese. At the 2004 Games in Athens, as one might expect, much was made of this heritage link at every promotional opportunity.

The city of Olympia in ancient Greece had functioned as a meeting place for politics and religious worship since the tenth century BC. 'The central part of Olympia was dominated by the majestic temple of Zeus, with the temple of Hera parallel to it. The ancient stadium in Olympia could accommodate more than 4000 spectators, while in the surrounding area there were auxiliary buildings which developed gradually up until the fourth century BC and were used as training sites for the athletes or to house the judges of the Games' (International Olympic Committee, 2004).

The ancient Greeks were very much followers of the cult of Zeus and there is a close link between this and the Olympic Games – although the Games were not part of a religious rite or ritual, they did aim to demonstrate the performing and physical capabilities of athletes, which was a form of offering to the gods. The Games also had one further purpose, to bring the various warring towns and cities of Greece closer together in the context of this unique and historic occasion so that they could, at least for a short time, put their differences behind them and focus on what they had in common; this process had a gradual but positive effect.

Winners had flowers thrown at them by the cheering crowds, a palm branch was placed in their hands and on their heads and their hands were tied with red ribbons as a mark of victory. The official award ceremonies were held on the final day of the Games at the temple of Zeus and the overall winner had a sacred olive tree wreath placed on his head; a similar practice was adopted for the Games in 2004 in Greece.

In ancient times, women were not officially allowed to enter the Games but some dressed up as men to do so and took the risk of being thrown off the mountain of Typaion, which was the punishment stipulated in the rules for such subterfuge.

The Olympic Games are divided into those sports that take place in the summer and others in winter, and have been held almost every four years since 1896, as shown in Table 5.10.

The next winter games will be held in Torino in 2006 and the summer games in Beijing in 2008.

For many years the Olympic Games, because of their enormous global profile, have attracted many organizations who wish to promote a product, brand or service through either advertising at the event or sponsorship of it, but they have also been keen to use it as a 'testing ground' for new ones. Multi-nationals with a worldwide brand portfolio, in particular, have long been associated with this event; Coca-Cola, Mars and McDonalds are just some examples.

The year 2004 saw not only the Olympic Games but also other significant sporting events, such as the Euro 2004 Football Championships and the annual Wimbledon Tennis Championships. Coca-Cola's UK subsidiary had a planned spend of £6 million (a combination of advertising and sponsorship) in 2004 to help sales of its isotonic Powerade brand. GlaxoSmithKline supported its Lucozade Sport brand with a £2 million promotional push but

Table 5.10 Locations of Olympic Games since 1896

Location	Year
Summer Games	
Athens	1896
Paris	1900
St Louis	1904
London	1908
Stockholm	1912
Antwerp	1920
Paris	1924
Amsterdam	1928
Los Angeles	1932
Berlin	1936
London	1948
Helsinki	1952
Melbourne	1956
Rome	1960
Tokyo	1964
Mexico City	1968
Munich	1972
Montreal	1976
Moscow	1980
Los Angeles	1984
Seoul	1988
Barcelona	1992
Atlanta	1996
Sydney	2000
Athens	2004
Winter Games	
Chamonix	1924
St Moritz	1928
Lake Placid	1932
Garmisch Partenkirchen	1936
St Moritz	1948
Oslo	1952
Cortina d'Ampezzo	1956
Squaw Valley	1960
Innsbruck	1964
Grenoble	1968
Sapporo	1972
Innsbruck	1976

Continued

Table 5.10 Locations of Olympic Games since 1896 (continued)

Location	Year
Lake Placid	1980
Sarajevo	1984
Calgary	1988
Albertville	1992
Lillehammer	1994
Nagano	1998
Salt Lake City	2002

mainly focused on the Euro 2004 Championships; both brands used a range of mass-market communication channels as the products were aimed not only at the professional sports target market but also at the general public.

Coca-Cola

The Coca-Cola Company is the world's largest beverage company with approximately 400 different beverages in its portfolio. Along with Coca-Cola, recognized by many consumers and often quoted as the world's best-known brand, the company markets four of the world's top five soft drink brands, including Diet Coke, Fanta and Sprite, and a wide range of other beverages including diet and light soft drinks, waters, juices and juice drinks, teas, coffees and sports drinks.

The company has the world's largest distribution system and consumers in more than 200 countries drink the company's beverages at a rate exceeding 1 billion servings each day. For many years it has used the strapline 'Always' and 'The Real Thing', which consistently emphasizes its heritage, linked firmly to the past, whereas the Pepsi company, Coca-Cola's closest competitor, associates its brand with technology and the future.

Coca-Cola was invented by Dr John S. Pemberton and registered as a trademark in 1895, by which time this syrup (that had to be mixed with carbonated water) was being sold in every state in the USA. The Coca-Cola brands are now available in virtually every country of the world.

In 1990, the Coca-Cola company opened a visitor attraction in Atlanta, USA (the location of the international headquarters of the company) to demonstrate the unique heritage of this product and its development through time – 10 million people have visited the site.

In March 2004, to coincide with the ceremonial Olympic flame lighting in ancient Olympia, The Coca-Cola Company unveiled its plans to celebrate and share the experience of the Athens 2004 Olympic Torch Relay, presented by Coca-Cola with local communities in the 27 countries on the first truly global Relay in history. A supporter of the Olympic Movement since 1928, in 2004 Coca-Cola served for the fourth time as a Presenting Partner of the Olympic Torch Relay, although this was the first occasion for any Olympic Games' sponsor to present the Olympic Flame in so many countries. Coca-Cola's extensive local operations around the world helped to present the Olympic Flame in their communities during this historic Relay.

'For millions of people in countries along the international Olympic Torch Relay, this will be their first personal encounter with the unique spirit and tradition of the Olympic Games', said David Brooks, Olympic Torch Relay Director, The Coca-Cola Company. 'The deep local connections we have in each Relay city enable us to create a genuine, community-based approach to this worldwide event.'

'In each city, Coca-Cola will help create festive Relay moments and special memories of the Olympic experience', said Petros Karachalios, general manager, Coca-Cola Athens 2004 Olympic Group. 'Coca-Cola will refresh spectators along the route and provide commemorative pennants. The Company is also contributing to the city celebrations that will cap each day's Relay event, often in the form of renowned entertainment and cultural performances.'

Local torchbearer programmes centred on the themes of 'unity' and 'inspiration' were at the heart of Coca-Cola Relay activities. The Coca-Cola Company offered torchbearer slots to local people who are an inspiration to others or have helped build bridges among individuals, cultures and generations. Following are a few examples of Coca-Cola programmes in local markets around the world.

- *Beijing, China* – Coca-Cola China extended the torchbearer opportunity to people across China – a first for the world's most-populous country. In local provinces, Coca-Cola formed judging panels made up of local education commissions, sports bureaus and the media, ensuring that those selected to carry the Olympic Flame in Beijing represented local regions across China.
- *Cairo, Egypt and Cape Town, South Africa* – Egypt and South Africa were the first African countries in history to welcome the Olympic Flame. In Egypt, in addition to locally nominated torchbearers, Coca-Cola opened the Torch Relay experience to people representing Sudan, Tunisia, Morocco, Cameroon, Ivory Coast and Nigeria, who travelled to Cairo to carry the Olympic Flame.
- *South Africa* – Coca-Cola shared Olympic heritage and the flame's uplifting story through the accounts of four inspirational citizens featured in a 'Real Heroes' campaign. The four were Vusi Mahlanze, who developed polio as a child and later entered the Coca-Cola 'Popstars' talent

competition on television; Mpeki Maepa, a community mother who looks after more than 116 AIDS orphans; Elizabeth Petersen, who runs the St Anne's Homes in Cape Town, which offers shelter and hope to abused and homeless women and their children; and Andre Botha, who helps subsistence farmers unite to produce commercially viable crops.

- *London, England* – for the Relay's first appearance in England in 56 years, Coca-Cola Great Britain sought torchbearers from the Personal Best Challenge Park programme, a pilot playground project that encourages physical activity during school break times.
- *Moscow, Russia* – Coca-Cola partnered with the Moscow Education Committee to identify young athletes as torchbearers for the 3 July Relay in the Russian capital. In each of Moscow's ten administrative districts, Coca-Cola established selection juries of city officials and famous Russian athletes to review nominations. The selected torchbearers were announced in January at the Moscow Young Athletes Ball, sponsored by Coca-Cola.
- *Greece* – Coca-Cola connected in several ways with local Greek communities to celebrate the unique heritage in the country where the Olympic Games were born. One of the most-engaging activities, 'Follow the Flame,' invited five young people, each with four of their friends, to visit one of five cities outside Greece hosting the Olympic Torch Relay. Each group of friends – or 'parea' as they are called in Greece – experienced once-in-a-lifetime moments taking part in the Torch Relay in either Sydney, Australia; Beijing; Cairo, Egypt; New York; or Amsterdam.

Acknowledgment: by kind permission of The Coca-Cola Company, Atlanta, USA, 2004.

Religious heritage and food and drink

Once again, there are many associations between religious heritage and food and drink heritage on which comment could be made. I have therefore been very selective, but I would urge students with an interest in this area to look in the many excellent books available, on the Internet and in journal articles, which can usually be easily accessed through academic (and other) libraries; this is a fascinating subject.

Firstly, what does religion mean? Is it an institutional definition or a personal one that we should follow? Unfortunately it is beyond the scope of this book, never mind this chapter, to engage with such philosophical debates, so the best that I can do is to offer some illustrative examples of the link between an aspect of religious heritage and food and drink.

In Insight 5.6 we made reference to the Greeks and will therefore use this as a starting point for my examples.

For the Greeks, food had all sorts of religious and philosophical meaning. One illustration of this is that they never ate meat unless it had been sacrificed to the gods, after having been caught in the wild, i.e., they did not believe in rearing animals for personal consumption. This concept even extended to vegetables, some of which they believed were 'cleaner' or 'dirtier' than others and which they also firmly believed were either 'accepted' by the gods, or not.

I am not sure how far this idea is practiced in modern Greece but it is analogous to the religious practice of some Hindus, notably in India but in other countries too. For example, a particular type of Hindu, especially the 'Jain's', believe that eating onions and garlic arouses 'passions' that are inconsistent with the worship of God, therefore they adhere to a strict vegetarian diet prepared without these ingredients. Hindus in general do not eat beef as the cow is considered a sacred animal and indeed the vast majority, especially in India, do not eat meat at all, as the killing of animals for food is thought to be inappropriate in terms of one's devotion to God.

The production and consumption of alcohol in most parts of the Indian sub-continent was almost unheard of until the last century and certainly alcohol was never consumed in the company of women. However, today, there are several internationally well-known Indian beers such as 'Kingfisher' and 'Cobra' aimed at both the female and male target markets.

The Islamic and Jewish religions both forbid the eating of pork as the pig is considered to be an unclean animal. This idea has its roots in ancient biblical times when diseased animals were all too evident and was therefore enshrined in later religious doctrine as a way of protecting people.

In China, Taoism believes that curing disease and eating food are for maintaining health and restoring energy, and the purpose of cooking food is for perennial youth and long life. There is therefore a strong relationship between the use of herbs and the religious heritage of China.

Japanese dietary culture has also been influenced by religious beliefs. The two major religions, Buddhism and Shinto, had an effect on Japanese people and their food preferences. Buddhist teachings are very firm on the concept of preserving life and therefore prohibit the consumption of any living thing. The idea of not eating either meat or fish was adopted by emperors and shogun throughout Japanese history, as they had been influenced by the teaching of Buddhism, consequently if people ate meat they had to hide from the law. However, people started to eat meat again after the Meiji Restoration in 1867, as food was gradually introduced into Japan by visitors from Europe. The Japanese also have a long heritage of producing alcoholic drinks, originally made from cereals and consumed with any meal. The best-known product is 'Sake', which is a rice-based drink, 15 per cent of which is alcohol.

'Shojin-ryori' has a deep meaning and was a dish introduced by a high priest after he came back from China during the Kamakura Period. 'Shojin-ryori' was cooked by Buddhist priests and this was considered part of their Buddhist training. The dish is strictly vegetarian and, for the same reasons mentioned above in relation to Hinduism, some vegetables such as the onion, garlic and leek cannot be used in the dish because they are too 'strong'. Further, no cooking spice is used in preparing the dish because each vegetable is considered to have a unique taste.

The 'Shojin-ryori' is thought to be the mother of the Japanese table style, because Kaiseki-ryoti and Hucha-ryori were based on 'Shojin-ryori'; it is also one of the reasons why there are many recipes for vegetable dishes in Japan, never more popular than today because of their health properties.

Recipes and food heritage

In the age of the 'celebrity chef' (a largely UK phenomenon) and his or her 'signature dish', heritage is being created, as both food writers/critics and the consuming public will associate a particular recipe with one person or restaurant. However, even when specific dishes or recipes are not associated with a certain individual, there are thousands with a unique heritage, for a whole variety of different reasons and these can be used as promotional tools to stimulate demand.

For example, many people have heard of 'The Waldorf Salad' and it is generally well-known that this dish originated at The Waldorf Hotel in New York. Therefore, the combination of ingredients that goes into this salad has a heritage, even though it may have spawned many variants under the same name, over the years.

However, certain dishes can have a contested heritage and, in the end, it is up to the individual to select the version that suits his or her personality. One example of this is the Caesar Salad. The salad is made up of a specific type of lettuce, the romaine, which is topped with a dressing. The dish is believed either to have been invented by the Romans (notably at the time of the Roman Emperor Julius Caesar) because of their admiration for this vegetable (they believed it to have unique health benefits) or that its origins are much more recent, being invented in 1924 by Caesar Cardini, a Tijuana restaurateur. A further view is that Caesar Salad was created in 1906 in the USA.

Chicken Cordon Bleu, which is made by stuffing chicken breasts with ham and cheese, is often associated with the French but this recipe has never (until very recent times) appeared in any of the standard French cookbooks. While its origins are difficult to trace, the dish was probably created in New Orleans by a chef who once trained at France's world-famous cooking school, Le Cordon Bleu.

Every country around the world has issues with the heritage of some of its food and drink, and it is probably part of the cultural heritage to relate these stories to successive generations, which is why they are still known today. The following are some examples from China (these have been chosen because the Chinese believe that a dish that is named after an important person gives it more prestige).

- *Beggar's Chicken* – this is a story about a homeless, starving beggar who is wandering along a road when he catches sight of a chicken. The beggar, desperate for food, kills the chicken by wringing its neck and as he has no stove on which to cook it, covers the chicken in mud, makes a fire and bakes it. During the wait, an Emperor passes by with his staff and, attracted by the aroma of the baked chicken, stops and dines with the beggar, demanding to know how he created such a delicious meal. The signature dish of this beggar (!) was subsequently added to the list of dishes served at the Imperial Court and has always been known as 'Beggar's Chicken'. However, not everyone is entirely comfortable with the title of this recipe and it is now sometimes called 'Fu Guai Gai' or 'Rich and Noble Chicken'.
- *Lion's Head Meatballs* – this dish contains huge meatballs (roughly the size of tennis balls) that are often served with cabbage to represent the lion's mane; they have been made and served for hundreds of years in exactly the same way.
- *Kung Po Chicken* – this dish is named after an official, in some versions a General, who lived during the Ching dynasty. In other stories he is a crown prince who discovered this dish while travelling and brought it back to the Imperial Court and there is further confusion about whether the dish originated in Shanghai or Szechuan. 'Kung Po was the title given to the person charged with protecting the heir apparent, as Kung meant castle and Po meant to protect. During a certain period the Kung Po was a man whose favourite dish happened to be spiced chicken with peanuts and thus over time it was named after him' (Chen, 1994).

CASE STUDY 5.1: Buccleuch – Scotland's first heritage brand

The Buccleuch name is granted only to selected authentic and original food and drink products made by family and small businesses in and around the Scottish estates of The Duke of Buccleuch. As Scotland's first heritage food and drink brand, it is providing an appropriate showcase for some of the region's best locally produced fine foods.

The range currently comprises seven conserve relishes, classic Scottish biscuits, jellies, preserves, mustards, pickles, chutney, ales and handmade chocolates.

With a rich heritage dating back 700 years of Scottish history, the Buccleuch family is well-known for judicious stewardship of its fertile lands, a pedigree of expert husbandry and committed support for the rural community. More recently,

Buccleuch Estates has established a first-class reputation among Britain's top chefs, including Gordon Ramsay, Anton Edelmann at Allium and George Fuchs at the Savoy, for producing the finest Scottish beef and fresh produce.

The Earl's family is one of the largest landowners in Europe, with 270 000 acres and three stately homes, plus a multi-million-pound commercial property portfolio and an impressive collection of art.

The introduction of a range of locally produced foods and drinks bearing the name is a vital element of the family's integrated approach to rural development in Dumfries & Galloway and the Scottish Borders. Accordingly, The Duke of Buccleuch and Queensberry and his son, The Earl of Dalkeith, are both taking a close and personal interest.

Local producers are selected for the excellence of their food and drink but must also demonstrate the knowledge, skills and passion to maintain the quality of every existing product and to develop new ones. They are also required to meet the high standards of production and food safety imposed by Buccleuch Heritage Foods.

Ensuring product excellence and originality

The heritage brand can be seen on both traditional and original Scottish products and recipes. The initial ranges will evolve to include new products and new ranges will be introduced.

The company has recruited experienced professionals from the food and drink industry to ensure the necessary quality control and innovation; these include Anton Edelmann, Mizie Wilson (editor-in-chief of new quality food magazine *Delicious*) and Jayne Stanes (director of the Academy of Culinary Arts). The work of these people is complemented by meeting regularly in the seventeenth-century kitchen at the Duke's Dumfriesshire home, Drumlanrig Castle with members of the Buccleuch family and with some of Britain's leading chefs and food experts. These 'Buccleuch Kitchen Clan' gatherings are hosted by the Duke's son, The Earl of Dalkeith. The mission of the 'Kitchen Clan' is to taste, refine and select existing and original products for the Buccleuch Estates range and discuss recipes, processes, skills and ideas with the local producers.

Behind the brand

The Buccleuch producers who make the different foods in the Buccleuch range from their original or favourite recipes are:

1 Fiona Hesketh and her family, who run a food manufacturing facility in Gatehouse of Fleet. They make pickles, chutney, mustards, conserves and preserves, and latterly, conserve relishes.
2 John Mellis is an experienced bee keeper who produces the Buccleuch honeys.

3 Robert and Christine Irving and their son Keith run the family bakery in Castle Douglas, which produces the biscuits in the Buccleuch range.
4 Gillian Houston is a Scottish chocolatier who makes the luxurious handmade chocolates.
5 The Henderson family runs Sulwath Brewery in Castle Douglas, Scotland's most southerly micro-brewery, which produces the real ales.
6 A number of other local businesses are currently working on developing traditional or new ranges in a variety of product areas from honeys, preserves, ice cream and porridge to chilled products such as smoked salmon, sausages, haggis, cheese and smoked meats.

Buccleuch Estates

The Buccleuch Estates are owned by His Grace, the Duke of Buccleuch and Queensberry and this 'family business' has always maintained a careful and consistent balance between commerce, stewardship and countryside. Their philosophy is that 'we are simply the managers of a piece of countryside in which the most essential ingredients are the people who live in it'.

The Estates' latest venture, Buccleuch Heritage Foods, will help family and other small food and drink producers from Dumfries and Galloway and the Scottish Borders to find new and/or wider markets for their locally made products. Like the Buccleuch Estates generally, Buccleuch Heritage Foods is in the business of adding value to the region and its people and is committed to an on-going investment in this part of Scotland.

Buccleuch Heritage Foods has strong links with Scottish Enterprise Dumfries and Galloway and Scottish Enterprise Borders, built up during the business development of Buccleuch Scotch Beef. Buccleuch continues to work in close partnership with the Enterprise Companies to support and encourage the small fine food and drink businesses operating on the Estates.

Covering some 400 square miles of beautiful Scottish countryside in Dumfries and Galloway and the Scottish Borders, the Buccleuch Estates are steeped in a rich history dating back 700 years to Robert the Bruce. Nevertheless, the Estates have had great success in moving with the times, initiating ventures and finding new markets that support the rural economy.

The Buccleuch Scottish Beef story is a good example. Since its inception as a business to market beef from the Buccleuch Estates and locality in 1996, the company has grown in size and stature and now employs 30 people. According to The Duke of Buccleuch, 'Buccleuch Estates is part of a community that ensures the land is sufficiently productive to provide its people with a worthwhile living and, at the same time, present a beautiful environment for the present and future enjoyment of everyone; that's why our plans for foods that carry the Buccleuch name are long term and must be synonymous with quality, integrity and authenticity'.

About the range

- *Buccleuch Scottish Beef* – Buccleuch Scottish Beef is already well established as the first choice of the UK's leading chefs and restaurants and it is now available to the general public. All Buccleuch cattle are grass fed and traditionally reared in the glorious Scottish countryside. Buccleuch Butchers then take over, using traditional craft skills to ensure all cuts are expertly prepared. Each cut of premium quality Buccleuch Scottish Beef is fully traceable from the farm where the cattle are born to the outlet in which it is sold.
- *Pickles and chutney* – Buccleuch Poacher's Pickle, Hot Tomato Pickle and Spiced Peach Chutney are made by Fiona Hesketh (see above) and this company is also making mustards, a marmalade and a jelly for the Buccleuch brand. They are all presented in attractive and distinctive 312 g screw-top jars.
- *Mustards* – Buccleuch Scottish Crunchy Mustard and Original Galloway Mustard are both made to original Scottish recipes. The mustard seeds are ground by Fiona Hesketh and her colleagues at the Gatehouse of Fleet mill. Both mustards are presented in attractive and distinctively packaged wide-mouth, screw-top 280 g jars.
- *Preserves and jellies* – Buccleuch Bramble Jelly is made from a unique Scottish recipe, using locally grown brambles that are pressed by hand. These are cooked slowly in small pans to produce a distinctive and exceptional-tasting jelly; it is presented in attractive and distinctively packaged 340 g jars.
- *Conserve relishes* – Apple and Ginger, Chilli and Honey, Spiced Rhubarb and Ginger, Plum and Port, Spiced Apricot and Banana, Mulled Cranberry, and Rhubarb and Dill conserve relishes offer seven varieties of this delicious and distinctive product innovation. The conserve relish range was awarded a Scottish Enterprise Award in 2004 at the time of its launch for 'outstanding' flair and innovation. Created by Scottish chef consultant and writer Liz Ashworth especially for Buccleuch, the recipes were inspired by traditional Scottish expertise with conserves, chutneys and pickles. The conserve relishes can be served hot or cold as a sauce or used as a savoury spread or chutney; they are equally versatile when used as an ingredient in recipes and meals.
- *Conserves* – Gooseberry and Strawberry, Raspberry and Redcurrant, Raspberry and Heather Honey, and Rhubarb and Elderflower conserves are based on combining natural local produce to create luxurious recipes. The conserves are developed exclusively for Buccleuch and all the ingredients are hand-stirred in small pans to ensure products that are comparable with the very best home-made preserves. They are all available in 340 g jars. The four conserves are based on traditional recipes and fruit combinations that were developed at the end of the eighteenth century by Joseph Florence, the celebrated chef at Drumlanrig Castle, the ancestral home of The Duke of Buccleuch.
- *Honey* – Buccleuch Scottish Heather Honey and Scottish Blossom Honey are both pure and natural. John Mellis produces both types of honey from bees

that are kept on and around the grounds of the Buccleuch Estates. In July of each year, John moves his bees to the Scottish moors in order for the bees to collect from ling heather, giving them the best opportunity to make honey in a natural and fertile environment. Buccleuch Scottish Heather Honey has a strong smoky flavour, which is not overly sweet, reflecting a traditional Scottish taste; it is packed in a 350 g jar. Buccleuch Scottish Blossom Honey is harvested throughout the summer and includes nectar from Scottish clover, willow herb, wild raspberry, bramble and lime to give it a mild, sweet flavour; it is also packed in a 340 g jar.

- *Special Scottish Biscuits* – Scottish Butter Shortbread; Original Galloway Oat Cakes; Perkins; Sultana Drops and Galloway Oat Crunchies are made by the Irving family and their colleagues in Castle Douglas. Robert and Christine Irving farmed for many years close to Castle Douglas and the family began selling their home-baked products from their modest farm shop in the mid 1980s. These proved so successful that they soon moved to a small bakehouse in Castle Douglas in 1988. Subsequently, when their son Keith joined them in the business some 10 years ago, they invested in a state-of-the-art bakery in the town. The Irvings pride themselves on producing biscuits of the same quality and recipes as those that they hand-produced and baked on their farm when they first started selling to friends and farm-shop customers nearly 20 years ago. All Buccleuch biscuits are attractively packaged in 200 g traditional, tall biscuit 'tins' with a lid and the Galloway Oat Cakes also come in a 70 g pack.

- *Chocolates* – Buccleuch Whisky, Cherry, Banoffee, Raspberry Flower Dome, Cointreau Milk Swan and Mocha Coffee Bean – a selection of six flavours, the Buccleuch family's favourites are handmade by Scottish chocolatier Gillian Houston exclusively for the heritage sub-brand. Buccleuch Whisky is a blend of milk chocolate and Buccleuch malt whisky; Cherry consists of a fresh Amarena cherry enrobed in a white chocolate ganache blended with cherry juice; Raspberry Flower Dome is a combination of fresh raspberry puree and a raspberry liqueur blended with milk chocolate ganache; Banoffee is a delicious blend of banana and vanilla ganache with soft caramel topping; Cointreau Milk Swan is a milk chocolate blended with Cointreau liqueur; and Mocha Coffee Bean is a milk chocolate ganache blended with coffee liqueurs.

- *Real Ales* – Bold Buccleuch Premium Lager, Auld Wat Premium Ale, Black Ormiston Porter and Redcloak Premium Ale are the four real ales produced exclusively for Buccleuch Heritage Foods by Scotland's most southerly microbrewery, Sulwath Brewery in Castle Douglas, which is run by the Henderson family. Bold Buccleuch Premium Lager is a 100 per cent natural, 5 per cent ABV lager beer; it is named after the sixteenth-century Scott of Buccleuch who was nicknamed 'Bold' when he made a commando-style raid on Carlisle Castle in 1596. Auld Wat Premium Ale is a 100 per cent natural, 4.6 per cent ABV beer. 'Auld Wat' of Harden, whose legend inspired the brew, was a fierce, big-bellied reiver. Reivers were the warrior-like families who lived in the 'Debateable Land' on the Scottish/England border at the end of the sixteenth century and into the seventeenth century, who enjoyed nothing better than a good bout of cattle-rustling south of the border. Black Ormiston is a 4.4 per cent ABV and 100 per cent natural Premium Porter. 'Ormiston' was known as both an outlaw of Scotland and a murderer, despite being recorded by the Scottish Parliament as 'clean exempted'; like Auld Wat, he was a typical reiver. Redcloak Premium Ale is a 100 per cent natural, 5 per cent ABV beer. It is named after 'Redcloak Bell', an ally of the Buccleuchs at the time when these and other families living in the 'Debateable Land' on the Scottish/England border, prior to the crowns of both countries being united in 1603, 'debated' issues by rustling, raiding and skirmishing. The beers are presented in traditional 500 ml bottles and will be sold both individually and in gift packs comprising all four types.

Distribution of Buccleuch products

Buccleuch products were sold in a limited number of 'premium' retail outlets in Scotland in their first year but are now being launched in the rest of the UK and will soon be available in selected food stores, delis and independent food specialists.

The public are now able to buy any of the range of Buccleuch Estates products and Buccleuch Scotch Beef and other Buccleuch fresh meat, fish or seafood direct, either by telephone or via their newly launched website.

Acknowledgment: by kind permission of Morag Mclachlan, Buccleuch Heritage Brands Ltd, Castle Douglas, Scotland, 2004.

Questions

1 Briefly explain the difference between a traditional food or drink and one that is original.
2 How does the connection with aristocracy help this organization?
3 Identify at least two further foods and beverages that could be added to the Buccleuch range in the next three years.
4 Comment on the philosophy of this company: 'we are simply the managers of a piece of countryside in which the most essential ingredients are the people who live in it'.
5 Which market development opportunities exist for the sub-brand of Buccleuch Heritage Foods that have not already been exploited?
6 What are the added-value benefits of the Buccleuch Heritage Foods sub-brand?
7 Comment on the flavours of the chocolates marketed under the Buccleuch Heritage sub-brand.
8 Look at the logo of this company in Figure 5.3, how is the concept of heritage evident?

Figure 5.3 Two short marketing communications used by Buccleuch Foods. Courtesy of Buccleuch Estates, Scotland.

Figure 5.3 continued

Figure 5.4 An advertisement to celebrate the 2004 Scottish Food and Drink Excellence Award presented to Buccleuch Foods.

CASE STUDY 5.2: Hamble Valley – The Strawberry Coast

The Hamble Valley lies on the Hampshire coast and in 2004 celebrated its third food and drink festival, which is part of the countywide Hampshire Food Festival.

Festivals, as we saw in Chapter 3, are or can become part of the cultural heritage of an area and this is the case with the Hamble Valley Food Festival, which despite being only three years old has come to be regarded as an important heritage event.

The celebration of food at the Hamble Valley Food Festival explores both traditional and new types of food and many related concepts, such as the food of ethnic communities.

The event ran from 26 June to 11 July in 2004, and included a very wide range of events. Some examples are:

1 *Mediaeval Meals and More – food heritage in Hampshire.* The church of St Nicholas was the setting for many different activities that took place during the festival, all of which had a heritage connection either with the church itself or, for example, with a famous local person from the past. The activities ranged from a talk about the heritage of food locally and across Hampshire (this coincided with the launch of a new information leaflet from the council entitled *Hampshire's Food Heritage*); a demonstration of period dishes in the context of a

re-enactment of mediaeval village life; and information about quinces and spices that were brought to England by sailors and tradespeople in the past.

2   *Sausage Feastleigh* was a musical barbecue feast held on the Green outside the original farm that occupied the area for hundreds of years. There were 25 varieties of sausage on offer supplied by a local award-winning butcher, together with relishes and sauces made by local producers, all served with local beers – a real celebration of local culinary and cultural heritage.

3   *A Merrie Feast in Chandler's Ford* was a walk to this heritage village, which is surrounded by age-old woodland and fields, finishing with a meal at Hiltonbury Farmhouse pub.

4   *'Mr Darcy's Dinner' in the company of Jane Austen* was an event hosted by the Marquis of Lansdowne at his country estate Botley Park. The main idea was to provide a dinner of fine food and drink in the company of a Jane Austen actor and therefore, to recreate the ambience of that Regency period, diners were encouraged to dress up as 'Jane Austen characters'.

5   *Memories of D-Day Tea Dance* was hosted in conjunction with the local history society with the aim of '[taking you] back 60 years in time'. The event included music by the Earl Grey Ensemble and an exhibition of war memorabilia. Guests to this event were invited to dress up from the period.

6   *Special Open Day at Burlesdon Windmill.* The special open day enabled visitors to explore Hampshire's only working windmill, built by Phoebe Langtry in 1813, and to purchase stoneground flour from the mill as well as speciality bread, cakes and biscuits made from the mill's own flour.

7   *Wine and Cheese Tutored Tasting and Talk.* The local Wickham Vineyard was the venue for this tutored tasting of their wines, together with a talk about winemaking and an insight into the life of Wickham vineyard. Lyburn Farmhouse Cheesemakers, a local firm, supplied the accompaniments.

8   *William Cobbett's Botley* was a guided walk of the area to illustrate why the eighteenth-century author and political commentator described Botley as 'the most delightful village in the world' and also to explain why it has such a rich pub heritage.

9   *French Street Market on Hamble Quay.* 'The atmosphere of France' was created by inviting Normandy suppliers to offer their patisserie products, olives, dried fruit, coffee, jams, confectionary, charcuterie and other goods such as jewellery, handbags and soaps.

10   *Gales Beers Tutored Tasting.* Gales are the oldest independent family brewing company in Hampshire who produce prize-winning ales. Their brands include HSB, Festival Mild and Gales Best Bitter, each of which was on offer at this tutored tasting by the head brewer, Derek Lowe.

11   *A Taste of Bollywood* was a celebration of Indian culture and included a cookery demonstration of Indian heritage foods such as samosas and naan breads, together with dance performances and readings from Indian literature, which also has a long and rich heritage.

12   *Farmers' Produce and Craft Market on Hamble Quay* was a representation from local producers of a wide range of foods and drink, including soft fruit,

vegetables, pickles and preserves, free range eggs, smoked fish and meat, cheese, garlic, bread, biscuits and fudge.

Acknowledgment: website: http://hamblevalley.com, 2004.

Questions

1   In general, who are the main target markets for an event such as the Hamble Valley Food Festival?
2   Identify at least one specifically profiled target market for each of the events listed above.
3   Look at the information relating to the specific events carefully and identify the heritage aspects.
4   If you were to add another heritage event, what would be the theme and who would be the target market?
5   The use of an information leaflet on the wider Hampshire Food Festival and the website identified above are two communication vehicles used. Identify at least two other marketing communications possibilities.
6   Food festivals, together with many other substitute events, take place in the UK, Europe and most other places throughout the year. Identify at least two events that could compete with a food festival for consumers' time and money.
7   If you were given the brief for differentiating this food festival from others that take place, what would be your unique selling proposition(s) (USP)?

CASE STUDY 5.3: Twinings – a tea for every taste

The exact date of the first-known tea drink remains a mystery but the Chinese were the first to savour its pleasures 5000 years ago (around 2737 BC). Tea did not arrive in Europe until the middle of the sixteenth century when Portugal established a trading centre in Macao (China) and began to send this product back. Because it was so rare, it was very expensive and consequently it was only consumed by royalty, nobility and aristocracy. Coffee, however, was consumed in vast quantities by all sections of European society.

Tea arrived in England around 1653 during Cromwell's protectorate. It was originally marketed as a medicinal draught – an advertisement in a London gazette from the time stated 'That Excellent and by all Physicians approved China drink, called by the Chineans Tcha, by other nations Tay alias Tea'.

Thomas Garaway, a tea merchant, sold it at his London coffee house, Garaways, and also made much of its medicinal properties, advertising it as a cure that '... maketh the body active and lusty ... helpeth the head-ache, giddiness ... cleareth the sight ... vanquisheth heavy dreams ... easeth the brain ... is good for colds, dropsies and scurveys'.

However, despite these unique selling points (!) it did not really become popular until 1660 and in particular until Charles II married the Portuguese Princess Catherine of Braganza in 1662 – she bought with her a large chest of tea as part of her dowry and the drink subsequently became fashionable.

Initially tea was drunk 'green' (the original colour of the hand-picked leaf) without milk or sugar and was served at that time in handless 'cups' from brown stoneware pots, just as it was custom to do so in the Orient. 'Tea was blended at a little table by the mistress of the house in a pleasingly graceful ritual. Liqueurs like orange-brandy, ratafia and "Barbadoes-waters" frequently accompanied or followed the tea' (Simpson, 1986).

By the eighteenth century tea was immensely popular throughout England although it remained expensive, mainly because of the tax levied on it by governments who saw this as an easy way of generating revenue. However, in spite of the cost, it gradually came to replace gin as the drink of the 'common man', thereby slowly improving public health over a period of time.

The British government attempted to levy this tax on tea in American colonies also but to no avail, indeed this proposition saw one of the most famous uprisings ever known, that of the 'Boston Tea Party' when, in 1773, 'guests' came dressed in Red Indian outfits to renounce tea in favour of American independence. Following this, Pitt the Younger reduced the tax on tea, which further stimulated the demand.

The demand for tea led to the creation of two 'themed' 'tea palaces' at Vauxhall in London and Ranelagh in Essex. Visitors were charged a small entrance fee and then allowed to participate in a range of events: tea-drinking in mock-Chinese houses, suppers, firework displays and lantern-lit walks were just some of what was on offer and every layer of society might be represented at any one time.

However, one of the most significant contributors to the rise in tea-drinking was Josiah Wedgewood, who kept the prices of his tea sets low enough to allow all (but the poorest) to purchase one. Tea at that time was a social event, to be taken with friends, and therefore it was best served on an elegant tea service.

During the Victorian era, tea had been discovered growing wild in India and was soon being exported in vast quantities from this British colony; this tea, however, was black. The profile and popularity of tea was maintained by well-known figures at the time, including William Gladstone, Lord Wellington and Queen Victoria, who had a special Balmoral tea service made by Minton. This was the start of the 'souvenir era' and tea services in particular were embossed with themes to commemorate special events or anniversaries.

> In 1826, honest Quaker John Horniman started to measure tea leaves into sealed paper packets with a guaranteed net weight before selling them ... he was eventually bought out by two orphaned teenage brothers, the Tetleys, who had made some money peddling tea to inaccessible Yorkshire villages.
>
> (Simpson, 1986: 23)

Further into this century, fast three-masted ships called clippers were specially built in order to transport tea to Europe from the colonies. Their races across the oceans and into the Thames, bringing with them the new season's teas, led to gambling on a national scale. The use of these ships came to an end with advances in technology that created the steam ships, which used the newly opened Suez Canal in 1869.

In the Edwardian era the time for tea had moved to 5p.m. and the ritual had become an even more full-blown eating and drinking affair than had hitherto been the case (see Insight 5.2 on The Ritz Hotel). All manner of advice on tea drinking rituals began to appear and, for the first time, dedicated 'tea shops' began to do brisk business. The first of these was The Aerated Bread Company (ABC shops) in 1864, which enabled people to drink tea and eat cakes on the premises. The success of these ABC shops was enormous, which gave rise to further tea shops managed by Express dairies; J. Lyons and tea shops in department stores such as Whiteleys in London and, of course, The Ritz Hotel.

Although the Second World War and many changes in trends and fashions for food and drink have had an effect on the concept of afternoon tea, tea in itself '... has still not lost its symbolic or emotional status in England. Whenever anything momentous occurs, whether matter for celebration or tragedy, a pot of tea is produced' (Simpson, 1986: 23).

'Tea enters the twenty-first century more popular than ever ... the consumption of tea increases and the conditions of the people who pick it continue to improve' (R. Twining and Company Ltd, 2001). In the developed world demand is increasing, particularly in the last few years for 'speciality teas' (see below), such as those offered in the Twinings' range. The demand for tea from the developing world is also increasing but for reasons more similar to those that established tea drinking in England in the sixteenth and seventeenth centuries.

The amount of tea harvested worldwide each year is approximately 3 million tonnes and there are increasing moves by producers and suppliers to consider all the ethical issues involved. The Tea Sourcing Partnership is one example of such a move; it is a long-term initiative to continuously improve the conditions under which tea is produced and is entirely funded by major UK tea companies.

Acknowledgment: R. Twining & Co. Ltd, 2005.

Questions

1 From the narrative above, identify and briefly explain three aspects of tea heritage in the context of marketing.
2 What do you think are the main ethical considerations in relation to the production, distribution and marketing of a product such as tea?
3 From the list of 'speciality' teas marketed by Twinings, choose three and briefly explain who you think might be the target market for this sub-brand.
4 Twinings has asked you to design new packaging for the 50 tea bag variants of their tea. Briefly describe what the considerations might be and suggest a packaging design.

Summary

This chapter has been the most complex of all, as not only are there significant links to be made with topics and issues in the previous chapters but there are also numerous new ideas that can be explored. Unfortunately, publishing limitations have restricted me to the above analysis only.

However, we can clearly see that food and drink plays a vital role in establishing part of the heritage of most (if not all) countries around the world. Many countries are busy marketing what they have to offer, in order to encourage either inward tourism or the consumption of brands in consumers' home countries. The export markets for many food and drink manufacturers are worth millions, if not billions of dollars, pounds, euros, etc.; the branding and marketing of food and drink, more often than not associating it with its country of origin (heritage), is a global industry that can only be measured in terms of currency billions.

Discussion questions and activities

1   Identify a food and/or drink festival that takes place in a country of your choice and select at least two aspects of heritage that are associated with this event. Briefly explain and describe each one.
2   From a country of your choice choose a product that has a unique heritage, such as the Scotch Whisky example given above. Describe and explain the heritage of this product and its significance to the economy and individuals who live in that country.
3   Identify a target market at which a heritage food or drink product or brand is aimed. What are the psychographic or behavioural characteristics of this group that makes them particularly likely to consume such a product or brand?
4   Choose a retail organization that has a heritage in its own right but is particularly associated with food and/or drink. Critically evaluate the relationship between this organization and the brands it offers.
5   Buy a food or drink brand that is clearly marketed because of its heritage. Critically evaluate the packaging or labelling – how could this be improved for the target market at which the brand is aimed?

Recommended reading

Bainbridge, J. (2003) Whisky innovation mustn't be at cost of existing values. *Marketing Magazine*, December, 4, 15.
Chen, H. (1994) *Helen Chen's Chinese Home Cooking*. William Morrow.
Dickens, C. (1837) *Oliver Twist*. Penguin Classics, London.
Hall, M.C. and Mitchell, R. (2001) Wine and food tourism. In Douglas, Norman, Douglas, Ngaire and Derret Ros (eds) *Special Interest Tourism*. Wiley, Sydney.
King, E.B. (2003) *Are French wines screwed?* http://www.brandchannel.com
King, E.B. (2004) *Engaging the Aging: Marketing to Europe's Seniors*. http://www.brandchannel.com
Reuters Business Insight and TNS (2003) *The Older Consumer*.

Ritson, M. (2003) Parma Ham maintains heritage as EU strikes blow for branding. *Marketing Magazine*, 13, 11.
Simpson, H. (1986) The London Book of Ritz Afternoon Tea. The Art and Pleasures of Taking Tea. Random House, London.
Yin-Fei Lo, E. (2001) *The Chinese Kitchen*. Random House, USA.

Chapter 6

Company heritage marketing

Introduction

We have seen in previous chapters that whether it is long-haul holidays, business travel, short breaks or food and drink, there is a growing global social phenomenon where the common theme and demand is for all aspects of heritage. The heritage industry has not only grown to unprecedented levels, but has come to develop sectors (such as heritage tourism) and create demand that was not necessarily predicted. In this fascinating scenario we have another emerging trend, that of business organizations attempting to capture their corporate heritage and to use this for marketing, especially to create a point of differentiation for competitive purposes; this applies equally to small, medium and large (even 'multi-national') organizations. 'In a world of increasing over-choice and globalisation, or Americanisation, consumers are seeking out brands (and companies) with genuine history and authenticity' (Stewart-Allen, 2002).

This chapter is therefore about the relationships that customers are now seeking with organizations. One way for organizations to respond is by incorporating aspects of their heritage in different types of marketing communications as, at the very least, this usually has the effect of **reassuring** customers and therefore makes commercial sense. The deeper perspective is that by emphasizing certain values, the organization can build **reputation and trust**, which has the positive effect on consumers of an increased perceived quality of the firm and its products, brands or services and creates a 'goodwill' bank that leads consumers to become more positively disposed towards it, creating an **evoked mind-set** that would take some significant 'wrong doings' to change.

Consumers are increasingly assessing organizations on their ethical values, behaviour and stance in society, which has a direct effect on the value of the corporate brand or the brand(s) of that firm. 'As consumerism develops, so the consumer demands on companies grow. In an era when customers expect more and more from companies . . . they are also becoming more cynical about the corporate sector as a whole, and multi-nationals in particular. Companies need to understand this . . . they need to engage in a much more proactive way with society and its citizens . . . they need to become "citizen brands". Post-Enron, this has become even more important' (Willmott, 2002).

In the previous chapter, and also in Chapter 1, we have identified that a nation's general perception of itself (its identity, as expressed by consumers when they are asked how they 'see' themselves in terms of a nation and also with respect to the types of benefits sought in the consumption of certain goods and services) can be an important determining factor in the choice of products and services. The perception of other nations can also be an influential factor in the choice of certain goods and services.

> Recent studies by the UK's British Brands Group, amongst others, claim that this [British] heritage can make a difference in global markets because of the positive impact 'Britishness' makes in international markets.
>
> (Stewart-Allen, 2002)

For example, the positive perception of Americans in relation to British goods and services is largely the result of associations that they make in their minds between these brands (or organizations) and the heritage of the country as a whole, or specific aspects of its heritage. In a recent large-scale consumer study, the evidence gathered confirmed this view and concluded that Americans are 30 per cent more likely to buy British today than they were ten years ago; heritage branding can therefore be a useful tool for **developing new markets**.

The study found that Americans have a generally positive perception of high quality for all British goods and services, but in particular luxury men's goods, for which they are price insensitive and do not perceive any notable risk associated with the consumption of these premium-priced brands. This is an ideal marketing scenario for British manufacturers/traders, particularly in New York, where consumers have a very high affinity for all things British; more on this concept, below.

The quote above reinforces a view held by many authors on business in international markets and which we have begun to establish above, i.e., that consumers are increasingly in the market for brands with a 'history' and are authentic (the latter is an issue that we have covered in previous chapters). However, promoting this point of differentiation is not without its problems, as consumers in different countries range in their perceptions of the same issue. For example, the Japanese perceive British brands as leading-edge, innovative and inventive, whilst Americans have a greater sense of tradition and history associated with the same brands. However, the Japanese will often also look to the heritage of Britain or the UK to reinforce brand preference.

In short, marketers need to observe the fundamental relationships between consumers, the organization and its brands and the society in which all operate. 'The challenge for brands is great. While maintaining their traditional roles as guarantors of quality and instruments of identity they need also to embrace the individualism, complexity and wider concerns of the modern world. In particular, they need to embrace more social values' (Willmott, 2002).

In this chapter I want to look specifically at how companies use either themselves and/or their brands with associated aspects of heritage for competitive advantage. There are many examples, insights and case studies in the previous chapters that have (sometimes tentatively) explored this notion but the marketing cornerstone on which I wish to focus on in this chapter is **branding**.

The structure of this chapter is slightly different to previous ones as I have put forward all the theoretical arguments first, followed by a range of insights and then the case studies.

What exactly is a brand?

Branding is currently defined as a set of expectations and associations evoked from experience with a company, product or service, i.e., it is about what customers feel and think of the company and/or its products or services. If this perception is positive, it is likely to lead to advances in market share and profitability. The associations made in the minds of consumers, whether positive, negative or neutral, combine to create the **brand's equity**, which can be measured in financial terms.

In 2001, the American Marketing Association (AMA) suggested 'the brand represents the culture of all who touch the business, [including] its employees, its alliances, its suppliers and its consumers'. In 2002, an article in the *Journal of Consumer Marketing* argued '. . . customers do not have a relationship with a product or service; they have a relationship with a brand'. The product or service therefore is generic, but the brand has a **soul and personality**. The brand can give meaning and identity to its user; thus its benefits can be functional, symbolic and psychological, i.e., feelings, view of self, experience, trust and loyalty.

The concept of trust (often linked to the heritage of an organization) seems to have captured the creative imagination of many in management and is being increasingly used as a point of leverage or differentiation. 'Insurance giant New York Life will seek to leverage a $43 million advertising campaign built on a strong heritage and values message' (Kenneth, 2002). Executives at the firm called this the 'Heritage' initiative and advertised the message on both network and cable television. The concept of building trust across different cultural markets was also a top priority for the firm and they planned to use the same message ('The company you keep') but translated into different languages. The company spent US$3 million on advertisements in the first six months of 2002, US$30.2 million in 2001 and US$41 million in 2000 but, despite the scale-down in activity year-on-year, the revenue generated was showing an annual increase of approximately 12 per cent.

The soul of a brand, then, is its unalterable essence that incorporates **the values of the organization**. In 2003, BMW decided to embark on a relationship marketing exercise in order to develop long-term ties with its consumers by launching a direct marketing initiative that could be rolled out across the range of cars in the portfolio. Initially, the company launched a direct marketing campaign for its 5-series cars, which focused and used as a theme the heritage of the BMW brand, namely by charting its genealogy – this was a new departure for the company in terms of advertising.

The vast majority of writers on branding also argue that a brand has a personality, i.e. a character (analogous to that of a human). The brand's personality reflects the organization's culture and heritage. A **brand's attributes** (again, just like the case of a human individual) are those images or perceptions that people store in their minds and associate with the brand, for example whether it represents and evokes a particular 'section' of society (see the example of Burberry in Singapore, below).

In short, the value proposition of any brand is made up of the attributes shown in Figure 6.1.

Another term commonly used to describe the above is **brand franchise**, because the values of a brand can be transferred on to a range of (different) products and services, something that many organizations do incrementally. One example is Benetton, originally in the market for the sale of

FUNCTIONAL BENEFITS

+

EMOTIONAL BENEFITS

+

SELF-EXPRESSIVE BENEFITS

+

RELATIVE PRICE

Figure 6.1 The value proposition of a brand.

Italian-designed clothing (mainly woollen jumpers), over a period of time they successfully used the strong and positive association that consumers had with this brand and franchised it on to other types of clothing and accessories, followed by perfumes and toiletries, luggage, etc.

The brand franchise is the organization's essential link with customers and is therefore the life-blood of the business. Let us look at the estimated value of some well-known brands from all over the world (Table 6.1).

Undoubtedly, it is critical that senior personnel understand how to manage a brand appropriately in the context of the market in which it competes and also how to develop the brand (and customers in relation to it) in order to enhance the brand's equity.

Brands can also fall foul of the market, for a variety of different reasons. This, too, needs to be managed, especially if that brand is to either stay in the market or be bought back at a later stage. One example of a marketing communications activity that is frequently used to counteract injury to the brand (which might be of the organization's own doing) is PR – much can be said and claimed in order to try and limit the damage and re-develop/ re-launch the brand, as appropriate.

Many authors on branding argue that large organizations can afford to invest in a 'logo cop' in order to make sure that their logo is being displayed correctly, using the right colours, in the right proportions and to be aware that an organization can become 'unbranded' very quickly if the logo is mistreated. Brands can also become unintentionally connected to things that are negatively perceived by consumers. For example, recently in the USA a well-known restaurant was named after its owner, 'Osama's', this would have meant next to nothing before 11 September 2001.

There is also a strong potential correlation between the brand (at this point the brand's identity will have developed beyond the logo recognition and/or advertising strapline) and price. That is, when appropriately positioned in the consumer's mind, the brand can more often than not charge a **premium price** and use its existing platform to develop a long-term relationship/loyalty with the customer that will ultimately lead to enhanced financial performance of the brand.

Table 6.1 **The estimated values of some well-known brands**

Company/brand	Brand value (US$, billions)
Coca-Cola	469.6
IBM	51.2
Nike	7.7

Source: 100 Best Global Brands, compiled by BusinessWeek and Interbrand, 2004.

A Consumer Branding Study by management consultants Kuczmarski & Associates in the USA showed that 72 per cent of customers will pay a 20 per cent premium for their brand of choice over the closest competitor. Moreover, price is inconsequential to 25 per cent of customers when buying a brand that 'owns' their loyalty. Obviously, that translates into higher price points and higher profit margins.

(Leiser, 2003)

The other way to enhance the bottom line, in particular if a premium cannot be charged (or it is negligible), is to encourage repeat purchase. This is something that will happen automatically if customers are loyal to a brand, and will have the added effect of maintaining or increasing market share.

In 2002, Bloomberg Business News in the USA reported that an eight-year study of 400 brands showed that 70 per cent of sales increases from advertising came from increased loyalty of existing customers.

In summary:

1 strong brands are profitable and may be the organization's most valuable assets;
2 brands can create loyalty through establishing direct relationships with consumers;
3 most brands are able to charge a premium price;
4 the entire supply chain may be more supportive of a (strong) brand;
5 the brand's values can be perceptually franchised on to other products and services;
6 brands are a weapon in the competitive marketplace.

There is no standard formula for creating a successful brand but long-term investment and nurturing should pay dividends. However, the reputation of a brand can be destroyed overnight.

We have seen above that there are a number of elements to a brand, all of which must work **synergistically** for the value proposition to be realized, although it may be one or another of these elements that can be identified as having been the key that unlocked the door to the consumer's heart.

The brand planning process

The brand planning process can be represented as a series of logical questions that need to be both asked and (more importantly) answered:

1 Where are we?
2 Why are we here?
3 Where could/should we be?
4 How do we get there?
5 Are we on schedule?

1   Where are we?

The first of these questions examines closely the values of the organization and how they impact on the brand in relation to its target markets, both internal and external. This examination may lead to changing or fine-tuning the overall **mission statement** of the organization and is therefore a critical analysis.

The sub-questions that will lead to the formation of an answer to the overall question are as follows:

1   What is the brand's position in the marketplace at the present time?
2   What are the strengths and weaknesses of this brand?
3   What are the core functional components of this brand?
4   What are the key (and secondary) images that consumers associate with this brand?
5   What is the position of this brand in the product life-cycle?
6   What is the key attribute of this brand that motivates the majority of consumers?
7   What core functional component discriminates this brand from competitors?
8   What position(s) do its competitors hold in the marketplace?
9   What are the strengths and weaknesses of the competitors?

2   Why are we here?

The second question requires an understanding of how the brand's current position was reached and, crucially before the next question can be answered, whether at this juncture there are any gaps in the market or marketing research that need to be filled. The research can, of course, be of a **quantitative** or **qualitative** nature, but either takes time and money, both of which need to be planned for.

The sub-questions that will enable an answer to be framed in relation to the bigger picture are as follows:

1   What are the most important macro- and micro-environmental factors that affect this brand and its performance in the marketplace?
2   What are the current important new paradigms in the market, such as social phenomena that might be a source of advantage for the brand?
3   What is the brand's personality and which aspect(s) should be preserved, nurtured or changed?
4   What type of image does this brand have in the marketplace and does this need to be preserved, nurtured or changed?
5   The brand makes certain claims or promises in the marketplace, are these really being met?

6   Could a competitor have successfully manipulated their (or our) brand to his/her advantage?

7   What is the current view of the brand's value proposition amongst its target market?

8   What about non-users and lapsed users of the brand, what might their view of it be now?

3   Where could/should we be?

The aim of this analysis is to identify a number of alternative strategic scenarios that will enable the brand to advance in the marketplace. The analysis usually takes place in what is known in management as a **synectics** session, where both **divergent and convergent thinking** will be revealed; both are equally valuable in forming a direction for the brand.

The next steps for a brand's development that usually emerge out of a synectics session are as follows:

1   develop the strategic scenarios such that they can be tested;
2   test the main concepts by engaging qualitative-type research;
3   review and refine the main concepts;
4   finally, produce and present a cost-benefit (quantitative) analysis based on an evaluation of the concepts that have been discussed.

4   How do we get there?

Based on the above findings it will now be significant to do the following:

1   Produce and present a new or revised **brand strategy** for the marketplace that takes into account many of the variables identified above. That is, an outline of the brand in terms of its functional/physical attributes; the significance of the organization for the brand or the organization as the brand itself; a description of the brand's personality; a presentation of the symbol (such as a logo) that represents the brand; an explanation of the target market for the brand; its overall value proposition and brand positioning.

2   Develop a marketing communications strategy. The marketing communications strategy will take into account (and present in the form of a plan, complete with analysis of target market(s), timescales, etc.) the quantitative and qualitative objectives of the overall brand strategy; the theme for the campaign (for example, this could be a heritage theme as was used in the summer of 2004 by Ireland, notably using the strapline 'this island of memories' and associated images of its heritage, in particular views of the landscapes) and how the consumer is expected to respond (for example, this may be to encourage an online response for

more information or through a 'cut-out' coupon in a magazine or news-paper).
3   The next step will be to brief the advertising agency, in particular to review the following:
    1   the market and marketing, quantitative and qualitative research presently at the disposal of the organization and/or agency;
    2   the new brand strategy;
    3   the specific advertising/and/or wider marketing communications strategy;
    4   creative strategy for the forthcoming campaign.

We can summarize this section with a quote from Sir John Egan, Chief Executive for BAA, who recently said '. . . defining the experience that customers want becomes a criterion by which you can judge the design work you commission'. In short, the organization needs to ask itself whether the advertising effort will contribute to brand image and equity; will it dilute brand position; will it enhance consumers 'experience' of the brand?

4   Assuming that satisfactory responses have been gained in relation to the questions in (3), the final step will be the advertising launch, although this may not necessarily take the form of paid advertising, either because it is too expensive or is inappropriate. For example, in the early 1990s, the National Trust wanted to both raise the awareness of and generate funds to preserve some of Britain's coastlines that are eroding and will therefore be lost forever. The result of this sub-branding strategy was a themed campaign entitled 'Enterprise Neptune' and initially took the form of an invitation to journalists of newspapers and magazines with which the target audience would be familiar, such as the *Daily Telegraph* and *Country Life* magazine. Coaches were laid on to take these editors and writers out of London and to the coast in order that they might see for themselves the plight that the National Trust wanted to highlight. Many stories appeared in a variety of written media and were followed up by an interest in the broadcast media that ultimately generated thousands of pounds in funds for this cause at relatively little cost, relative to advertising in those media in order to reach the same audiences. The National Trust have used this strategy on numerous occasions since that ground-breaking event.

The way in which advertising works (if indeed it can be *proved* to do so – this can be problematic) is in any one of four different ways, according to the following models.

1   **The Sales Response Model** is one of these models that specifically sets out to demonstrate that advertising can cause short-term changes in consumer behaviour. The constructs or variables associated with this

model (and indeed the brand it is advertising) stimulate direct interest in (and therefore sales of) a brand; for example, through initiating a price promotion (such as a 'sale') or engaging in reminder advertising to encourage consumers to buy at a particular time, such as at Christmas. The Sales Response Model is reputed to be the first model to demonstrate advertising effectiveness.

2 **The Persuasion Model** uses advertising to persuade consumers about the brand's functional strengths and, in particular, any one(s) which may be *superior* to that of the competition. For example, this model is commonly used to demonstrate the attributes of one fmcg good compared with another, such as washing powder, and is becoming more popular as a form of advertising in the UK. The Persuasion Model developed alongside brands and the mass market, in particular from the 1950s onwards.

3 **The Involvement Model** aims to get consumers to respond positively to the brand's values, i.e., a (set of) value(s) with which the consumer wants to be associated (see the examples of Pepsi and Coca-Cola, below). The brand does not necessarily perform (or taste) better but the **perception** of it is more favourable than that of a competitor brand. Heritage (or an aspect of it) is one value that can be advocated to get consumers to buy a brand, therefore advertising in this context is about what the brand stands for and who uses it. The Involvement Model developed from the mid-1960s onwards as advances in the understanding of both advertising and branding gained ground.

4 **The Salience Model** is the most recent model, dating from the 1980s. The purpose of this model is to use a set of advertising variables that will emphasize the *radical difference* of this brand, but not based on its performance attributes or competitive ones. The brand is one that is self-assured.

5 Are we on schedule?

The aim of this question is to address the control aspects of the plan, i.e., to know at any point in time whether the plan is likely to succeed in terms of the qualitative and quantitative objectives that have been set. There are a number of different ways in which **brand auditing** can take place, for example on-going (even online) qualitative research of the target market (perhaps a focus group needs to be set up for on-going monitoring of (changing) attitudes). There are many, or all, aspects of the brand that can be investigated but the main ones to keep on track are its awareness, both through aided and unaided recall; its image and the perceptions of this amongst the target market, in particular; its positioning in the marketplace; its personality aspects; loyalty and the nature of the target market.

Specifically, marketing communications or advertising tracking can also take place to check that the themes resonate appropriately with the target market and that what the brand represents is relevant to their needs, and finally that the correct combination of media are being used to reach the desired audience.

Finally, no plan is complete without a **feedback loop**, which in this case will lead us back to question (1). However, before the brand planning process begins all over again, useful input will come from a review of the brand strategy, the advertising strategy used to project the brand into the marketplace and specifically the way in which this was executed, i.e. the type, timing and frequency of media used. One further set of information that will also prove helpful is an appreciation of any new opportunities in the market that have presented themselves and any new ideas to enhance the brand and its profile.

The key elements of a branding strategy

From all that we have learned above, we can conclude that there are certain associations that consumers make in their minds with respect to a brand that are reinforced by certain 'drivers'. These are as follows (*Source:* Leiser, 2003).

1 *Strategic Brand Drivers* – these are the most relevant (to the consumer) aspects of a brand's equity; they have strong and unique associations with the brand and are therefore a powerful influence on the customer's decision to buy the brand.
2 *Potential Drivers* – these can be described as elements of a brand's equity that have yet to develop as powerful an association as strategic brand drivers; these too need to be nurtured and protected as unique selling propositions.
3 *Category Antes* – these relevant equity elements have strong associations with the brand and all competing brands in the category; they are 'must-haves' if a brand expects to participate in the category, but cannot serve as a platform for differentiation. These are usually the basic product functions or service aspects that customers have come to expect.
4 *Neutral Associations* – these equity elements are unique and highly associated with a brand but play a minor role in the customer's decision to purchase. For example, the 'Shell' logo is instantly recognizable and associated strongly with the brand but does not necessarily mean that a purchase will be made at that particular fuel stop.
5 *Brand Barriers* – these are issues that must be addressed if the brand is to be leveraged for optimal business performance; they may be customer-relevant equity elements that are not actively associated with the brand or are negative associations that are uniquely associated with it.

The key elements of a heritage branding strategy, whether for an organization or a specific brand, takes one or more of the following descriptors and uses them in marketing communications activities in order to build a long-term relationship with the customer. These are: history, tradition, recognition, familiarity, loyalty, quality, value, trust and dependability.

The premise of heritage branding need not necessarily apply only to long-term brands (i.e., those that have been in existence for some time) but can also apply to new ones. A new brand can develop a heritage by pursuing a long-term, quality (differentiated) or cost-leadership approach; this means sustaining a consistent position and image in the marketplace that is reinforced by one or more of the descriptors identified in the paragraph above.

Branding – art or science?

The arguments about whether branding is an art or science (or both) are beginning to rage, but in an article by Edwin Colyer entitled *The Science of Branding* (2004), he concludes with scientific evidence that branding really works, as consumers, even though they might prefer the taste of one product to another, usually select the 'stronger' brand.

The experiment was conducted with two well-known cola brands, Pepsi and Coca-Cola, in the USA at the Human Neuroimaging Laboratory at Baylor College of Medicine. The Director of the study, Read Montague, carried out the well-known 'Pepsi Challenge' (where respondents almost always state that they prefer the taste of Pepsi to Coca-Cola – the alternative brands are not revealed until after the taste testing) but scanning the activity of the brain at the same time. Using a non-invasive technique called functional magnetic resonance imaging (fMRI), the scans reveal which parts of the brain are active in real time. The conclusions of the 'Pepsi Challenge' were as expected, that respondents preferred the taste of this brand to that of Coca-Cola. However, when the interviewees were told which brand they were tasting, nearly all the volunteers said they preferred Coca-Cola. 'Moreover, different parts of the brain fired as well, especially the medical prefrontal cortex, an area associated with thinking and judging. Without a doubt the subjects were letting their experience of the Coca-Cola brand influence their preferences' (Colyer, 2004).

The evidence from this study provides proof that branding can establish a preference in the consumer's mind but needs to resonate with the individual in terms of self-perception. 'The work of Montague and other studies prove that branding goes far beyond images and memory recall. The medical prefrontal cortex is a part of the brain known to be involved in our sense of self; it fires in response to something – an image, name or concept – that resonates with who we are. Something clicks and we are more likely to buy' (Colyer, 2004).

The idea that a **brand name** is the trigger that unlocks the door to the consumer's heart and mind has been advocated by many management and marketing authors. The arguments are that when it is said, read or thought, all the experiences and promises of the brand are brought to mind. Thus, the name should fit the company, the product or the service and should connote favourable associations and convey the essence of the brand – in short, it should be memorable, unique, pronounceable, timeless and exclusive to the organization.

Brand names can be derived in a number of different ways:

1 *Surnames* – for example, family names (see Insights 6.2 on Morgan and 6.4 on Scobie McIntosh) but there is no reason why a name should not be fictitious, as long as it carries a certain connotation favourable to the organization, or the product or service. However, the evidence is that real family surnames can take a long time to become established in the marketplace although there are some well-known ones such as Johnson & Johnson, Heinz, etc.

2 *Geography* – brand names can be established from a geographical area, such as a state, region, city or town. However, if the product or service is to be marketed beyond a specific geographical area, will the brand name based on geography be as synonymous far afield as it is in the locality?

3 *Initials and acronyms* – most initials used in corporate branding are based on the names of organizations that are too long for repetition purposes, for example, IBM (International Business Machines), RCA (Radio Corporation of America) or BBC (British Broadcasting Corporation). The initials mean nothing until they have been (long) communicated and there is familiarity with them in the market.

4 *Numeric and alphanumeric* – these are brand names that have at least one numerical value, for example 7-Up or the 7-11 shop. Although there is a trend to have a combination of letters and numbers to synonimize a brand, the combination must evoke a positive response, otherwise there is no point using it.

5 *Description and benefit* – the idea with a brand name that describes or evokes a benefit is that it should be strong, memorable and easily associated with a positioning statement and brand strategy.

6 *Classic and historic* – these names can be used to evoke mythology or history and, again, should be both positively perceived and non-controversial. Products or services that require a heritage-linked name can draw from this category. One example mentioned in the previous chapter was the use of 'Penny Bazaar' by Marks & Spencer in the branding strategy of foods sold exclusively at Christmas time, which has since been dropped. The images that reinforced this brand name were of 'Victorian England', particularly in winter time, and those of the upper social classes.

7   *Humourous/whimsical* – the main aim of using these types of brand name is to raise awareness and generate an interest in the brand. However, there may be a danger that the brand is not taken seriously, something that many organizations have found to their cost. This type of brand name will also only work in certain sectors of the market, such as toys and possibly some food and drink.

8   *Foreign* – sometimes organizations will adopt and present brand names from outside the country of origin. This is usually to impart an aspect of heritage (for example, history) but, in order to be sustainable, the culture of the organization must reflect the branding.

9   *Suggestive and symbolic* – these brand names use 'borrowed interest' in order to impart a positive connotation for the organization or its products or services, such as the use of animals. For example, whales are often used to symbolize 'freedom' on company logos.

10 *Arbitrary* – these are brand names that are radically different in order to stand out and gain the attention of potential customers, such as 'Blue Tooth' or 'Apple'.

Using heritage branding for marketing

In recent years, whilst travelling to the Far East, I have been struck by the 'reproduction' of aspects of UK life, particularly in retail outlets, the idea of which is to create a certain ambience which adds value to the brand. For example, Burberry, which sells a range of indoor and outdoor clothing, has a small retail concession in the complex that was once just the Raffles Hotel, Singapore. Raffles now has a range of 'luxury' shops, most of which are marketing British brands. In the Burberry showroom the atmosphere and setting of a 'period country house' has been created as the backdrop for the clothes and accessories, complete with real log fire (in an air-conditioned shop!) with the head of a large deer above it. I might have been amused by this sight but the point was not lost on me and, more importantly, the customers, i.e., much of what we purchase is not based on need but on **aspiration**, which is an emotional state and can be triggered for commercial advantage in any number of different ways, nostalgia being just one example. This was being reinforced in the retail ambience and undoubtedly in related marketing communications, such as in magazines aimed at this type of target market.

One further example of how heritage can be used by organizations is the case of airlines. British Airways (and most other countries' main airline) reinforce their **brand identity** by using aspects of heritage associated with the country of origin (for example, through the use of an indigenous work force, foods served, etc.) but particularly the country's flag, or at least its colours, especially on corporate livery and more often than not on the tail fin of the air-craft. In the late 1990s, British Airways took a first and radical step of changing from the use of the 'Union Jack' on its tail fins to a range of artists' drawings and paintings, which came from individuals all over the world. The idea was to reinforce the trans-national routes served by the airline and that it was the 'World's Favourite Airline', evidence which had been gathered through con-sumer and trade surveys and which was quickly used on a range of marketing communications, including mass-market television advertising. The fallout from this change was equally unprecedented, resulting quickly in a significant loss of market share and consumer confidence. 'We wanted BA to be seen as a diverse, cosmopolitan brand and positioned as a world airline, but we missed the fact that our core customers choose us because we are British – the per-spective of the British is that we are responsible, calm in a crisis, and in control, which are great traits for an airline to have' (George, 2004: 13).

The re-branding exercise, therefore, far from paying dividends, resulted in losing customers. This was not just from the UK but overseas, too, as inter-national travellers previously loyal to the BA brand moved away; they felt that the brand's attributes of reassurance, heritage, tradition and reliability, as evident in the crest, which was one of the most attractive and comforting aspects, could no longer be guaranteed. The **brand's asset value/equity** became severely reduced.

However, the traffic is not all one way. There are many organizations from countries all over the world that will use their heritage for branding. For example, in the previous chapter I discussed French wine as both a generic product with a heritage that is reinforced in marketing activities but increas-ingly is also being branded under the umbrella of a specific organization and its heritage, especially for the export market – something that the 'New World' wine producers have been doing successfully for some time and which effectively has eroded some of the French market share.

From the USA, in the UK and Europe there are now many well-known 'American brands', i.e., brands with an American heritage, such as 'Gap' clothing, 'AOL' (the computer Internet provider), Disney (see Case study 6.1), Ralph Lauren and, of course, the best-known of them all, featured in the previous chapter, Coca-Cola.

The future of branding

There is much debate on this topic but many authors seem to be of the view that 'brand-interaction' is the way forward. Brand-interaction is a combina-tion of brand building and direct response marketing. The advantage of this approach is that incentives, such as special offers, can be used to create *meas-urable* leads, sales, interactions and loyalty; more and more organizations want to know how the brand strategy has contributed directly to profitability.

In terms of branding strategies, six significant shifts in organizational behaviour are predicted, these can be summarized as follows.

1 Many organizations will position themselves around philanthropic causes.
2 Global images and messages will be redesigned for local markets.
3 There is a trend towards authenticity – many firms will try to re-associate themselves with their heritage, tradition and stability.
4 There will be increased investment to find new uses and applications for existing products.
5 Employees will become more involved in the branding strategies of organizations.
6 The value of branding will come under scrutiny and therefore research and measurement will be more commonly used.

There are many organizations, in addition to those discussed above, that use heritage branding in their marketing. We shall take a look at some further examples.

Insight 6.1: Royal Worcester, Worcester, UK

The Worcester Porcelain factory (the first of its kind) was founded in 1751 by a group of 15 men, led by Dr John Wall who was an eminent physician and worked, notably with his colleague William Davis, who was a chemist. It is the oldest continuous producer of Porcelain in Britain and is now one of the largest manufacturers of Fine Bone China and Porcelain. In 2001 the factory celebrated its 250th anniversary. Royal Worcester is the only porcelain company to have held a Royal Warrant continuously since 1788.

Worcester was chosen as a site for the factory for its proximity to the River Severn, which was used for the transportation of fuel, raw materials and finished goods, and because the City needed a new industry to replace the decline of trade in cloth.

The factory quickly gained an excellent reputation for its products and by 1756 the first London showroom had been opened in Aldersgate Street. At this time, the company rapidly began to attract skilled artists and also managed to perfect the transfer printing process. The actual origin of the process is controversial and there are several contenders for the honour of having discovered it. However, the man who first applied it to the decoration of porcelain was the engraver Robert Hancock. By 1756 Hancock had arrived at Worcester and the process was soon mastered. These very pleasant wares, so characteristic of early Worcester production, are today eagerly sought by collectors and exist in considerable variety.

Blue Backgrounds were also introduced at this time to surround hand painted scenes on exquisite vases. These pieces were further enhanced by skilfully applied gilding. The result was rarely copied by competitors and these pieces are some of the most famous of the 18th century.

(John Guy, Royal Worcester Publication, 2002)

The art of painting on the glaze in enamel colours was also mastered and, although a smaller part of the early production, the examples that have survived are of an unusually high quality.

One of the first Royal services made at Worcester towards the end of this period, around 1770, was for the Duke of Gloucester. Each piece of the service was painted with different groups of fruit of a very distinctive style.

Following the retirement of Dr John Wall in 1774, his partners continued the manufacture until their London agent, Thomas Flight, purchased the factory in 1783 for £3000. The famous Flight and Barr periods in their various forms firmly established the factory as one of the leading porcelain manufacturers in Europe. By 1789 the quality of their work at Worcester was held in such high esteem that, following a visit to the factory, King George III granted the company the prestigious 'Royal Warrant' as Manufacturers to their Majesties.

During the reign of Queen Victoria, the company achieved great success. Manufacture was consolidated on the current factory site in 1840 and, following a programme of major modernization in 1862, the 'Worcester Royal Porcelain Company Limited' was formed. The Managing Director, Richard William Binns and his colleague W.H. Kerr led the company until the end of the century and under their control the number of employees increased from 80 to 800.

During the second half of the nineteenth century, Royal Worcester produced a new material, Parian, which was to revolutionize figure making. Dramatic steps were also taken to develop new decorative skills and techniques. Apprenticed at 14 years old, boys were instructed in Anatomy and Botany and were encouraged to study old master paintings; they were taught skills such as gilding, groundlaying, printing and painting before specializing in one area, many traditions being passed down from father to son. New decorative styles introduced included Painted Fruit, Blush Ivory ware and the perforated porcelain of George Owen with thousands of tiny holes cut out by hand. Many rich and extensive dinner services were also made during this period for the British Royal Family and the European Aristocracy including Queen Victoria and the Prince and Princess of Wales.

Royal Worcester was successfully displayed at major exhibitions of Art and Manufacture throughout the world, and in the tradition of Dr John Wall, every effort was made to surpass all technical and aesthetic thresholds. Unique exhibition pieces were created, such as the Norman Conquest Vases, the Potters' Vases and the giant Chicago Vase, now on show at the Museum of Worcester Porcelain.

In 1891 Charles William Dyson Perrins (of Worcester Sauce fame) became a director. Dyson Perrins invested extensively in the company and even purchased the factory museum collection in 1927 at a greatly inflated price in order to ease its financial difficulties. In 1934 he purchased Royal Worcester outright and became its chairman. In 1946 he set up a Museum Trust and opened a new Museum in 1951.

During the early years of the twentieth century Royal Worcester took a traditional approach to shapes and decoration. Artists such as the Stinton family, Harry Davis and Frank Roberts produced meticulously painted landscapes, flowers and fruit on richly gilded vases and decorative services. Superb table services continue to be made, many of which are special orders individually designed with crests or monograms, as in the past.

The policy of Dr Wall for artistic and technological innovation continues to the present day and has led to the production of a Fine Porcelain ideal for oven cooking. These newer products have been met by an increasing demand, resulting in a new, modern factory on the banks of the River Severn to satisfy the needs of customers today.

A profound technological revolution has taken place since the company first started its activity so many years ago. However, sensitivity to changes in taste has made Royal Worcester products throughout the years some of the most sought after by important collectors and museums all over the world. The company continues to make 'classics', which are ever-popular with its customers, and frequently updates ranges with designs that are either based on 'old favourites' or are entirely new innovative designs in modern styles for both existing and new target markets.

The market research process for a new product range includes consultations with its customers, retailers and overseas distributors, initially to determine the product(s) parameters. Assuming the costs and benefits are in order, the designers then begin their part of the overall process of bringing a new range to market.

Royal Worcester has a sales and distribution company in the USA and has engaged with specific marketing opportunities both in the UK and overseas, some examples are:

1   Royal Worcester's fine bone china is used as the exclusive table setting on the Royal Scotsman Train;
2   since 1977, Royal Worcester has produced an exclusive design sold only by Tiffany & Co., New York;
3   since the early 1990s, staff retiring from the Surrey Constabulary receive a personalized Royal Worcester constable figurine;
4   throughout the 1990s, the winner of the Adelaide Cup has received a specially commissioned prestigious vase depicting a racing scene;
5   in 1997, one of the largest silk manufacturers in Thailand launched a range of ceramics using Worcester's famous blue elephant design.

The Royal Worcester site now provides a complete 'day out' for visitors. Its facilities include:

- the Museum of Worcester Porcelain;
- a range of associated retail shops;
- a film of the history and development of Royal Worcester;
- guided factory tours.

In 1990 a charitable trust was established called The Queen Elizabeth Scholarship Trust whose primary aim is to further the advancement in the UK of modern and traditional crafts and trades by using income from a fund to make grants of between £2000 and £15 000 to individual craftsmen and women.

By kind permission, Rachel Digger, Royal Worcester, Worcester, 2004.

Insight 6.2: The Morgan Car Company, Malvern, Worcestershire

Morgan is often associated with British heritage generally but specifically with the heritage of craftsmanship in the quality build of handmade cars from 1910 to today; an activity unique in this sector. The uniqueness of these cars and the long heritage of this organization (from very humble beginnings) are the two most important **unique selling points** used by the firm in its branding strategy.

Morgan is a car manufacturer that was established as a private limited company in 1912 by the Reverend H.G. Morgan and his son, who was the first Managing Director. It continues to be a family business.

A local man, H.F.S. Morgan was born in Herefordshire in 1881 but educated at classic English public schools, Stone House in Kent and Marlborough College in Wiltshire, and at Crystal Palace Engineering College in London. The career of the man who was to become a pioneer of quality, unique cars, began as an 18-year-old pupil of the Chief Engineer of the GWR Railway Works at Swindon, where he was employed as a draughtsman in the drawing office for seven years.

In 1906 he left the GWR and opened his first car garage in Malvern Link. The first initiative in making his own brand of car arose out of the purchase of a 7 hp twin-cylinder Peugeot engine, which was raised on to a light three-wheeled tubular chassis – this was the prototype of the first Morgan Runabout. 'The first design was successful due to its rigid frame, light weight and independent front suspension. Another important factor was the unusual power-to-weight ratio of 90 brake horsepower per ton, which enabled this little vehicle to accelerate as fast as any car being produced at that time' (website: http://www.morgan-motor.co.uk 2004).

H.F.S. Morgan had no initial intention of marketing his car, but many compliments led him to consider making a few more, all of which were sold and gained capital to enable machine tools to be bought and the creation of an extension to the garage. The design of the car was patented and manufacturing began in 1910. In the same year, several different designs of car were shown at the Olympia Motor Show where it became quickly evident that not only were they commercially viable but that the preferred model was for a two-seater variant; this was first shown at Olympia in 1911. During this show, the response for orders was so overwhelming that Morgan approached several existing car manufacturers to produce his models; they all refused. He therefore purchased further machine tools and again extended his garage in order to make the cars himself.

The site of the first factory was in Great Malvern, next door to the small terraced house in which lived the owner and his wife. Initially, very few cars were produced, as all are handmade and the site had a limited capacity for production. This was further reduced during the First World War when the machinery was used for manufacturing arms and munitions. However, after the First World War, on the strength of marketing the four-seater 'family Runabout', sales increased and a new factory was built at Pickersleigh, enabling 50 cars to be produced per week. Morgan was one of the largest British car manufacturers at that time.

The name 'Morgan' first became known in racing circles in 1913 (a heritage sport with which it has always been associated) when Henry Martin won an International Cyclecar Race. The cars have since won many prestigious awards for speed and efficiency.

In 1918 a new factory was opened on the Madresfield estate, which is the site of the present factory and is known locally as the 'Works'.

Acknowledgment: The Morgan Motor Company, Worcestershire, 2004. Website: http://www.morgan-motor.co.uk

---

Insight 6.3: The Classic Mineral Water Company. Natural Irish Water

In 1948 the late James McKee founded the Classic Mineral Water Company – the business has remained in the family ever since.

The business originally traded by selling premium-quality drinks directly to consumers by home delivery, but in 1990 it developed the market potential by supplying shops and supermarkets. Also in 1990, the firm was the first in Northern Ireland to achieve Mineral Water Status, an accolade that reinforced its commitment to quality products and to which its existing customer base responded extremely positively – they had been asking for more natural product drinks and the company had been listening.

During the 1990s the firm engaged in more market development by supplying its products to UK multiples (supermarkets), which saw a steady growth in sales. However, in 2000, they decided to commission an extensive market research exercise in order to understand what the consumers thought about the range of products and the brand. The research was carried out amongst a sample of the target markets in Northern Ireland, the Republic of Ireland, England and Europe.

The research revealed that consumers enjoyed the range of products but identified that the brand image needed to be developed more clearly, in particular to reflect the Irish heritage and identity of the company. The company responded by investing in new label designs and branding to confirm their positioning in the market as a supplier of premium-branded Irish Mineral water; this was reinforced by using Celtic fonts and an associated logo with a 'knots' design.

Sales expectations were exceeded as a result of these branding initiatives, so much so that the company acquired more state-of-the art manufacturing machinery and added additional warehousing in order to meet this surge in demand, mainly from new customers rather than existing or lapsed ones.

The company is now in the process of product development and is adding to the existing range with flavoured variants of mineral water and a new health-boosting variety.

Acknowledgment: The Classic Mineral Water Company, Co. Antrim, Northern Ireland, 2004.

Insight 6.4: Scobie McIntosh, Bakery Engineers Ltd. Over 120 years of heritage

Scobie McIntosh has been supplying specialist machinery to the baking industry for nearly 120 years. The company brand has come to be associated with quality and a friendly service.

The company was started by two colleagues, Mr Scobie and Mr McIntosh, but Scobie left soon afterwards leaving McIntosh to develop what has become a family business.

The company was first set up in Niddrie Street, Edinburgh, and then moved to 53 Cockburn Street with a works at Greenside Place. The first products made by Scobie McIntosh were cake tins for bread, fermenting tubs and a range of hand tools with product names such as Dockers, Peels, Hozzles and Chains. The product range developed into ornate copper tea and coffee urns and early types of machinery for the baking trade. However, the First and Second World Wars required the factory to produce goods of a different kind, namely aerial vanes for torpedoes and marine radios.

In 1922 the company moved to Fountainbridge but, during the recession of the 1930s it was taken over by McIntosh's brothers-in-law, James and John Brown, who were ironfounders and owners of the Forth & Clyde & Sunnyside Ironworks in Falkirk, Scotland. James put up the loss-making company as a dowry against his daughter marrying locally but the challenge of this was taken up by Peter Alderson, a practising lawyer from London.

Alderson slowly changed the image of the company into a respectable national supplier and, in the 1950s, added catering equipment to the existing product range. The factory subsequently moved to Annandale Street and began producing goods in stainless steel. The company expanded and opened new branches in Aberdeen, Glasgow, Belfast and Newcastle. In 1965 Peter's son, Geoffrey, joined the company, specifically to develop the English market. He returned to Edinburgh in 1979 as Managing Director, a role he continues in today.

In 1988, the company moved to Sighthill, opening a new factory and showroom where it hosted an international conference. The main line of business developed into self-service display counters, which are used by all major supermarkets and in kitchen installations on oil-rig galleys, hotels, schools and hospital kitchens. The company also had the foresight to tap into a significant emerging market, that of the in-store bakery, to whom they began supplying equipment, alongside the existing market of craft bakers.

The development of the business resulted in two separate divisions being created to serve the two distinct markets, Scobie & McIntosh (Catering Equipment) Ltd, which is located in Livingston, West Lothian and Scobie & McIntosh (Bakery Engineers) Ltd, which has remained in Edinburgh but also has service facilities in Leeds.

In recent years the company has undertaken a thorough review of its brand and, after engaging in a re-branding exercise, the vast majority of its functions moved to new premises at Birstall near Leeds, in 2003.

Acknowledgment: Scobie & McIntosh, Scotland, UK, 2004.

Insight 6.5: Crayola, USA

The Crayola organization, which spawned the now widely used term 'crayoning', began as Binney & Smith, Peekshill NY, USA in 1885. The two gentlemen who began the business were cousins and their earliest products included a red oxide pigment for painting red barns and carbon black for use on car tyres.

In 1900 the firm moved into the production of pencils from paints, in particular slate pencils for use in schools. These were manufactured at the company premises in Easton, Pennsylvania, USA. In 1902 Binney & Smith manufactured the first dustless school chalk on the request and recommendation of the school teachers whom they served; the product was so successful that it won a Gold Medal award at the St Louis Exposition.

The Crayola brand was launched in 1903 after the two partners recognized the need in schools for affordable wax crayons. Crayola crayons were initially in the form of a box of eight crayons. The colours available at that time were black, brown, blue, red, violet, orange, yellow and green, exactly the same as can be bought today.

The brand name was constructed by Alice Binney, wife of one of the founders, Edwin Binney, and is derived from 'craie', which is the French word for chalk and 'ola', which means oily.

Product development continued and by the 1920s, the range grew to include Crayola Rubens crayons and Perma Pressed fine art crayons for art students. By this time the Arista branded paints has also been launched.

In 1936 Binney & Smith became founding members of the Crayon, Watercolour and Craft Institute, which is now known as the Art & Creative Materials Institute and has the main aim of promoting the safe production of and use of art materials. This is a classic example of the philanthropic nature of many organizations that were founded as small family businesses and which serves to create a unique heritage for them.

By 1948 the company had not only expanded its product lines but also further philanthropic gestures were made, notably the teacher workshop programme, which offers in-school training across the USA to help art teachers learn about the many different uses for Crayola products; this programme continues today.

1958 saw the launch of a product that has become a leading one in the range, the Crayola 64 Box complete with built-in sharpener. During the same year, teachers requested that the name of one of the crayons should be changed as pupils could not relate to this period of history; 'Prussian blue' subsequently became 'Midnight blue'; this was the first name change to take place. In 1962 another name was changed: the crayon entitled 'Flesh' became 'Peach', a recognition by the company that not everyone's flesh colour is that indicated on the crayon.

Further product development continued and in 1978 the company introduced it's first box of colour marker pens in a box of eight different colours.

In 1984 there was a significant change for the company when it was acquired by Hallmark Cards Inc., USA, a world leader in the sale of greetings cards and associated products. During the same period, the company continued with its plans to support schools and launched the Crayola Dream-Makers programme, which had the aim of encouraging art in all curriculum areas. The result of this programme is that Binney & Smith owns one of the world's largest collections of children's art.

1990 was a landmark for the company as this year saw the first ever withdrawal of colours from the Crayola range: those that were no longer deemed to be appropriate for the needs of the market. The eight colours 'retired' were: maize, lemon yellow, blue grey, raw umber, green blue, orange red, orange yellow and violet blue. However, they can still be seen in the company's 'Hall of Fame'.

In 1992 the company launched the first Crayola multicultural crayons, which are an assortment of skin-tone based colours that enable children to more accurately reflect themselves and others when drawing and colouring. 1992 also saw the launch of another product innovation, the first set of Crayola crayons that were able to be washed off walls.

The company was 90 years old in 1993 and to celebrate this event, consumers were invited to identify 16 names for a new range of colours. These included purple mountain's majesty, razzmatazz, timber wolf, cerise and shamrock.

In 1996 the 100 billionth crayon was produced and, in honour of this occasion, American celebrity Fred Rogers of *Mister Rogers' Neighborhood* was invited to name it 'blue ribbon'. During the same year, the company opened 'The Crayola Factory Family Discovery Center' at their headquarters in Easton, Pennsylvania. The highlight of the opening ceremonies was a 'ColourJam parade', the largest gathering of people with colour in their names.

New crayon colours were launched in 1997 to commemorate eight 'true blue' heroes of children. The new colour range included: outer space, mountain meadow, fuzzy wuzzy brown, brink pink, shadow, banana mania, torch red and purple heart.

In 1998 the company decided to re-launch the Crayola 64 Box using the same packing as for the original, together with the built-in sharpener. The same year saw the Smithsonian Institution's National Museum of American History add a 1958 64 Box to its collection.

The company had been in existence since 1885, yet in 1999, for the third time only, another crayon was re-named, this was 'Indian red', which became 'chestnut'.

In 2000 the company carried out its first ever 'census' of consumers, an online poll to identify their favourite colours. The results included Blue at Number 1 with a further six shades of blue in the 'top ten'; these were cerulean, midnight blue, aquamarine, periwinkle, denim and blizzard blue.

During 2003, Crayola won the accolade for 'Best Toy of the Year' by *Child* magazine in the USA for its product entitled the Crayola Crayon Maker, which enables crayons to be melted down and new ones made. Further significant product innovations have been launched since that time, including Crayola Twistables (crayons in plastic tubes that twist up when more is needed); Window FX Markers which can be applied to windows and mirrors, and 2004 also saw the opening of an interactive retail store in Baltimore, USA.

2003 saw the 100th anniversary of the company and, once again, they invited consumers to name four new colours. These were: mango tango, wild blue yonder, inch worm and jazzberry jam. In order to enable these colours to become established, the company decided to withdraw blizzard blue, magic mint, mulberry and teal blue. The celebrations ended with the unveiling of the world's largest Crayola crayon, which weighed 1500 lbs, was 15 feet high and 16 inches wide; the colour was blue.

The total number of colours presently available is 120.

Acknowledgment: Binney & Smith, USA, 2005.

CASE STUDY 6.1: Disney, USA

In 1994, a survey by Total Research identified Disney as the premier brand amongst USA consumers. 'Disney is just one of the brands that seems to do everything right. It's wholesome, high-tech, nurturing, kid-friendly, escapism, sentimentalism all wrapped up in one brand' (J. Alleborn, 1994).

The heritage of Disney goes back to the early 1920s when Walt and his brother Roy arrived in California in order to start an animated film company, a venture that failed. In 1923 they made another attempt, created their own film studio and, in 1928, made the first ever silent cartoon called *Plane Crazy*, which featured their unique creation, Mickey Mouse. Although Mickey Mouse has won the hearts and minds of people all over the world, initially the idea of cartoon films was not without its critics, in particular that poor Americans would pay hard-earned money to watch a cartoon film during the Depression. However, when they made *Snow White and the Seven Dwarfs* in 1937, they finally managed to win over most of the sceptics because the film was very successful. This was followed by further successes in the form of *Fantasia, Pinocchio, Dumbo* and *Bambi*. 'That first big success also became the symbolic beginning of one of the most powerful and enduring brand identities in the world. The Disney name would forevermore be associated with the hope, the inevitable triumph of good over evil, the "magic" that audiences saw come to life in *Snow White*' (Alleborn, 1994).

The brand began to go from strength to strength with the development of related new 'products'. In 1955, the brothers progressed into television production and launched their own show entitled *The Mickey Mouse Club*, which was extremely successful, in particular for the generation of American 'boomers' who were in grade school at that time – this vehicle became an emotional meeting place (metaphorically speaking) for this group of target consumers.

The Disney brothers almost monopolized American television channels on Sunday evenings, showcasing various Disney shows continuously for 29 years – they provided deliberate escapism and Americans responded to this favourably.

The capital raised from the activities thus far enabled them to build themed parks, the first of which was Disneyland in Anaheim, California which opened in 1955. Walt Disney died a year after the completion of what has been described as 'the happiest place on Earth'. Roy Disney died in the same year that Disney World opened in Orlando, Florida, USA, in 1971.

The Disney Corporation, part of which is the original Walt Disney Company, generates annual revenues that are measured in billions of dollars – it is a global industry with further theme parks in Japan and France, frequent releases of films (both in cinemas and for the home viewing market in the form of VCRs and DVDs) and merchandizing of the characters featured in films, both recent and from the past. 'Their business comes down to protecting and capitalising on the value of the Disney brand identity, although a number of their ventures have spun off into non-Disney related areas, such as Touchstone Pictures. The Walt Disney Company knows how to use its brand identity to leverage a winner when it gets one' (Alleborn, 1994).

In the late 1980s, partly as a result of important social changes that saw the mass cinema-going audiences of the developed Western economies rapidly switch to the concept of watching video recordings of films in the comfort of their own homes, the Disney company launched a series of new cartoon character led feature films and also re-releases of 'old favourites' – this was another hugely successful enterprise. In 1993 alone, *Pinocchio* sold 13.4 million tapes, *Beauty and the Beast* 22 million in 1992 and *Aladdin* has made over US$50 million. The main 'hit' of 1994 was *The Lion King*, which may end up as the biggest money-making film in history. The re-release of *Snow White* in late 1994 sold 17 million tapes in three weeks, which generated an income of approximately US$300 million; there seems to be no danger of the various releases **cannibalizing** existing ones, which in itself is almost a unique phenomenon.

The Disney brand is clearly positioned as the symbol of happiness and well-being in whatever venue it appears. The brand's personality is most often revealed in the eclectic group of characters that inhabit the Disney landscape: Mickey and Donald, Pinocchio and Snow White, Roger Rabbit and Annette Funicello, Tinkerbell and Dumbo, the stormy elegance of *Fantasia* and the laughable silliness of *Honey, I Shrunk the Kids*. The brand specializes in likeable, loveable, everybody-has-a-good-time characters, a toon-town full of luminaries, real and animated, who, in a swirling blend of fantasy and wizardry, have been fused into a single brand personality of unparalleled potency.

In order to maintain consistency of the brand and especially one that resonates appropriately with consumers, the 'Brand Image Group, USA' is used to engage respondents in telephone surveys which elicit information on aspects of branding.

The training techniques used by the Disney Corporation (in particular those used at theme parks where employees are trained as 'cast members') are studied and adopted by all types of service organizations, all over the world.

Critics argue that Disney creates synthetic experiences, in particular at theme parks, but the Board has responded by saying that they have actually managed to change the overall perception of 'pleasure parks'/fun-fairs, away from dirty places operated by dubious characters to that which is wholesome and safe – as a result, the whole industry has benefited.

In 1992, Disney took another strategic branding move in order to further strengthen the brand and expand the number of people who might associate with it; they re-branded an Anaheim-based NHL hockey franchise by calling them the 'Mighty Ducks' (a branding concept that is popular in the USA), after the successful film of the same name. Disney's consumer products division branded a complete range of sport's clothing with the brand name and logo, hats, shirts, etc.; these are now sold in over 200 Disney retail outlets (together with many other merchandized items and memorabilia) and have proved successful amongst consumers, whether they support the team or not. Disneyland's Imagineering Group creates associated entertainment for use during matches; the Disney Development

Corporation designed the Ducks' offices; Disney employees are often required to sell tickets for forthcoming contests and Disneyland sponsors and conducts a Mighty Ducks sweepstakes. Disneyland package tours include Ducks tickets – all these activities serve to strengthen and further the brand franchise.

However, the Disney brand has not been without its problems, many of which affect most organizations and can have devastating and long-lasting consequences: power struggles, boardroom skirmishes, sudden death of key figures and unpredictable changes in the external environment in which it operates – all of these were features of what happened to the Disney Corporation, mainly from the mid-1980s to the early 1990s, at which time, at last, it once again began its ascent. The transformation has been slow, not least because new people have had to be bought in at senior level and it takes time to assimilate the culture of an organization.

Questions

1 How is Disney positioned as a brand?
2 What are the limitations of the Disney brand?
3 Describe how Disney engages in cross-selling and synergistic brand building.
4 How do you think that Disney controls and manipulates brand contacts?

CASE STUDY 6.2: Mulberry

Mulberry was founded in 1971 by Roger Saul and began by manufacturing leather fashion accessories in Somerset, where it is still based. The company states that its mission is 'To make Mulberry the English lifestyle brand, competing globally with the best luxury brands, using our strength in accessories as a foundation'.

Today, it is a worldwide brand name, associated with the symbolic aspects of 'luxury', quality and style but also a sense of the UK's past. The company began by making luxury leather accessories but has expanded into Womenswear, Menswear and Home Collections, over a period of time.

There is no doubt that the production facilities are specifically designed (as are the products) to ensure high quality, with each item undergoing vigorous checks before it leaves the plant, from the tannery and hide inspection to the detail of stitching and final polish; the Mulberry stamp of approval is not given unless each product passes through each stage of the production process.

The company has always had a reputation for craftsmanship, which stems from the early beginnings when Roger Saul designed and produced his first collection of belts and bags, working from a small outbuilding at the bottom of his parents' home in Bath. Demand for these products was so overwhelming that he decided to employ local craftsmen with traditional leather-working skills in order to make the goods; many of these people still work for the firm. The products were always intended for the premium/luxury end of the market and consequently were initially stocked by Harrods, Fenwick, Stirling Cooper and Biba.

In 1972, Saul decided to develop his market by going overseas to France, coming back with an order for 1000 belts from the famous Printemps department store in Paris, which now has branches in other parts of the country. The strength of these successes led Saul to open his first factory in Chilcompton, in 1973, at a cost of £10 000, which subsequently became the first Mulberry Factory Shop; even then he was ahead of his time as this concept is now very popular in the UK and Europe.

During 1974, Mulberry exhibited at the Pret-a-Porter exhibition in Paris for the first time and also established agents in Germany and France in order to distribute its goods. Another interesting development was the design by Saul of accessories for existing fashion houses such as Kenzo, Enrico Coveri and Facconable.

1976 was a landmark year for the company with the creation of the Mulberry Leather Accessories range, which was based on a hunting, shooting and fishing theme. In the same year, retail outlets providing a show case for the goods opened in London and New York. Also during this year Saul was commissioned to design belts for Ralph Lauren.

In 1977, the USA became Mulberry's biggest market and Saul was elected Chairman of the London Designer Collections.

During 1978, Mulberry opened 'in-store concessions' in Joseph and Harrods in London and Neiman Marcus in the USA, whilst at the same time a trip to Japan led to a three-year supply contract with Shisheido. 1978 also saw the launch of the first Ready To Wear Collection for Women. In 1979, the Mulberry Company was awarded the Queen's Award for Export, but in 1980 the firm suffered as a result of the US stock market crash and the worldwide recession. However, by 1981, all things considered, the company celebrated its 10th anniversary and declared a revenue of £900 000.

In 1982, the firm, now confident of its place in the market, opened Mulberry House in Gees Court, London, which accommodated a showroom, shop and offices. During this year, they also opened the first of their own shops in the fashionable Place de Victoires, Paris; together with the launch of the Men's Shoe Collection, the turnover increased to £1.5 million.

1985 saw further market development with the opening of a franchise in Stockholm, Sweden and, in 1987, Mulberry was presented with the British Knitting and Clothing Export Council Award; turnover in this year reached £4.3 million. In 1986, new shops were opened in Amsterdam and Pukeva in Finland, and Germany became Mulberry's leading export market.

By 1988, Mulberry had become the largest producer of high quality leather accessories in Britain and was exporting 80 per cent of its production; turnover continued to rise and stood at £6.8 million; the company was now employing 220 people. Further market development followed with shops opening in the UK, Scandinavia and the Far East – the year culminated with another export award.

In 1989 further product developments were launched, namely the Men's Toiletries Collection and a new headquarters and factory were opened at Chilcompton in Somerset. The company also developed and formed 'Mulberry Europe' in order to strategically develop and launch new retail shops in key cities, the first of which were in Paris and Milan.

A further separate company entity was formed in Japan, using £3 million of capital in order to launch 15 Mulberry shops over a period of three years. Another set of awards followed, the Queen's Award for Export (second time) and Best Consumer Product into Europe.

In 1990, Roger Saul was nominated as Accessories Designer of the Year by the British Fashion Council, for the second time.

During 1991 Mulberry once again won the Queen's Award for Export and in the same year launched the Mulberry Home Collection with a dedicated Mulberry Home department in Harvey Nichols, London.

By 1992, worldwide turnover had reached £50 million and Mulberry won Classic Designer of the Year Award. Further market development took place with the opening of retail shops in Oslo and Istanbul. In 1994, Mulberry launched the All Weather Collection with a dedicated corner at Harvey Nichols. New shops also opened this year in Lyon, Salzburg and Athens. Mulberry was also nominated for Classic Designer of the Year Award.

By 1995, the company had paid sufficient attention to its people management and was therefore awarded the 'Investors in People' kitemark. During this year the Mulberry Watch Collection was launched at a heritage sporting event, the Goodwood Festival of Speed, which Mulberry co-sponsored for the second year. Another sporting event with which it is associated is the Mulberry Pro-celebrity Challenge, a charity tennis tournament held at the Queen's Club in London.

1996 was Mulberry's 25th anniversary and saw it win the British Apparel Export Award for Accessories. The company was floated on the stock exchange. 1998 was notable for many further events, notably the launch of the Mulberry Flight Luggage Collection and hosting, for the second year, the Mulberry Classic at the Hurlingham Tennis Club. In 1999, Mulberry was invited to decorate Eltham Palace for English Heritage and launched the Mulberry Silver Millennium Collection.

In the year 2000, Roger Saul and associate Scott Henshall launched the Mulberry Capsule Collection and the red 'Islington bag', which sold out completely, three times over. One further significant development and departure was the invitation to Christina Ong, the millionaire entrepreneur, to join the Board of Mulberry. Christina Ong of Club 21 had developed a Singapore-based fashion and hotel empire that extended into Europe and the USA, as well as other parts of the Far East. Christina Ong, together with her husband, invested £7.6 million to develop the Mulberry brand, which has been themed as the 'Renaissance of Mulberry'. The main activities have been to thoroughly review the brand and its presentation formats, together with the creation of a new flagship store, which opened in New Bond Street in London in October 2001 and was followed by stores in Brampton Road, Knightsbridge, London, Copenhagen, St Petersburg and The Hague.

In 2002, an out-of-town discount outlet opened at the 'Bicester Village' complex in Oxfordshire, together with a concession in the Selfridges Store in London. The company also launched a 'Bottletop' campaign in order to raise funds for AIDS education in Africa and Roger Saul became President of Mulberry.

Acknowledgment: Mulberry, 2004.

Questions

1   What aspects of the UK's heritage are symbolized by the Mulberry brand and how do you think these are reinforced in the consumer's mind?
2   Why do you think designers design goods for other organizations? Is there a danger of brands cannibalizing each other?
3   Examine the timeline of Mulberry's development and identify what events have taken place to develop the brand's equity.
4   Why do you think New York was chosen as the first (alongside London) city in which to open a retail outlet?
5   Why are 'luxury' goods likely to suffer disproportionately if there is a downturn in consumer confidence as a result of events such as a stock market crash?
6   Why do you think Paris and Milan were chosen as the first cities for new retail shops under 'Mulberry Europe'?
7   Why do you think Mulberry sponsors heritage sporting events such as the Goodwood Speed Challenge?

CASE STUDY 6.3: Hershey, USA

Hershey, a company whose headquarters are in North America, began by producing chocolate bars over 100 years ago and has gradually moved into related and unrelated product lines over its history.

The Corporate Philosophy of Hershey is as follows:

In seeking to balance our desire for profitable growth with the obligations which we have to various other constituencies, we shall strive to:
1   Protect and enhance the corporation's high level of ethics and conduct.
2   Maintain a strong 'people' orientation and demonstrate care for every employee.
3   Attract and hold customers and consumers with products and services of consistently superior quality and value.
4   Sustain a strong results orientation coupled with a prudent approach to business.

The Hershey confectionary company was started in the USA by Milton S. Hershey, who was born in 1857 in Central Pennsylvania. Hershey's forefathers had arrived in the USA from Switzerland and Germany in the 1700s. He started work at a printing company after having completed only the fourth grade, but it soon became clear that this was not the sector for him.

Milton Hershey went to work for a sweet-maker and in 1876, still only 18 years old, he opened his first sweet shop in Philadelphia, but only after six years in business the venture failed. Undeterred by this setback, Hershey moved to Denver, Colorado where he took up a post as a caramel manufacturer.

In 1883, Hershey moved to Chicago, then to New Orleans and later to New York City, having tried to establish his own confectionary business in each city. He returned to Lancaster, Pennsylvania in 1886 and there set up the Lancaster Caramel Company.

Chicago hosted an International Exposition in 1893 where Milton Hershey became fascinated with German chocolate-making machinery which he subsequently purchased for his caramel manufacturing company. The range of products at this time was very limited, consisting of chocolate coatings, breakfast cocoa, sweet chocolate and baking chocolate.

The Lancaster Caramel Company was sold in 1900 for US$1 million but Hershey retained the chocolate-producing equipment and the legal rights to manufacture chocolate as he still firmly believed that there was a potential mass market for low-priced chocolate confections.

Hershey's next physical move was back to the place where he was born, Derry Church in Pennsylvania, an area abundant in dairy cattle, producing in particular fresh milk, of which he would need vast quantities in order to make fine chocolate.

In 1903 Hershey began to build one of the world's largest chocolate manufacturing plants, part financed from the proceeds generated from the sale of the caramel business. The plant was ready for business in 1905 and began to produce chocolate for the mass market; at this time Hershey was an industry in his own right.

The business was a success and Hershey used revenue and profits to establish a community around the plant, similar in principle to that of Bourneville near Birmingham, UK, which was an entire village set up by the Cadbury family. Hershey had banks, department stores, schools, parks, churches, golf courses, zoos and also a transport system to bring workers to the plant from surrounding areas. The philanthropic approach of sharing one's good fortune did not stop there. Hershey began a second phase of building in 1930 and, although this coincided with the Depression, he kept workers on the payroll but moved them into building projects such as a grand hotel, a community building, a sports arena and a new office block for the chocolate factory.

Hershey and his wife Catherine had no children so in 1909 they set up the Hershey Industrial School, which is now called the Milton Hershey School. Catherine Hershey died in 1918 and, shortly afterwards, Hershey left his entire fortune to the school.

The fortune of the company continued to grow, despite no advertising of any of its products for the first 66 years. Hershey's view was '. . . give them quality and that's the best kind of advertising in the world'. However, by the 1970s much had to be done as Hershey was rapidly losing market share to its new rival, Mars, mainly a result of the fact that they had not advertised nationally.

In the present climate, Hershey is one of the largest advertisers in the USA and has created strategic alliances with film distributors, such that pictures of films like *Jurassic Park: The Lost World, Godzilla* and *Small Soldiers* have been used on chocolate wrappers on fast-selling lines of chocolate bars. Hershey has also sponsored NFL, NASCAR racing and the NCAA in order to reinforce the values of the brand in the consumer's mind. The company also used to conduct factory tours in order that consumers could see the chocolate manufacturing process and also gain a unique, first-hand insight into the heritage of this organization; however, increasing competition led them to postpone these for the time being.

The company has also acquired the Leaf North American Confectionary business which has enabled them to have a complete product range without having to develop some lines. Further advantage has come from gaining control of popular and well-known products such as Jolly Rancher, Milk Duds, Whoppers and Payday.

Product development is on-going, as is continuous review of its packaging, advertising strategies, etc. Hershey is also considering the move into confectionary ice-cream products, many variants of which, mainly from the Wall's/Mars alliance are available in the UK.

The majority of Hershey's products are distributed through wholesalers but a breakthrough in terms of supplying retailers directly has come with the launch of a low-fat chocolate bar.

In terms of the international market, Hershey's is a relative newcomer, only entering in the 1990s with varying success in different countries; the most disappointing region has been Europe. The products were branded in the same way as in the USA for the export market but in Germany the company also manufactures and markets chocolate and confectionary products under the Gubor brand, and in Italy under the Sperlari, Dondi, Scaramellini and other brands. The products are also made under license by other manufacturers, particularly in South Korea, Japan, the Philippines and Taiwan. The Philippines is one of the strongest markets outside North America. In 1995, Hershey International opened offices in Shanghai and Moscow, which were part of a strategy to expand into 17 new export markets.

Prices of the brands are kept as stable as possible, in spite of the fluctuations of the commodities markets on which purchases of raw materials such as cocoa and sugar have to be made. The confectionary sector in the USA is worth approximately US$28 billion and, today, Hershey and Mars control three-quarters of this between them.

Acknowledgment: The Hershey International Group, USA.

Questions

1 The first company was named after a geographical location; what are the strengths and weaknesses for an organization in using this branding approach?
2 The sale of the company in 1900 was a strategic move. Briefly explain what this means in the context of this case.
3 Explain the sentence taken from the case that in 1905 '. . . Hershey was an industry in his own right'.
4 Briefly argue whether Hershey's view '. . . give them quality and that's the best kind of advertising in the world' would be sustainable in any confectionary market today.
5 Why do you think that films such as *Jurassic Park: The Lost World*, *Godzilla* and *Small Soldiers* have been used on chocolate wrappers?

6   What do you think might be the critical success factors that would enable Hershey to compete in Europe?

Summary

The aim of this chapter has been to demonstrate that there is a new paradigm in marketing which is taxing the minds of anyone associated with business, namely branding and, in particular, brand strategy and the creation of brand equity.

The relationship between branding and heritage is that a brand can espouse certain values and more and more organizations are looking to embed aspects of heritage either into the organization and its profile and marketing activities or in its products or services.

We already know that anything can become 'heritage' as long as someone wishes this to be the case, but beyond this philosophical stance is the fact that values such as trust, authenticity, reliability (perhaps as a result of the organization and/or its products or services having been around for 'some time') can create added value or a point of differentiation that might be well worth having in the competitive marketplace. However, organizations have to balance carefully that the (ubiquitous) use of words such as 'promise' and 'trust' can lead consumers to become cynical about the organization and/or its products.

However, in general and at least for the moment, most aspects of heritage evoke favourable responses amongst the vast majority of consumers and I believe that this concept will be more widely used by organizations in the future.

Recommended reading

Alleborn, J. (1994) Total Research Equitrend Survey, USA.

BusinessWeek and Interbrand (2004) *100 Best Global Brands*.

Colyer, E. (2004) *The Science of Branding*. http://www.brandchannel.com

George, M. (2004) Heritage branding helps in global markets. *Marketing News*, 4, 13.

Kenneth, H. (2002) A Matter of Trust. *Brandweek*, 43(31), February.

Leiser, M. (2003) *Understanding Brand's Value: Advancing Brand Equity Tracking to Brand Equity Management*. http://www.brandchannel.com

Stewart-Allen, L. (2002) Heritage branding helps in global markets. *Marketing News*, 36 (16), 7.

Willmott, M. (2002) *Citizen Brands: Corporate Citizenship, Trust and Branding*. The Future Foundation, London.

Willmott, M. (2003) *Citizen Brands: Putting Society at the Heart of Your Business*. John Wiley & Sons, Chichester.

Bibliography

Amery, C. and Cruickshank, D. (1975) *The Rape of Britain*. Routledge, London.

Appandurai, A. (ed.) (1986) *The Social Life of Things: Commodities in Cultural Perspective*. Cambridge University Press, London.

Ashworth, G. (2003) *Heritage: Management, Interpretation, Identity*. Continuum Books, London.

Ashworth, G. and Howard, P. (eds) (1999) *European Heritage Planning and Management*. Intellect, Bristol.

Bainbridge, J. (2003) Whisky innovation mustn't be at cost of existing values. *Marketing Magazine*, December.

Blythe, J. (2001) *Essentials of Marketing*. Prentice-Hall, London.

Boniface, P. and Fowler, P. (1993) *Heritage and Tourism in the 'Gobal Village'*. Routledge, London.

Boswell, D. and Evans, J. (2003) *Representing the Nation: A Reader*. Histories, Heritage and Museums. Routledge, London.

Cohen, E. (1988) Authenticity and commoditization in tourism. *Annals of Tourism Research*, 15, 19.

Colyer, E. (2004) *The Science of Branding*. http://www.brandchannel.com/features_effect.asp?pf_id=201

Cormack, P. (1978) *Heritage in Danger*. Second edition. Quartet, London.

Crouch, R., Entringer, M., Frank, E. and Post, J. (2004) *Elizabethan Food and Drink*. http://www.springfield.

de Beer, J. (2004) *Community Aspiration and Authentic Expression*. de Beer Marketing and Communications, Auckland, New Zealand.

De Chernatony, L. (1998) *Creating Powerful Brands in Consumer, Service and Industrial Markets*. Second edition. Butterworth-Heinemann, Oxford.

Department of the Environment (2000) *Power of Place: The Future of the Historic Environment*. London.

Department of the Environment (2001) *A Force for Our Future*. London.

Dibb, S. and Simkin, L. (1996) *The Market Segmentation Workbook: Target Marketing for Marketing Managers*. Thomson, London.

Dibb, S. and Simkin, L. *et al.* (2002) *Marketing Concepts, Techniques and Strategies*. Houghton Mifflin, London.

Doswell, R. (1997) *Tourism*. Butterworth-Heinemann, Oxford.

Douglas, N. (ed.) (2002) *Special Interest Tourism*. Wiley, Sydney.

Drummond, S. and Yeoman, I. (eds) (2001) *Quality Issues in Heritage Visitor Attractions*. Butterworth-Heinemann, Oxford.

Edensor, T. (1997) National identity and the politics of memory: remembering Bruce and Wallace in symbolic space. *Environment and Planning: Society and Space*, 29, 23.

Engel, J.F., Fiorillo, H.F. and Cayley, M.A. (1972) *Market Segmentation: Concepts and Applications*. Holt, Rineholt and Winston, New York.

Engel, J.F., Blackwell, R.D. and Miniard, P.W. (2001) *Consumer Behaviour*. West, Fort Worth, TX.

Evans, J. (1999) Nation and representation. In Evans, J. and Boswell, D. (eds) *Representing the Nation: A Reader: Histories, Heritage and Museums*. Routledge, London.

Finn, M., Elliot-White, M. and Walton, M. (2000) *Research Methods for Leisure and Tourism*. Longman, London.

Food & Drink Europe.com.

Frechtling, D.C. (2001) *Forecasting Tourism Demand*. Butterworth-Heinemann, Oxford.

Goodey, B. (2002) Re-visioning the past for the future. *Interpretation Journal*, **7** (2).

Gunn, C. (2002) *Tourism Planning*. Routledge, London.

Hall, M. (2000) *Tourism Planning*. Prentice-Hall, London.

Hall, M.C. and Mitchell, R. (2001) Wine and food tourism in special interest tourism. In Douglas, Norman, Douglas, Ngaire and Derrett, Ros (eds) *Special Interest Tourism*. Wiley, Sidney, Australia.

Henderson, J.C. (2002) Conserving colonial heritage: Raffles Hotel in Singapore. *International Journal of Heritage Studies*, **7** (1), 7–24.

Herbert, D.T. (ed.) (1995) *Heritage, Tourism and Society*. Pinter, London.

Hetherington, L. and Andrews, P. (2002) Connecting people through place. *Interpretation Journal*, **7** (2).

Hobsbawm, E. (1983) *The Invention of Tradition*. Cambridge University Press, London.

Hooley, G. and Saunders, J. (1998) *Marketing Strategy and Competitive Positioning*. Prentice Hall, London.

Hooper-Greenhill, E. (2004) *The Educational Role of the Museum*. Second edition. Routledge, London.

Howard, G. (2003) *Heritage: Management, Interpretation, Identity*. Continuum Books, London.

Huffman, K. *et al.* (1994) *Psychology in Action*. Third edition. Wiley, USA.

Jennings, G. (2001) *Tourism Research*. Wiley, Sydney.

Karmowska, J. (2004) *Cultural Heritage as an Element of Marketing Strategy in European Historic Cities*. Centre for European Studies, Jagiellonian University, Krakow, Poland.

Kenneth, H. (2002) A matter of trust. *Brandweek*, **43** (31), 9 February.

King, E.B. (2004) *Engaging the Aging: Marketing to Europe's Seniors*. http://www.brandchannel.com/features_effect.asp?pf_id=228.

Kirshenblatt-Gimblett, B. (1998) *Destination Culture: Tourism, Museums and Heritage*. University of California Press, Berkeley CA.

Leiser, M. (2003) *Understanding Brand's Value: Advancing Brand Equity Tracking to Brand Equity Management*. http://www.brandchannel.com/papers_review.asp?sp_id=301

Lowenthal, D. (1996a) *The Heritage Crusade and Spoils of History*. Viking, London.

Lowenthal, D. (1996b) *The Past is a Foreign Country*. Cambridge University Press, London.

MacInnes, L. and Wickham-Jones, C. (eds) (1992) *All Natural Things: Archaeology and the Green Debate*. Oxbow Books, London.

Middleton, V. (1998) *Sustainable Tourism*. Butterworth-Heinemann, Oxford.

Millar, S. (1999) Co-ordination, co-operation and collaboration: operations management – the neglected heritage profession. *Interpretation Journal*, **4** (3).

Moore, K. (ed.) (2004) *Museum Management*. Routledge, London.

Morgan, N. and Pritchard, A. (2001) *Advertising in Tourism and Leisure*. Butterworth-Heinemann, Oxford.

Morgan, N., Pritchard, A. and Pride, R. (2003) *Destination Branding*. Wiley, London.

Museums, Libraries and Archives Council (2004) *A Manifesto for Museums: Building Outstanding Museums for the 21st Century*. MLA, London.

Myers, J. (1999) *Measuring Customer Satisfaction: Hot Buttons and Other Measurement Issues*. American Marketing Association.

Pervin, L.A. and Oliver, J.P. (1997) *Personality Theory and Research*. Seventh edition. Wiley, USA.

Prentice, R. (1993) *Tourism and Heritage Attractions*. Routledge, London.

Richards, G. (1996) *Cultural Tourism in Europe*. CAB International, Wallingford.

Ritson, M. (2003) Parma Ham maintains heritage as EU strikes blow for branding. *Marketing Magazine*.

Robins, K. (2004) In Boswell, D. and Evans, J. (eds) *Tradition and Translation, National Culture in its Global Context in Representing the Nation: A Reader*. Routledge, London.

Ryan, C. (1997) *Exploring Perception*. Thomson International.

Samuel, R. (1989) *Patriotism: the Making and Unmaking of British National Identity. Volume 1*. Routledge, London.

Shackley, M. (ed.) (1998) *Visitor Management*. Butterworth-Heinemann, Oxford.

Simpson, H. (1986) *The London Book of Ritz Afternoon Tea. The Art and Pleasures of Taking Tea*. Random House, London.

Sorrell, M. (2002) Heritage branding helps in global markets. *Marketing News*, **36** (16), 7.

Swain, H. (ed.) (1993) *Rescuing the Historic Environment – Archaeology, the Green Movement and Conservation Strategy for the British Landscape*. Routledge, London.

Swarbrooke, J. (2002) *The Development and Management of Visitor Attractions*. Butterworth-Heinemann, Oxford.

Tunbridge, J.E. and Ashworth, G.E. (1996) *Dissonant Heritage: The Management of the Past as a Resource in Conflict*. Wiley, London.

Urry, J. (1995) *Consuming Places*. Routledge, London.

Wahab, S. and Pigram, J.J. (eds) (1998) *Tourism, Development and Growth*. Routledge, London.

Wedel, M. and Kamakura, W. (2000) *Market Segmentation: Conceptual and Methodological Foundations*. Kluwer Academic Publishers, Boston MA.

Wilkie, K. (2000) *Indignation*. Available at www.kimwilkie.com/pages/issues/iss_indign.html.

Willmott, M. (2002) *Citizen Brands: Corporate Citizenship, Trust and Branding*. The Future Foundation, London.

Willmott, M. (2003) *Citizen Brands: Putting Society at the Heart of Your Business*. John Wiley & Sons, Chichester.

Wilson, I. (2003) *The Economics of Leisure*. Heinemann, Oxford.

Wind, Y. (1978) Issues and advances in segmentation research. *Journal of Marketing Research*, 15.

Wong, J.L. (2002) Who we are. *Interpretation Journal*, **7** (2).
Yin-Fei Lo, E. (2001) *The Chinese Kitchen*. Random House, USA.
Zikmund, W.G. *et al.* (2003) *Customer Relationship Management*. Wiley International.

Index